RECONSTRUCTING THEOLOGY

RECONSTRUCTING THEOLOGY

Essays in Honour of
Rev. Prof. Dr. J. A. David Onesimu's 65th Birthday

Edited by

Samuel Jayakumar
K. Vijayan

Madras Theological Seminary & College

&

Christian World Imprints

First Published in 2020 by

Madras Theological Seminary & College
14 Waddells Road, Kilpauk
Chennai 600010
mtsc@vsnl.com
www.mtsc.co.in
Phone: +91 44 26413178

&

Christian World Imprints
Christian Publishing & Books from India
C-3, Wazirpur Industrial Area
Delhi-110052
cwidelhi2017@gmail.com
www.ChristianWorldImprints.com
Phone: +91 11 41526079

ISBN: 978-93-5148-434-9 (HB)
ISBN: 978-93-5148-435-6 (PB)

The Cover Design Arranged by: *Rev. K. John Dinakaran, ECI Hope City*

About the Cover Design: 'Both' the ***Banyan*** 'and' the ***Cross*** symbolize unity and power; in the sense that in ***reconstructing theology,*** the binaries go beyond a mere critique of the old structures, but to develop a new alternative community, an open *koinonia* (fellowship), which is new creation in Christ where all share their resources, respect each other's dignity, live in peace and harmony, and work towards justice for all.

Printed in India.

Rev. Prof. Dr. J. A. David Onesimu

CONTENTS

Part II: THEOLOGICAL

Part III: HISTORICAL-MISSIOLOGICAL

Part IV: RELIGIOUS

Part V: MINISTERIAL

FOREWORD-1

On behalf of the Korea Evangelical Holiness Church (KEHC), I pray for the grace of the Lord to be in the Evangelical Church of India (ECI) family and Madras Theological Seminary and College (MTSC) in Chennai, Tamilnadu, India.

Congratulations to Dr. Onesimu, who will be finishing and retiring from the Principal position of MTSC in May 2020. The principal Dr. Onesimu has served as the coordinator between KEHC and ECI for more than two decades and as the principal of MTSC for thirteen years. I am pleased that MTSC faculty will publish a retirement memorial papers with respect and gratitude for Dr. Onesimu.

I would like to bring a few things about Dr. Onesimu in this congratulatory message. Rev. Dr. Onesimu is a well-known personality among the Korean Evangelical Holiness community since his Th. M. studies at the Seoul Theological Seminary in 1984. He is our Evangelical Seminary product, a fine prepared evangelical instrument for God's mission in India. Onesimu has been ordained by the Korean Evangelical Church General Conference in the year 1986 December 08. He is the first foreign person ordained by our denomination. Further, our KEHC had sent him to Yonsei University to study the Korean language from 1983-1985 where he has completed 6 levels of Korean Language. This training is very useful for the translation of sermons and discussion in the time of need. Dr. Onesimu is serving as the bridge between KEHC and ECI. We are praying for all success to him.

In *Changing Minds*, Howard Earl Gardner, a professor of Educational Psychology at Harvard University, says that one of the seven levers to change one's mind is "representational re-descriptions". When a message or content is repeatedly provided in a variety of formats, the formats reinforce each other and finally help to change the mind of those who read or listen to it.

The title of the Papers is *Reconstructing Theology*. I believe that it can strengthen the truth by re-describing the gospel of creation, fall, and redemption to be suitable to the present age and change many people's minds. I do not doubt that *Reconstructing Theology* will make fresh impacts and academic contributions to churches scattered across India and the world. Once again, I congratulate Dr. Onesimu with all my heart as a representative of the KEHC.

In His Holiness Ministry,

Rev. Dr. Jeong Ho Ryu
The President of the 113th General Assembly of Korea Evangelical Holiness Church

FOREWORD-2

I come to know that Madras Theological Seminary & College (MTSC) Faculty have taken a worthy initiative to bring out a 'FESTSCHRIFT' in honour of Rev. Dr. David Onesimu, Principal, Madras Theological Seminary & College. It gives me immense pleasure to pen this Foreword to the Festschrift to be released during the MTSC Annual Convocation 2020.

I have known Rev. Dr. David Onesimu for more than four decades, as my Pastor in ECI Nungambakkam church, as a faculty and later as Principal of MTSC, fellow faculty of Laymen's courses and a trusted co-worker in the vineyard of ECI. He is an erudite scholar, prolific writer, and an able administrator. Under his leadership, MTSC has seen great strides in terms of academic as well as infrastructural developments. I had the privilege of visiting South Korea twice hosted by him. He is very fluent in the Korean language.

His scholarly presentation in several theological conferences and workshops is noteworthy and he has a passion for preaching and evangelism. He has earned the trust of our Father Bishop Most Rev. Dr. M. Ezra Sargunam and Bishop-President Most Rev. Dr. D. Sundar Singh.

I commend Rev. Dr. Samuel Jayakumar, Rev. Dr. K. Vijayan and the team of MTSC faculty for thinking about bringing Festchrist in honour of Rev. Dr. David Onesimu. May God bless him and take him to greater heights in the coming days (Psalms 91.14).

In His Mission

Rev. Dr. S. J. Kingsley
Chairman, MTSC Board
Director, ECI Prayer & Revival Dept

PREFACE

In the highly pluralistic context of India, the search for relevant theology/ model of mission and evangelism in most cases is also an encounter between the Christian faith and other faiths, raising questions of Gospel and Culture at the theological level. The fundamental relation between *religion and culture* also thus becomes central to our search for new theological paradigms/ paradigms of mission and evangelism. The *Modern Period* which is that the Enlightenment in eighteenth-century Europe, where human and reason and the scientific approach to the study of natural phenomena predominated in the thinking of man. This phase may, therefore, be referred to as the *Age of Reason*. The *Postmodern* phase is the emergence of a new and revolutionary system of thought in the last decades of the twentieth century. This phase may be to call it the *Age of Subjective Relativism.*[1]

The word *Postmodernism/Postmodern* could be described as a philosophical concept and *Postmodernity* as a time or period concept. The same distinction can be applied also to *Modern-* as a philosophical concept and *Modernity* as a time concept. Charles Jencks, in his book, *What is Post-Modernism*, (London: Academy Editions, 1996), distinguishes 'Postmodernn'- as an outright rejection of Modern- from 'Post-modern'- which is an attempt to appropriate whatever is good in Modern.[2] In the above context, postmodernism as a paradigm shift provides necessary tools to both the people who have been categorizing and those who have been categorized by the modern Christian mission as 'the reached-unreached'; 'the civilized-uncivilized'; 'the developed-undeveloped'; 'the evangelized-unevangelized'; 'the Christian-non Christian'; 'the insiders-outsiders' and the like.

1 R. H. Duncan Lyngdoh, "Postmodernism: Challenges and Prospects" in *Indian Theological Journal* 2/2 (July- December 2008), 7- 8.

2 cf. Alex Kalathikattil, *Postmodernity, Globalization and the Sacrament of Reconciliation: Social Reconciliation and the Reconciliation of the Sacrament of Reconciliation* (Bangalore: Kristujyoti Publication, 2010), 29. However, the editor must admit that in this work these distinctions are interchangeably used.

Jacques Derrida was one of the most well-known twentieth-century philosophers. He developed a strategy called "deconstruction" in the mid-1960s. Although not purely negative, deconstruction is primarily concerned with something equivalent to a critique of the Western philosophical tradition. Deconstruction is generally presented via an analysis of specific texts. It seeks to expose, and then to subvert, the various binary oppositions that undergird our dominant ways of thinking-presence/absence, speech/writing, and so forth. Deconstruction has at least two aspects: literary and philosophical. The literary aspect concerns the textual interpretation, where an invention is essential to finding hidden alternative meanings in the text. The philosophical aspect concerns the main target of deconstruction: the "metaphysics of presence," or simply metaphysics.

The deconstructive postmodernism shows that Western thought is characterized by dichotomies or binaries like mind and matter, soul and body, nature and history, nature and culture, male and female, good and evil, etc. The binaries are arranged in a hierarchical order in which the first terms in the binaries have primacy over the second terms, which are considered to be inferior. It is an attempt to *deconstruct* the missiological 'selfishness'/ 'otherness' of the modern Christian mission and to *reconstruct* a relevant and viable missiological paradigm for doing mission in the postmodern context of India.

The term 'reconstruction' needs to be given particular attention and especially what is and what is not involved in the process. Though the term coined in 1768, associated with rebuilding, only in the aftermath of the American civil war, and means to build a new, to restore, to construct again, rebuild, makeover and to recreate, in the mind from given or available information.[3] Reconstruction is an attempt to explore doing mission/theology with commitment in Christ, to bring a change in human relationship through Liberative praxis and to listen to other voices in order to correct ourselves and also our mistakes in doing mission/theology.[4] The Christian mission in which Christ at the centre of the mission in whom there is neither Jew - nor Gentile; neither rich - nor poor; neither men - nor women; neither Christian - nor people of other faiths; neither saved - nor unsaved.

---

3 Cf. Michael N. Jagessar, "Living in multi-faith landscape: Some Thoughts on Reconstructing Mission" in *Bangalore Theological Forum,* 52/1 (January 2010), 175; K. G. Pothen, "Margins in Conversation: Postmodern Methodologies" in Joseph Prabhakar Dayam and P. Mohan Larbeer eds., *Margins in Conversation: Methodological Discourses in Theological Disciplines,* (Bangalore: BTESSC, 2012), 87.

4 cf. Joshua Raja, "Mission as Creating Common Spaces of Peace" in Joshua Raja, et al., *Towards a Reconstruction of Mission Stories: Building Communities of Hope and Peace,* (New Delhi: ISPCK, 2010), 31.

Missiologically, the term "reconstruction" means to develop alternative communities in Christ that would share their resources, respect each other dignities and work towards justice for all. When the dominant communities feel threatened through this deconstruction or critic of their narratives key they tend to defend them in every possible way. This leads to narrative confrontations. At times, insiders tend to feel superior to the outsider or tend to confront the other by repeating belief in such narratives or identifying the challenging narratives as a threat to them. The mission of God is not only for the oppressed but also for the oppressors to liberate in and through Christ. Mission in Christ's way is not only a liberating but also a reconciling mission.[5] Therefore, 'reconstructive postmodernism' is an attempt to explore doing theology/mission with commitment in Christ, to bring about a change in human relationship through reconciliation and to listen to "other voices" in order to correct ourselves and also our mistakes in doing theology/mission.

As Rev. Prof. Dr. J. A. David Onesimu, the Professor of Christian Theology celebrating his 65th Birthday, it is fitting for the members of the faculty of ECI Seminaries and other scholars known to Dr. David Onesimu to contribute academic papers in terms of topics from the Biblical, Theological, Historical, Religious, Contextual, Strategic disciplines in his honour to bring out a compendium of essays titled as *Reconstructing Theology*. We really appreciate and thank each and every one of the contributors to this volume for their sincere co-operation to contribute in the form of Academic papers written in a multi-disciplinary and multi-dimensional approach. Our special thanks to Rev. Arpit Simon Mathews, Assistant Professor of Christian Theology and Faculty in-charge of MTSC library and Mr. Sudhanshu Kanda, the Chief Executive Officer of the Christian World Imprints (CWI), New Delhi for their team spirit and commitment in jointly publishing this volume with the Madras Theological Seminary and College, Chennai in a very short period of time.

Samuel Jayakumar
K. Vijayan

5 Joshua Raja, "Mission as Creating Common Spaces of Peace…, 28-29.

BIOGRAPHICAL SKETCH OF REV. PROF. DR. J. A. DAVID ONESIMU

I am Epsi Beulah, wife of Rev. Dr. David Onesimu and I am pleased to pen this brief biography of my beloved husband. I got married to David Onesimu on 4th September 1989 and God has blessed us with a son Ezra Leander Santhosh, who is doing his final semester M.Tech. course in VIT Vellore.

David Onesimu was born on 27th May 1955 at Virudhunagar, a town in southern India. His granddad David, a mission school teacher from a tiny hamlet called Kulakattakuruchi near Kovilpatti town in the Tirunelveli District of Tamil Nadu married Gnanamani hailing from Thirupuliankudi, a nearby town called Srivaikundam. My father-in-law, John Albert was the first son in the David family and was married to Dorothy Kovilammal. John Albert was a teacher at a Strict Baptism Mission (SBM) school and a catechist. My mother-in-law served as a Bible Woman. Later, my father-in-law had been Ordained by the SBM missionaries and became the Superintending Pastor of the Tamil Baptist Mission churches in the then Ramnad District (now Virudhunagar District).

My husband grew up with six male and three female siblings, as the youngest among the boys. My mother-in-law, who was fascinated by the character of Onesimus found in Paul's epistle to Philemon, named my husband 'Onesimu', which is the Tamil version of the name. She came to know about 'Onesimu' while studying in the Bible Women Training Institute at SBM Mission Bungalow at Panaiyadipatti Village near Sattur, conducted by Mrs. W. H. Kurt, an SBM missionary. Mrs. Kurt, who was lovingly known as '*Missiamma*' (a reverent Tamil expression to connote a White woman) taught the students that 'Onesimus' meant 'useful'. Moved, my husband's mother immediately made a covenant with God that if He blessed her with another son, she will give him the name 'Onesimu' and dedicate him to be 'useful' for the Lord's ministry.

My mother-in-law's resolve to dedicate my husband for the Lord's ministry was further strengthened when he miraculously survived a fireworks accident in 1966 at a place called Thayilpatti close to the famous fireworks manufacturing hub Sivakasi in Virudhunagar District. He was in bed for nearly a month and his mother who took care of him rededicated him for God's ministry.

Right from his youth, Onesimu was drawn to God's ministry. He would often go out in the evenings with the youth of his church for 'field prayers' dubbed as *Kaattu Jebam* or 'jungle prayer' in Tamil. On Sunday evenings, he would be involved in open-air preaching and tract distribution in the surrounding villages with the evangelism team of the local church.

While he was pursuing his Pre-University Course (PUC) at VHNSN College in Virudhunagar District, he happened to participate in a gospel camp for Christian students during the Deepavali holidays held on the CSI Mallakinaru Church campus. It was at this camp that my husband accepted Jesus Christ as his personal saviour through I Timothy 1:15. After completing his PUC, he studied B Com at the same college. Though he was good at studies and completed all his assignments, he was forced to drop out due to financial constraints and sicknesses.

Circumstances compelled my husband to scout for a job and he eventually landed a temporary job as caretaker of the State Government's Divisional Development Office (DDO) in Kovilpatti, hoping that he would eventually secure a permanent job in the same office. Of course, the opportunity did come his way, pretty soon. The Collector of Tirunelveli District orally instructed the DDO to appoint him as a clerk but failed to follow it up with a written order. Though oral orders were not uncommon in those days, the DDO refused to carry out the oral order of the Collector and give him the job.

Later, he was called for a written test by Air India to shortlist a candidate for the post of Bookkeeping Clerk in their regional office. He did well in the exam, but his candidature was rejected because his signature in the Air India application did not match with his signature in his SSLC book.

After all his efforts to secure a job in a government department or the private sector turned futile, he was utterly dejected. When all the doors to a worldly job were shut, Isaiah 55:8 came to his mind where the Lord declares: "For my thoughts are not your thoughts neither are your ways my ways". My husband thought of Peter's failures that turned to success found in Luke 5:4-6 and acknowledged God's call and committed himself to the ministry. He surrendered himself totally to God asking Him to reveal His way for him in life. God inspired him from John 15:16 – "You did not choose Me, but I chose you and appoint you to bear fruits." – to pursue the call of God.

While Onesimu was helping a senior pastor in Kovilpatti from 1977-1978, he clearly sensed the Lord's call for full-time ministry. He right-away dedicated his life for full-time ministry and started working towards it. His dad directed him to the Madras Bible Seminary to study Diploma in Theology to equip himself for church ministry.

In 1978, he joined Madras Bible Seminary and thus began his theological career. After earning a diploma and bachelor's in theology, he was sent to South Korea to pursue his Th M in Mission by Father Bishop Ezra Sargunam, who was the President of ECI at that time. Once in Korea, he simultaneously studied the Korean language and the Lord enabled him to master it. He used to preach in the Korean language whenever he is invited to speak in the churches and other occasions. He has interpreted hundreds of sermons and lectures of Korean pastors and leaders into Tamil at church services and conferences. He won the *Korean Herald* English daily's Korean language contest for foreign residents in the summer of 1985. He enrolled for his Ph.D. at Asia United Theological University (formerly called ACTS), South Korea in 2002 and completed his doctoral studies in Systematic Theology in 2007.

My husband had the privilege to personally observe the principles of the Korean church growth while visiting the KEHC churches during his days in Korea for higher studies.

In May 2005, he went to the Full Gospel Church Prayer Mountain of Dr. David (Paul) Yonggi Cho for a week of fasting and prayer, where God strengthened him with the power of the Holy Spirit. He sensed God empowering him for his future ministry with Madras Theological Seminary and College. Years later, this tremendous prayer experience inspired him to create a small prayer area for his personal prayers in his office. The time at the Prayer Mountain also motivated him to construct a prayer chapel for students and pastors on the MTSC campus. The prayer chapel was dedicated during the Golden Jubilee celebrations of the Evangelical Church of India in 2016.

From June 1981, he has been serving the Lord in different ECI churches like ECI Vyasarpadi Church and ECI Nugambakkam Church in Chennai, ECI Mulund Church in Bombay, ECI Kotturpuram Church, ECI Trustpuram Church, ECI Maduravoyal Church, ECI Kadambadi Nagar Church, ECI Otteri Church, ECI Thiru Nagar Church and now in the ECI Nerkundram Church all in Chennai. He has been teaching at the Madras Theological Seminary and College since 1995. In 2007, God elevated him to the office of the Principal of MTSC, where he began his theological education almost three decades ago.

He has been extensively invited by the pastors of ECI churches as well as other denominations to speak in their churches or conduct prayer sessions.

Positions in ECI

1981-Till date	Pastor
1983 May	Licensing from ECI Tamil Nadu Area
1986 December	Ordination from General Conference of Korean Evangelical Holiness Church, Korea
1987-1988	Superintendent, ECI Schools, Chennai
1989-1991	District Chairman, ECI North Maharashtra, Mumbai
1992-1998	Director, ECI Overseas Department, ECI Headquarters, Chennai
1999-2002	Coordinator, East Asia Affairs, ECI Headquarters, Chennai
2005-2007	Dean, MTSC, Chennai
2007-2020	Principal, MTSC, Chennai
2020-	Coordinator, Korean Partnership, ECI Headquarters, Chennai

Secular and Theological Education

1972-1975	(B.Com.)	VHNSN College, Madurai University
1978-1982	Bachelor of Theology	Madras Bible Seminary, Chennai
1983-1985	Dip. in Korean Language	Yonsei University, Korea
1984-1986	Master of Theology	Seoul Theological Seminary, Korea
!992-1994	Master of Theology	Gurukul College (SSC), Chennai
1993-1995	M.A. History	Annamalai University, Tamil Nadu
2002-2007	Ph.D.	Asia United Theological University, Korea
2008	D.Th. (*Honoris Causa*)	Kernel University, USA

Books Published

Dr. Ambedkar's Critique towards Christian Dalit Liberation. ISPCK: New Delhi, 2008

Constructing Dalit Theology towards Dalit Liberation. ISPCK: New Delhi, 2010

Books Co-Edited

Towards an Integral Theology: Festschrift in Honour of Bishop Dr. Ezra Sargunam's 80th Birthday. New Delhi: Christian World Imprints/Madras Theological Seminary & College, 2018

Towards an Integral Spirituality: Festschrift in Honour of Bishop Dr. D Sundar Singh's 75th Birthday. New Delhi: Christian World Imprints/Madras Theological Seminary & College, 2019

Rethinking Mission: Essays in honour of Dr. Samuel Jeyakumar 65th Birthday. New Delhi: Christian World Imprints/Madras Theological Seminary & College, 2020

Korean Books Translated into Tamil

999 God's Promises
One to One Evangelism-Methods for Discipleship Training

Mrs. Epsi Beulah Onesimu
B.Ed. Assistant,
Advent Christian High School, Kottur, Chennai

THE REV. PROF. DR. DAVID ONESIMU
THE PERSON I KNOW

I am grateful to the family of MTSC and ECI, for both spiritual support and physical strength, who have shaped my life in India and helped me learn many things. I thank God and my brothers and sisters for the privilege of sharing my greeting essay in this article. Personally, the Rev. Dr. David Onesimu is A HALF INDIAN VS A HALF KOREAN, my dearest *Thambi* more than twenty-five years in India, There are the five issues of the purpose of our friendship and brotherhood;

Our Meeting Was Not Accidental But Inevitability

I strongly believe that God planned where we'd be born and where we'd live for His Purpose. Our race and nationality are no accident. God left no detail to chance. He planned it all for His Purpose. The Bible says, "From one man He made every nation of men, that they should inhabit the whole earth; and He determined the times set for them and the exact places where they should live" (Acts 17:26). Nothing in our lives is arbitrary. It's all for a purpose.

Developing Our Friendship With God

I have learned from Dr. Onesimu that we obey God, not out of duty or fear or compulsion, but because we love Him and trust that He knows what is best for us. We want to follow Jesus Christ out of gratitude for all He has done for us, and the closer we follow Him, the deeper our friendship becomes. However, the unbelievers often think Christians obey out of obligation or guilt or fear of punishment, but the opposite is true.

Experiencing Spiritual Journey Together

We also believe that the Body of Jesus Christ, like our own body, is really a collection of many small cells. The life of the Body of Christ, like our own body, is contained in the cells. For this reason, every Christian needs to be involved in a small group within their church, whether it is a home fellowship group, a

Sunday school class, or a Bible study. This is where the real community takes place, not in the big gatherings. For example, if we think of our church as a ship, the small groups are the lifeboats attached to it.

A World-Class Christian

We must shift from self-centered thinking to other-centered thinking. The Bible says, "Brothers, stop thinking like children. In regard to evil be infants, but in your thinking be adults" (1 Corinthians 14:20). This is the first step to becoming a world-class Christian. Children only think of themselves; grown-ups think of others. God commands, "Each of you should look not only to your own interests but also to the interests of others" (Philippians 2:4). Of course, this is a difficult mental shift because we're naturally self-absorbed and almost all advertising encourages us to think of ourselves. The only way we can make this paradigm switch is by a moment-by-moment dependence on God. Fortunately, He doesn't leave us to struggle on our own.

Living With Purpose

About twenty-five years back, I noticed a little phrase in Acts 13:36 that till now altered the direction of my life journey in India. It was only nine words but, like the stamp of a searing hot branding iron, my life was permanently marked by these words: "David had served God's Purpose in his own generation. No doubt, the Rev. Dr. David Onesimu dedicated his life to fulfilling God's purpose in MTSC and ECI. Our friendship and brotherhood will go together until the last breath on the earth."

Rev. Dr. Bong Tae Kim
The Director, Calcutta Bible Seminary

PART I

BIBLICAL

1

MOSES
A LEADER PAR EXCELLENCE

John Samuel[1]

I am very happy to write this article in honour of my friend and Professor Dr. David Onesimu. He is serving as the Principal of the Madras Theological Seminary, Chennai. He is a well-respected and a senior member of the Serampore fraternity. He has shown himself as a man of principles and leadership. He is kind, friendly and humble. We have developed excellent friendship between Madras Theological Seminary and Gurukul Lutheran Theological College during the time of his leadership. Whenever we invited him as a guest of honour in our college functions, he has always accepted our invitations with kindness and magnanimity. I appreciate the festschrift committee for this wonderful gesture to Professor Dr. Onesimu and wish you all the best. As a token of my love, I write this article on the leadership of Moses. All good wishes for Prof. Dr. David Onesimu.

A leader or a worker, one of the most difficult things – to maintain love and unity, friendship and fellowship. It can be both long term and short term. When there is a lack of trust, grace, generosity of spirit and the ability to respect and recognize others, there is divisiveness, rancour, back-biting, resentment, internal politics and a lack of coordination. We must always put the interests of the group (people) above those of any individuals in the group. We must care for, and inspire others to care for, the common good.

---

1 *Rev. Dr. John Samuel is the Principal of Gurukul Lutheran Theological College & Research Institute. He is the Professor in the Department of Old Testament.*

When the Bible says, 'Love your God', 'Love your neighbour,' it is said in a social context. When the people were suffering from the tyranny of the Pharaoh, Moses teaches them that the only way to get freedom was to Love God and the fellow brothers and sisters. Jesus will reiterate the same in the fierce Roman oppression. Prophets were teaching these words in their context. Love, friendship, fellowship will have to be determined in their social setting. The collective unity, love among the members of the community, will be necessitated by an external factor. The book of judges will show how the tribes come together again and again in order to confront a common enemy. Judges were leaders who brought the people together to keep their freedom alive.

Moses Engaging with his People

There are at least three events of Moses' intervention to rescue some weaker persons, recorded in the Bible. In the first event, when Moses saw an Egyptian abusing a Hebrew, he was overcome by a passion for his fellow Hebrew, quickly murdered him and buried him. The second time, when he saw two Hebrews engaged in a quarrel, one of whom is beating the other, he takes authority in his hands and tries to arbitrate among them. Moses acts as a judge in a polarized world filled with aggressors and victims. His intervention as an individual on behalf of the abused parties only shows that the protection he offers is as much protection he needs. Where there is no justice, nothing can be done. Without authorization or appointment, his role is presumptuous, his authority is disputable, no less than an encroachment than the one he thinks of him.

In the first episode, Moses kills the Egyptian because the Hebrew in Egypt had lost his civic status, the rights or obligations one might appeal on behalf of the Hebrew. To protect his people, if he is to follow the unforgiving Kenite Lamech, who wants to avenge seventy and sevenfold (Genesis 4:24), If that is the case, Moses might have to kill all the Egyptians for the sake of his people. In the second episode, Moses tries to bring the necessity of unity among the Hebrews, the right state of mind that should be exhibited, where one Hebrew will not rise against the other Hebrew. The story does not tell us how rights are got or from where rules of conduct derive their authority.

In the third event as narrated in Exodus 2:11-22, Moses is trying to defend the rights of the women who were vulnerable in that situation. Moses has not given up his passion to defend the suffering, it is the women. Moses still feels that he should take up the role of defender, but this time, his action seems to convey that he is more successful. He secures the use of the well for the daughters of Jethro. We suspect that the shepherds are the habitual offenders because Reuel questions the early return of his daughters. He implies that it takes a longer time to water the flock because we presume others were regularly permitted to take their turn before these women. They not only appropriate the women's turn but also rob the fruit of their work. Those shepherds were the only party who had the first rights over water.

Like the freedom of speech and the right to a free country, safe water defines a livable environment. Everyone aspires for the right to the available resources of the land. Moreover, he asserts the worker's rights to the fruits of their labor. For Moses, Moses is only in an interim place. He will go to Egypt only to come out of Egypt. He will walk towards the Promised Land only not to enter into it. In the meanwhile, Moses engages in the potential conflicts happening around him and tries to defend the weak. Moses does not belong to anyone. But he understands about himself that he belongs to everyone. The daughters of Reuel simply said, after all his deliverance from the shepherds, "An Egyptian delivered us" (Exodus 3:19).

Moses Resolving in a Crisis

The Israelites were on the last stage of their journey to the Promised Land. They were now situated on the east bank of the Jordan, within sight of their destination. Two of the tribes, Reuben and Gad, who had large herds and flocks of cattle, felt that the land they were currently on was ideal for their purposes. It was a good grazing country. So, they approached Moses and asked for permission to stay there rather than take up their share in the land of Israel. They said: "If we have found favour in your eyes, let this land be given to your servants as our possession. Do not make us cross the Jordan" (Num. 32: 5).

Moses was instantly alert to the danger. The two tribes were putting their interests above those of the nation as a whole. They would be seen as abandoning the nation at the very time they were needed most. There was a war – in fact, a series of wars – to be fought if the Israelites were to inherit the Promised Land. As Moses put it to the tribes: "Should your fellow Israelites go to war while you sit here? Why do you discourage the Israelites from crossing over into the land the Lord has given them?" (32: 6-7).

The proposal was potentially disastrous. Moses reminded the men of Reuben and Gad what had happened in the incident of the spies. The spies demoralized the people, ten of them saying that they could not conquer the land. The inhabitants were too strong. The cities were fortified. The result of that one moment was to condemn an entire generation to die in the wilderness and to delay the eventual conquest by forty years. "And here you are, a brood of sinners, standing in the place of your fathers and making the Lord even angrier with Israel. If you turn away from following him, he will again leave all this people in the wilderness, and you will be the cause of their destruction" (Num. 32: 14-15). Moses was blunt, honest and confrontational.

What then followed is a role model in negotiation and conflict resolution. The Reubenites and Gadites recognized the claims of the people as a whole and the justice of Moses' concerns. They propose a compromise. Let us make provisions for our cattle and our families, they say, and the men will then accompany the other tribes across the Jordan. They will fight alongside them. They will even go ahead of them. They will not return to their cattle and families until all the battles have been fought, the land has been conquered, and the other tribes have received their inheritance. Essentially they invoke what would later become a principle of Jewish law: an act is permissible if "one side gains and the other side does not lose."[1] We will gain, say the two tribes, by having land good for our cattle, but the nation as a whole will not lose because we will be in the army, we will be in the front line, and we will stay there until the war has been won.

Moses recognizes the fact that they have met his objections. He restates their position to make sure he and they have understood the proposal and they are ready to stand by it. He extracts from them an agreement to, a double condition, both positive and negative: If we do this, these will be the consequences, but if we fail to do this, those will be the consequences. He leaves them no escape from their commitment. The two tribes agree. The conflict has been averted. The Reubenites and Gadites achieve what they want but the interests of the other tribes and the nation as a whole have been secured. It was a model negotiation.

Quite how justified were Moses' concerns became apparent many years later. The Reubenites and Gadites did indeed fulfill their promise in the days of Joshua. The rest of the tribes conquered and settled Israel while they (together with half the tribe of Manasseh) established their presence in Trans-Jordan. Despite this, within a brief space of time, there was an almost civil war.

Joshua 22 describes how, returning to their families and settling their land, the Reubenites and Gadites built "an altar to the Lord" on the east side of the Jordan. Seeing this as an act of secession, the rest of the Israelites prepared to do battle against them. Joshua, in a striking act of diplomacy, sent Pinhas, the former zealot, now a man of peace, to negotiate. He warned them of the terrible consequences of what they had done by, in effect, creating a religious centre outside the land of Israel. It would split the nation in two.

The Reubenites and Gadites made it clear that this was not their intention at all. To the contrary, they were worried that in the future, the rest of the Israelites would see them living across the Jordan and conclude that they no longer wanted to be part of the nation. That is why they had built the altar, not to offer sacrifices, not as a rival to the nation's sanctuary, but merely as a symbol and a sign to future generations that they too were Israelites. Pinhas and the rest of the delegation were satisfied with this answer, and once again civil war was averted.

First Moses separates the people from the problem by making it clear to the Reubenites and Gadites that the issue has nothing to do with who they are, and everything to do with the Israelites' experience in the past, specifically the episode of the spies. Regardless of who the ten negative spies were and which tribes they came from, everyone suffered. No one gained. The problem is not about this tribe or that but the nation as a whole.

Second, he focused on interests, not positions. The two tribes had an interest in the fate of the nation as a whole. If they put their personal interests first, God would become angry and the entire people would be punished, the Reubenites and Gadites among them. This is quite the opposite of Korahrebellion. There, the whole argument was about positions, not interests – about who was entitled to be a leader. The result was a collective tragedy.

Third, the Reubenites and Gadites then invented an option for mutual gain. If you allow us to make temporary provisions for our cattle and children, they said, we will not only fight in the army. We will be its advance guard. We will benefit, knowing that our request has been granted. The nation will benefit from our willingness to take on the most demanding military task.

Fourth, there was an agreement on objective criteria. The Reubenites and Gadites would not return to the east bank of the Jordan until all the other tribes were safely settled in their territories. And so it happened, as narrated in the book of Joshua:

Then Joshua summoned the Reubenites, the Gadites and the half-tribe of Manasseh and said to them, "You have done all that Moses the servant of the Lord commanded, and you have obeyed me in everything I commanded. For a long time now—to this very day—you have not deserted your fellow Israelites but have carried out the mission the Lord your God gave you. Now that the Lord your God has given them rest as he promised, return to your homes in the land that Moses the servant of the Lord gave you on the other side of the Jordan" (Joshua 22:1-4).

This was, in short, a model negotiation, a sign of hope after the many destructive conflicts in the book of Numbers as well as a standing alternative to the many later conflicts in Jewish history that had such appalling outcomes.

Note that Moses succeeds, not because he is weak, not because he is willing to compromise on the integrity of the nation as a whole, not because he uses honeyed words and diplomatic evasions, but because he is honest, principled, and focused on the common good. We all face conflicts in our lives. This is how to resolve them.

Caleb

Caleb is mentioned twice in this text. Moses mentions to them that ten spies discouraged the people. But it was only Caleb who encouraged the people.

All the ten people went in the way Moses ordered not to go. It was the way forbidden by the Lord. Because the Lord taught that the people will be afraid of the Philistines and go back to Egypt. The ten spies went by the same way eastwards towards the sea. So they arrived at Nagev. Whereas Caleb arrived in Hebron. That is why it is mentioned in singular in Hebrew text, saying only Caleb came to Horeb,

They saw the land, fruits, people, city, forts, Nephilim, anakim. They thought that they appeared like grasshoppers to them. Whereas, Caleb came to Hebron, even closer to Machpelah, where father Abraham and mother Sarah, Isaac and Rebecca, Jacob and Rachel were buried. Caleb looked into the earth, into the tom, the fathers and mothers. He saw the promises of God attached to them. He came back with a different view about the future. We must see into the tombs of our faith fathers. We must see our Lord under the earth. That will guide us into our future.

Conclusion

The people of Israel had to be united. The people had to be reminded of their responsibility to be together. Whenever they were divided, they became weak and became prey to the powerful. The book of judges even explains how this collective spirit became weakened gradually. In the beginning, when they had to lead the battle, they ask which tribe should lead. When the responsibility felon the tribe of Judah, they led the battle collectively. Towards the end, it became one man to fight for the people, Israel. In the beginning, they went to battle together. In the end, the same tribe betrays Samson to live peaceably. In the middle of the book, at least, Gideon was able to gather 32000 men for war. But God showed that 22000 would leave even before the war began. However, Samuel brought the people together. There was no interference with the Philistines all the days of his life.

This is a time of divisiveness. People are being divided for various reasons. Hatredness is imbued into the hearts of people. Collective spirits are eroding day by day. This must be replaced by the spirit of love. By the spirit of friendship. By the festivals and celebrations of unity. Through the demonstrations of peace for nature and humanity. We must focus on love in our context. Our love of God and neighbor must be more localized. Relativisation of love may lead to the negation of love. Love will conquer all evil. God will be with us in our love for our brothers and sisters.

2

LEADERSHIP ROLE OF SELECTED PRE-CLASSICAL PROPHETS AND THEIR IMPLICATION FOR THE CHURCH IN INDIA TODAY

S. Duraiswamy[1]

Rev. Dr. J. A. Onesimu is the Principal of MTSC and I had the privilege to serve as the Dean of MTSC for 8 years during his tenure of leadership. It was a pleasure to work with him as he encouraged and motivated me. He is a kind and gentle man who takes decisions only after spending time in prayer. Under his able leadership, the Madras Theological College and Seminary has grown in all aspects. I thank God for giving me the opportunity to work with Dr. Onesimu. May God bless him on his 65th Birthday and may he see many more years with good health and cheer.

Introduction

Prophets in the Bible were the ones who spoke on behalf of God and they were giving leadership to the people of Israel in many instances. Prophets were charismatic figures, believed to be endowed with the divine gift of receiving messages from God and imparting them to the people. The early prophets were sometimes called "seers". They had a very good spiritual relationship with Yahweh. They could talk to God and listen to the still voice of God and

1 *Rev. S. Duraiswamy is the Director Partner Relations - Evangelical Church of India (ECI), the Bishop's Commissary, ECI Chennai Diocese. Currently he is a doctoral candidate at Sam Higginbottom University of Agriculture, Technology & Sciences (SHUATS), Allahabad.*

communicate God's word to the people of Israel with courage and boldness. Some of the pre-classical prophets like Moses, Elijah, Elisha, Ahijah, Nathan, and others played a major role in standing for justice in the Israelite society and we have many leadership qualities that we can learn from their life and ministry. An attempt has been made here in this research to understand the leadership role of three of the pre-classical prophets Moses, Elijah, and Nathan.

1. Understanding Pre-Classical Prophets

Prophets before the eighth century period are called as pre-classical prophets. These pre-classical prophets fearlessly rebuked the rulers and any kind of injustices in the society. The pre-classical prophets are referred to by four different names: "*hozeh*", "*roeh*" both meaning seer, "*ish-ha-elohim*", man of God and "*navi*" prophet. *Navi* is also the standard term for the classical prophets. The distinction or relationship between these titles is unclear. I Samuel 9:9 simply affirms that he who is called a prophet now was called a seer in the former times. Some of the pre-classical prophets like Moses, Elijah, Elisha, Ahijah, Nathan, and others played a major role in giving leadership for the Israelites and standing for justice in the Israelite society.

2. Leadership of Pre-Classical Prophets

Prophets in general, pre-classical prophets in particular exhibited leadership qualities that helped them to succeed in their ministerial journey. They were able to defend their faith and religion through their leadership abilities that are exhibited through their words and deeds. We can try to understand the leadership qualities of Moses, Nathan, and Elijah in this brief research.

2.1. Moses, the Deliverer

Moses was the one drawn from the water by Pharaoh's daughter, raised in Pharaoh's household, and who fled from all he had known in the land of Egypt to the land of Midian. We can see all these things in the first two chapters of the Book of Exodus.

However, Moses was Israel's leader who led them out of Egypt amid oppression and slavery at the hands of Pharaoh. God appears to Moses in the burning bush and explains to Him that he will bring God's people, the sons of Israel, out of Egypt (Exodus 3:10). Moses is known for then explaining to the Lord the reasons why he couldn't possibly be the leader to lead the children of Israel out of Egypt. The Lord wouldn't hear of it, and while Moses is the leader, his brother, Aaron, is the mouthpiece. There are several good lessons that we can learn from Moses' life regarding his leadership abilities.

2.1.1. Moses was Persistent

Moses continued to go before Pharaoh and persistently seek the release of the Israelites (Exodus 5). Despite the magic tricks of Pharaoh's magicians, Moses continued to make his way into Pharaoh's presence and ask for the Israelites' release. Though, Pharaoh repeatedly denied the request and made the task of brick making harder for the Israelites, Moses trusted God for what He promised – deliverance of God's people. How many times do we give up on something, even when we know the Lord promised? If the leader gives up, why shouldn't the people?

2.1.2. Moses was Patient

It is very interesting to read in the chronological Bible all the accounts of Exodus, Leviticus, Numbers, and Deuteronomy in the order that they occurred. When we read these stories in order, one thing stands out: the people complained, again, and again, and again. Seriously, if it wasn't one thing, it was another. People kept complaining for one reason or the other. As a leader, Moses was patient with the people. Granted, he had his moments of lack of patience and disbelief in the Lord, and this ultimately led to his inability to step a toe into the Promised Land (Numbers 20:8-13). He patiently stayed with the people and led them for forty years despite their complaints about the food, water, having a better life in Egypt, making a god for themselves and wanting a new leader. He patiently stayed the course to which God called him.

2.1.3. Moses was Teachable

Even though Moses led the people well, he didn't have it altogether and he learned from older, wiser people. One of those people was his father-in-law, Jethro. Jethro recognized that Moses was submerged with the disputes of the people – Moses handled all the disputes of all the Israelites (Exodus 18:13-16). Jethro saw this wasn't good – for Moses or the people – and encouraged him to delegate to able men who could help handle the disputes (Exodus 18:17-23). What Exodus 18:24 says is important, "Moses listened to his father-in-law and did all that he said." Moses could have easily told his father-in-law to leave him alone; God had appointed and chosen him as the leader of the Israelites and how dare Jethro to try to tell him how to lead. But, he didn't. He listened, discerned, considered, and applied the suggestion he had been given.

2.1.4. Moses was Faithful

Moses was faithful to the Lord and he was faithful to the people. God was always faithful to Moses, but the people weren't always faithful to him. When it would have been easy to leave the people in the desert, Moses continued to serve the Lord by serving the people. When Moses had frustrations with the people, he took them to the Lord – not the people. Numbers 11:1-9 shows us that the Israelites were complaining and took their complaints to Moses. Moses, in turn, takes the complaints of the people – as well as his own – to the Lord (Numbers 11:10-15). But, he never left the people – even amid all their complaints, their rebellion and their disloyalty. He faithfully led them in good times and bad.

2.1.5. Moses was Obedient

Though he had his moments of disobedience and disbelief, overall Moses was obedient to the Lord. Even when the people wanted to do something else, Moses was obedient to act upon what the Lord told him. In Numbers 14:1-10, we read of the reaction of the Israelites to the report that the 12 spies brought to the Israelites regarding the land of Canaan. Ten of the spies' report that people are big and there is no way to overtake them. But, two of the spies, Caleb and Joshua, told the people not to rebel but to trust in the Lord (vs. 6-10). Moses pleads before the Lord on behalf of the people (vs. 11-19) and the Lord pardons the people, but He said to Moses, "Surely all the men who have seen My glory and My signs which I performed in Egypt and the wilderness, yet have put Me to the test these ten times and have not listened to My voice, shall by no means see the land which I swore to their fathers, nor shall any of those who spurned Me see it…I, the LORD, have spoken, surely this I will do to all this evil congregation who are gathered together against Me. In this wilderness, they shall be destroyed, and there they will die" (vs. 22-3, 35).

Moses shares this news with the people and they mourn greatly (vs. 39). But, the very next morning they decide they are going to go into the land anyway, despite having sinned against the Lord. Moses, though, obediently stands his ground, "Why then are you transgressing the commandment of the LORD, when it will not succeed? Do not go up, or you will be struck down before your enemies, for the LORD is not among you. For the Amalekites and the Canaanites will be there in front of you, and you will fall by the sword, in as much as you have turned back from following the LORD. And the LORD will not be with you" (vs. 41-3). The people don't listen and they "heedlessly" tried to take the land and they are all killed at the hands of the Amalekites and the Canaanites (vs. 44-5). Moses, however, didn't go with them. He was obedient to the Lord's command rather than the people's desires.

In evaluating the leadership role of Moses, we can see highs and lows, good and bad, cooperative and noncooperative situations. But in the midst of all that he was persistent, patient, teachable, faithful and obedient. Most likely the same can be said of our leadership and lives. But, we learn from his life as he is one commended in Scripture who had faith (Hebrews 11:23-29). Moses remains as one of the models for contemporary Christians.

2.2. Nathan, the Just Prophet

Nathan was one of the pre-classical prophets who ministered to the people of Israel. Scholars are baffled over the logistics of how Nathan emerged into the position of being a prophet.[2] Some suggest that his political abilities enabled him to succeed Samuel as the next advisor.[3] While others speculate that his poetic talent ushered him into prominence. Bodner additionally asserts that biblical literature is relatively limited and consequently silent due to the lack of elaboration within the text. He is the prophet whom God sends to David to inform him that his and Bathsheba's child will die because David had Bathsheba's husband Uriah murdered. Bathsheba's next child is named Solomon, and one of three following sons is named Nathan, possibly after the prophet. Luke traces the genealogy of Jesus through this Nathan (Luke 3:31), Matthew goes through Solomon (Matthew 1:6).

Nathan's actions are defined in the books of Samuel, Kings, and Chronicles especially in 2 Samuel 7:2-17 and 12:1-25. According to 2 Samuel, he was a court prophet who lived in the time of King David. He announced to David the covenant God was making with him and he came to David to rebuke him over his committing adultery with Bathsheba while she was the wife of Uriah, the Hittite whose death the king had also arrange to hide his previous transgression (2 Samuel 11-12). Nathan wrote histories of the reigns of David and Solomon and was also involved in the music of the temple. We will try to understand a few insights from the leadership role of Nathan, the prophet.

2.2.1. Nathans Ability to be Open

Bodner's observation points toward some critical elements of the leadership of Nathan. First, the notion of Nathan being "rebuked for carelessly encouraging David" in II Samuel chapter seven, possibly points toward this prophet's ability to be open. This facet of openness or transparency can be a catalyst to organizational trust. This intangible element, according to Covey, effortlessly increase the speed (effectiveness) of an entity and lower overall cost. We could assert that the ability to be open to receive correction from God is not only a sign of wisdom (Pro 3:11-12) but a critical element in decision making (Pro 3:6).

2.2.2. Removal of Barriers

Nathan demonstrated the leadership mannerism of the "removal of barriers." This concept can be inclusive of addressing and implementing new systems

---

2 P. Kyle McCarter, "II Samuel: A New Translation with Introduction, Notes, and Commentary," in *The Anchor Bible* (New York: Doubleday, 1984), 210-31.

3 Keith Bodner, "Nathan: Prophet, Politician and Novelist," Journal for the Study of the Old Testament (2001), 43-54.

into an organization for the purposes of process improvement. To reiterate, Bodner suggests that "Nathan receives instructions that are minutely specific—even to the point whereby indirect discourse is employed." We would contend that such specific discourse from God to Nathan was a "divine" attempt to implement a system (a word from the Lord not an opinionate utterance from the prophet) that would proactively debunk barriers that could potentially hinder organizational productivity.

2.2.3. Encouragement of Creativity

The third leadership trait of Nathan is the encouragement of creativity. According to Merriam-Webster's Dictionary, creativity can be defined as, "the quality of being creative or the ability to create." According to Bodner's exegesis, "the prophet is given insight into the future promises to David's house." One could contend that such an insight enabled both David and Nathan to recast a vision large enough for generations yet to come, to grow. As such, according to Yukl, this construct is essential to corporations if they are to lead followers through change.[4]

In analyzing the leadership of Nathan, we can understand that he was one of the courageous prophets who could boldly talk to the King and remind him of his mistake. He demonstrated his spiritual leadership by pointing out the sin committed by the king and encouraging him to restore his broken relationship with God. Our country needs leaders like Nathan who not only pinpoint the mistakes of others but also pave a way for them to repent and reconcile with God and men.

2.3. Elijah, the Defender of Yahwism

In the biblical records, we read that Elijah confronted the violent killing of the prophets of Yahweh initiated by Jezebel. He also challenged Baalism and the prophets of Baal at Mount Carmel and asked the people to choose either Yahweh or Baal for worship. Elijah's service lay in the fact that he clarified the distinctiveness of Yahwism and Baalism and thereby prevented the gradual extinction of Yahwism through absorption into Baalism. Elijah's response to Baalism was based on the custom and law of his day. Among his generation, he stood for his faith and belief and challenged the violent attitude of Baalist followers.

The first chapter of the Elijah narrative (1 Kings 17) is a portrait of prophetic utopia. Elijah appears from an unknown location[5] and with no parents. Other than the need to eat, there seems to be little that is human

4 Gary Yukl, Leadership in Organizations (Upper Saddle River, NJ: Prentice Hall, 2002).

5 The only mention of Tishbe is in 1 Kings 17:1. James T. Dennison says that Elijah hailed from Tishbe and sojourned in Gilead. James T. Dennison, "Elijah the Tishbite: A note on I kings 17:1," *WTJ* 41/1 (Fall, 1978): 126.

about him.[6] Neil Glover says that the narrative of Elijah is scattered with the symptoms of a life that is dew, rain, bread, meat, oil, and water.[7] He is a prophet who "stands before the Lord." Elijah speaks without the need for divine warrant or authentication. He establishes no credentials for himself, there are no miraculous birth narratives, no battles won and no patriarchal heritage. He is simply the man who speaks for Yahweh. R. R. Wilson has suggested that Elijah was throughout his life a "peripheral prophet" attempting to reform the central cult.[8] Further, Steven L. McKenzie says that Elijah is the only pre-exilic prophet to call himself "the servant of Yahweh" (1 Kings 18:36).[9]

These things help us to understand that prophet Elijah is one of the great personalities of the Old Testament. In the Jewish expectation, it was believed that he would return to herald the messianic age[10] and we know that in New Testament times there were some who asked whether Jesus was Elijah.[11] In the story of the transfiguration of Jesus, Moses and Elijah appeared on the mountain with Jesus.[12] So, Elijah was a charismatic figure who stood for the faith of Yahweh and confronted the powers that worked against his monotheistic belief.

2.3.1. Commitment to Defend Religion

When Ahab married Jezebel, he did not restrict her in the worship of her native gods, rather he made a provision for her to worship her god in the land of Israel.[13] Jezebel was not contended with the worship of *Melqart* in Israel but interested in spreading her religion (worship of Baal *Melqart*) in the land of Israel. To fulfill her agenda, she killed many prophets of Yahweh and she also had some four hundred prophets of Asherah who ate at her table. So, Jezebel's character shows that she was an active proponent of her faith. On the other hand, Elijah has not been portrayed as interested in spreading Yahwistic religion in Phoenicia or other places. He was interested in defending his religion and his faith and not spreading his religion and his faith. Here we can find that Elijah

---

6 cf. I Kings 17:6, 11.

7 Dew and rain in 1 Kings 17:1, bread and meat in 17:7, meal and oil in 17:16, bread and water in 18:4 and grass and water in 18:5. Neil Glover, "Elijah verses the narrative of Elijah: The contest between the prophet and the word," *JSOT* 30/4 (June, 2006), 451.

8 R. R. Wilson, *Prophecy and Society in Ancient Israel* (Philadelphia: Fortress Press, 1980), 206.

9 Steven L. McKenzie, *The Trouble with Kings: The Composition of the Book of Kings in the Deuteronomistic History* (New York: Leiden, 1991), 86.

10 Mal 4:5; cf. Sir 48:1ff; Mt.11:14, 17:10ff.; Mk 6:15, 9:11ff.; Lk 9:8; Jn 1:21.

11 Mt 16:14; Mk 8:28; Lk 9:19.

12 Mt 17:3; Mk 9:4; Lk 9:30.

13 cf. 1 Kings 16:32.

did not want to impose or spread his monotheistic faith but he wanted to only safeguard his religious rights.

2.3.2. Courage to Confront the King

The context of 1 Kings 18 reveals that King Ahab and Jezebel were searching for Elijah because they considered that the drought in the land was because of Elijah and his prophecy. Moreover, this is the time, when Jezebel killed many prophets of Yahweh (1 Kings 18:4,13). During this period when violence against Yahweh prophets was high, Elijah appeared boldly and alone confronts the king. This shows that Elijah was risking his life and had the courage to point out the mistake of the king. Elijah's courage can also be manifested when he stands alone on Mount Carmel against four hundred and fifty prophets of Baal (1 Kings 18:22).

2.3.3. Builds a Platform for People to Decide who is God

Elijah, as Yahweh's prophet is not imposing any of his religious ideas on the people, rather he gives a call for the people to decide who is god through a contest, Yahweh or Baal. He also lays down the rules and regulations of the contest that is "God who answers by fire is God." At Mount Carmel, Elijah was very active until the end of the contest. Here Elijah builds a platform for the people to decide who their God is based on the outcome of the contest. After Yahweh answered through the fire, we see that people themselves proclaim "Yahweh is God."[14] This is not initiated by Elijah. It is people who had the choice to decide their God but Elijah builds a platform for the people to take decisions.

2.3.4. Aggression to Protect Yahweh Prophets

During the period of Elijah, the followers of Yahweh had decreased drastically and violence was used against Yahwistic prophets. Many prophets of Yahweh were killed and few who escaped went into hiding. During this period of violence, Elijah is using violence to respond to violence according to the practice of his day. This we can see when he kills the prophets of Baal after the contest at Mount Carmel (1 Kings 18:40). This shows the aggression of Elijah to protect Yahweh's prophets and his religion during his time.

2.3.5. Obligation to the Welfare of the Nation

Elijah risks his life and appears before Ahab for the welfare of his nation. There was a severe drought in the land and human beings and animals were suffering without food and water. If Elijah had been selfish, he could have not appeared before Ahab, because God had miraculously provided food, meat,

14 cf. 1 Kings 18:39.

and water for Elijah (1 Kings 17:6). Even though his basic needs are met, he was concerned about the entire nation and for their wellbeing. If Elijah's interest is to show who is God, he should have limited his role after the contest or after killing the Baal prophets. But he didn't do that. He goes beyond that and prays to God to send rain to end the drought in the land. This concern can also be witnessed by his persistent prayer for rain on the land. He asks his servant to go and watch outside seven times. It shows how committed Elijah was to the welfare of the nation and not simply interested in proving who is God or revenging Jezebel.

We can see that Elijah is portrayed as the defendant of Yahwism and the champion of Yahweh. Elijah confronted the violence of Jezebel and challenged the prophets of Baal to take a decision through a contest.

3. Pre-Classical Prophets Leadership Message for the Contemporary Indian Context

3.1. Leadership is in Speaking the Truth for the Powerless and Discriminated

Different scholars utilized to define the phrase "speaking truth" to "power". Powell refers to this concept as not being "afraid to challenge the pros, even in their own backyard." Whereas, Chaleff frames this process simply as *the courage to challenge*. Chaleff further explains that here one "gives voice to the discomfort they feel when the behaviors or policies of the leader or group conflict with their sense of what is right. They are willing to stand up, to stand out, to risk rejection, to initiate conflict to examine the actions of the leader and group when appropriate."

At the same time, Yulk states that "the term power is usually used to describe the absolute capacity of an individual agent to influence the behaviour or attitudes of one or more designated target persons at a given point in time." Hence, for the purposes of this article, the term *speaking truth to power* refers to a person not being afraid to challenge those agents that impact the behaviour or attitudes of one or more designated target persons at a given point in time. Both Nathan and Elijah were committed to speaking the truth for the powerless and discriminated against. So, our leaders need to develop an attitude to stand for establishing truth and seek justice for the poor and downtrodden in society.

3.2. Leadership is a Courageous Approach to Problematic Power

Approaching a powerful person with leadership issues can sometimes invoke creative tension. Scott amplifies this point in writing, "90 percent of workers are afraid to confront the boss. Getting fired isn't the biggest concern. Instead, people worry about being labeled troublemakers, being perceived as not being team players, suffering salary loss or career derailment or damaging future relations with the boss."[15]

One must find equal footing with the leader if the "approach" is to be received and such stereotypes defused. I define "*approach*" as the methodology in which a follower comes into the presence of a leader for the expressed purposes of speaking truth to power. Followers usually cannot match up to a leader's external qualities, such as the trappings of formal power, and must find their equal footing on intellectual, spiritual or moral ground. All the three prophets, Moses, Nathan, and Elijah were courageous in their approach of problematic power. These days we don't see leaders who are courageous to rebuke people in power. Biblically, a good leader should be courageous enough to stand for justice and promoting equality among the people of our land irrespective of caste, class, and creed.

3.3. Leadership is Creating an Atmosphere for Transformation

When we try to understand the story of Nathan and David, it unfolds the fourfold process; that is to enable the leader to see that he is the source of the problem, specifically identifying his errors, projecting the consequences of poor decision making, and doing it privately helped David to transform in his life. Verse 13 indicates that after this encounter, "David said to Nathan, 'I have sinned against the LORD.' Transformation occurs most readily in an atmosphere of 'tough love'—a genuine gratitude for the person and a steadfast attitude against the behaviours that are harmful to the person and the organization.

We could assert that the ultimate goal of a person who dares to speak truth to power is not to destroy the person but rather to usher them to a place within themselves to want to change. The fruit of such a broken state is inclusive of taking personal responsibility, changing one's thinking, remaining teachable, righting wrongs, and becoming accountable to someone else. This fruit can flourish within a garden that's cultivated by tough love. This was the case with David upon being challenged by Nathan; the king yielded the fruit of repentance and consequently wrote Psalm 51 as evidence to this. So, we need to understand that leadership is not power and position. But a good leader should create an atmosphere for transformation for his subordinates if they go wrong at any point in their lives. Leader should take initiative to restore relationships and create an atmosphere for transformation.

---

15 Nancy R. Scott, "How to Confront the Boss and Win," Nancy Rathbun Scott, http://www.nancyscott.com/page50/page33/page33.html

3

THE REINTRODUCTION OF THE HISTORY AND THEOLOGY OF THE FOURFOLD GOSPEL

Bill Vermillian[1]

A paper presented in honor of Rev. Dr. J. A. David Onesimu, the author of Constructing Dalit Theology for Dalit Liberation; Dr. Ambedkar's Critique Towards Christian Dalit Liberation, the Principal of the MTSC and the Professor of Christian Theology in his 65th Birthday in the year 2020. Given Dr. Onesimu's long and vibrant history with Korea and in keeping with the topic of Reconstructing Theology, I will focus this paper on the Fourfold Gospel which unfortunately was not part of the legacy passed along from OMS to ECI until recently. It is, however, part of the warp and woof of early OMS and still found strongly in the Korean Evangelical Holiness Church.[2] *The reintroduction of the history and theology of the Fourfold Gospel will be*

---

1 *Rev. Dr. William H Vermillion, PhD is a Team Member, and the Co-coordinator of Higher Theological Education of the Theological Leadership Education and Development (TLEAD), One Mission Society(OMS), USA.*

2 The Korean Holiness Church originated as an evangelical holiness movement through indigenous work and the American holiness mission. From its inception, the Korean Holiness Church believed that its primary task was not only to promote "scriptural holiness," as John Wesley and primitive Methodism had preached, but also to preach the "fourfold gospel," which may be summarized as regeneration, sanctification, divine healing, and the premillennial second coming of Christ. *The Rise of the Korean Holiness Church in Relation to the American Holiness Movement* argues that the theological foundation of the Korean Holiness Church can best be understood by analyzing the fourfold gospel in the history of the Korean Holiness Church and its internationally connected holiness movement. The brief, though rich, biographical accounts of the Korean Christians and

a significant contribution to reconstructing theology in a scripturally faithful positive Christ-honoring way.

Introduction

This study of the Fourfold Gospel will provide a definition of the Fourfold Gospel, examine its historical roots and its theological content. Practical application will be identified with a close focus on the influence on Oriental Missionary Society, now One Mission Society hereafter referenced as OMS. First, though it is crucial to clear up a misunderstanding when one uses the term fourfold gospel or googles it. The Fourfold Gospel is not to be confused with a study of the four Gospels of our Lord Jesus Christ which in itself is a very commendable study nor confused with a study of a denomination like the Foursquare. While both the Foursquare and the Christian and Missionary Alliances use the Fourfold Gospel in their theology, this paper will not directly study either of them or the permutations of these denominations.

Definition of the Fourfold Gospel

It is simply expressed as a summary of the basic teachings of the Bible: Salvation, Sanctification, Healing and the Lordship of Jesus Christ especially referencing His second coming. Another way of phrasing or presenting the Fourfold Gospel is Jesus is Savior, Jesus is Sanctifier, Jesus is Healer and Jesus is Lord and coming King. When presented in this manner one can easily see the Fourfold Gospel is indeed the Good News about Jesus. He receives the preeminence. He is the initiator of my relationship with God; the one who receives my consecrated life and makes me holy, Jesus is the one who heals me physically emotionally and spiritually, and Jesus is the one to whom all my allegiance is due as I serve Him in expectation of His return.

History of the Fourfold Gospel

As one can observe from the definition it is evident that the Fourfold Gospel is a way to look at the believer's relationship with Jesus and His actions on

---

American and British Missionaries woven into this book finally give these great men and women their due.

In deference to Dayton's seminal work, Theological Roots of Pentecostalism (1987), the author traces the "fourfold gospel" from its American inception in A. B. Simpson to one of its international expressions in the Korean Holiness Church (KHC). In doing so, Choi offers a thick description of how this message was transposed from Simpson to the American Holiness movement, particularly as manifested in Martin Wells Knapp, then to Charles Cowman, the Tokyo Bible Institute and the Oriental Missionary Society (OMS), and finally to KHC. The novelty of this work lays not so much in Choi's primary objective to recover the identity of KHC (which she does not discuss in great detail anyway) but in her synthesis of how Simpson's model lay the theological foundations of KHC, which, we are informed, constitutes about 25 percent of Korean Christians.

behalf of the believer. It presents a simple way of clearly identifying the basic elements of Jesus' ministry. As such one can say the seed of the Fourfold Gospel are presented in the scriptures. These manifestations of Jesus' ministry were discussed, taught and preached by the early church Fathers but not labeled as the Fourfold Gospel. Indeed, throughout the next centuries, these aspects of Jesus' life continued to be preached and taught but again without that label of Fourfold Gospel. Even within the reformers' emphasis on the five Solas: Sola Scriptura, Sola Gratia, Sola Fides, Sola Christus, and Soli Deo Gloria, one can easily see the elements of the Fourfold Gospel. John Wesley's writing, teaching, and preaching conveyed all these elements too but he never formulated them as the Fourfold Gospel.[3] In a recently published work by Dr. William Purinton, he elaborates on the development of the Fourfold Gospel: While we continue to view the last two decades of the nineteenth century as evangelical prolegomena for the twentieth century, one essential theological formulation rises to the forefront: The Fourfold Gospel. This topic is not well-known by all Christians, and only a minority of evangelicals are even familiar with the term "fourfold gospel." We will be using "fourfold gospel" to mean the four cardinal teachings of Christ as Savior, Sanctifier, Healer, and Coming King. These pillars were as early as Irenaeus (*c.*130-*c.*200) in relation to the four canonical New Testament gospels: Matthew, Mark, Luke, and John.

In broader terms, Donald Dayton describes these four "themes of the 'four-fold gospel' [as being] so pervasive in late nineteenth-century evangelicalism that one could almost speak of them as defining and indicating the boundaries of that subculture."[4] Dayton's claim should be taken seriously and will be the step upon which we stand to move to the next claim: That as evangelicalism reaches back through the centuries beyond the nineteenth and eighteenth centuries to the sixteenth-century Reformation, so the teachings of the Fourfold Gospel can be identified in antecedent theological formulations. Further, it will be noted that we can fit the fourfold Gospel within Christology—a broader theological category that includes Christ's person and work.

In some ways, the fourfold gospel is like the Apostles' Creed; it's not written word-for-word in the Bible, but flows entirely from the Bible, expressing clearly and powerfully what the whole Bible teaches. The end of the nineteenth century marked a big shift in the Wesleyan-Holiness movement when people began to change their millennial views from "post-millennial" to "pre-millennial." This may sound like a mere technicality, but the change to "pre" signaled a shift from trusting human-inspired visions and dreams to

3 *The Rise of the Korean Holiness Church in Relation to the American Holiness Movement*, 2008, Meesaeng Choi for more details.

4 Donald W. Dayton, "The Four-Fold Gospel: Key to Trans-Pacific Continuities," in *From the Margins: A Celebration of the Theological Work of Donald W. Dayton*, ed. Christian T. Collins Winn (Eugene, OR: Pickwick Publications, 2007), 362.

placing faith solidly in His Word that promised Pentecostal visions and dreams (Acts 2:17).

In the 1890s, holiness Christians began taking the Great Commission (Matthew 28:19-20) seriously by looking at the fields "white for harvest" (John 4:35, NKJV); they were at the same time keeping an eye on the eschatological clock. One verse that maintained this focus was Matthew 24:14: "And this gospel of the kingdom will be preached in the whole world as a testimony to all nations, and then the end will come" (NIV). Waiting for the Second Coming did not mean hiding in a monastic cave, praying and fasting until his return; it meant going to the nations and preaching to bring about the end. For many true believers, it was now the "eleventh hour;" time was running out and the mission remained to bring in the harvest from the farthest nations. Christ told his disciples that no one, not even himself as the Son of God, knew the exact hour when the Lord would return, but that we could all prepare for that time. Indeed, getting ready for the second coming became a theme of the holiness movement as it shifted from the nineteenth century to the twentieth century. The urgency of Christ's second coming became vivid to the point of seeming imminent. Since Christ could return any day, evangelicals were determined to train workers for the end-time harvest fields. Thus shows the connection between the first item (Savior, Regeneration) with the final one (Returning King, Second Coming).

As the fourfold gospel is in position, the church can survey means and ways of accomplishing the Great Commission to bring revival. For the radical holiness/evangelical, looking up meant understanding the events of the past simply as preparation for our current mission, asking questions such as: Where is our vision today? What is the focus of our affections? Are you so much in love with the Lord that your gaze is upon Him alone, the bride looking for her bridegroom? Now, we move to the second item: holiness/sanctification.

One of the New Testament texts on "holiness" is 1 Peter 1:13-16. It tells us we are to "be holy." It might appear as a common greeting in English, like: "Be nice" or "be happy." But "Be Holy" is a command, in the imperative mood. You *must* be holy, holy or else. William Baxter Godbey (1833-1920), an evangelical Methodist, wrote "*Holiness or Hell?*"[5] Hebrews 12:14 states clearly that "without holiness, no one will see the Lord." Not only is holiness a "must do," or a command, but it is also for all Christians, including all evangelicals.

We continue the fourfold gospel with the third point: Healing. Right after Jesus is tempted in the desert, he emerges with a message and a ministry. Matthew 4:23 outlines the full ministry of Jesus Christ. "Jesus went throughout Galilee, teaching in their synagogues, proclaiming the good news of the

5 W. B. Godbey, *Holiness or Hell?* (Atlanta: Foote & Davies, 1893).

kingdom, and healing every disease and sickness among the people" (NIV). Very simply, his ministry was preaching, teaching, and healing. The rules for his kingdom are set up in Matthew 5-7, called the Sermon on the Mount. Now that the new standards are announced, he begins putting them into practice. Jesus begins to display his authority, to take back from Satan, to demonstrate his power to rule over all the person: the body, soul, and spirit. He pushes back to sin, Satan, and sickness to bring healing and wholeness to hurting people. We will be looking at the healing ministry of Jesus more closely below in Matthew 8.

But this is not just a story about what happened 2,000 years ago; it is what we believe today and must also practice in our lives. Hebrews 13:8 says very clearly, "Jesus Christ is the same yesterday and today and forever." He hasn't changed, and his word remains true forever. We can witness the same Jesus, the Savior, Sanctifier, and the Healer, as he ministers through us as his body. We can say with confidence today in churches that affirm the truth of his word and the power of the Spirit, "Jesus the Healer is in the house today." Is a physician available for all of us: spirit, soul, and body? Yes; his name is Jesus.

First, Christ heals our bodies. Matthew 8 begins with healing. A man came to Jesus with leprosy. Jesus touched the unclean man, the kind you are not supposed to touch. Next, a centurion came to Jesus. His servant was sick at home. Jesus was ready to go there, but the centurion stopped him, saying, "Lord, I do not deserve to have you come under my roof. But just say the word, and my servant will be healed" (8:8). The third healing in Matthew 8happens when Jesus goes to Peter's house: "He saw Peter's mother-in-law lying in bed with a fever" (8:14). Already three healings have happened in Christ's ministry, within only 15 verses.

Today, in thinking of Christ the healer, three groups of people appear. First, the nonbelievers among Christian liberalism who affirm neither the miracles of healing nor the historical record of the Bible or in the world today. Second, the people who affirm the historical record of the miracles in the past but believe these ceased a long time ago, either with the completion of the New Testament or the death of the last apostle. We call this group cessationists. Third, are the people who believe all the miracles recorded in the Bible (Old and New Testaments) and hold to the reality of miracles today. We call this group fourfold gospel believers, full gospel, or even whole gospel believers.

After healing of bodies comes the healing of spirits and souls. 1 Thessalonians 5:23 describes God's will for our entire sanctification. His will is also for our total healing. Many people today suffer from mental and spiritual illnesses. Jesus was able to drive out evil spirits and heal with his word. In the twenty-first century, people, at least those people in parts of the world where such care is available and affordable, find bodily healing in medical science. But the real challenge for the church today remains the ministry of healing to the spirits and souls of hurting people in a broken world. The church today needs to minister divine healing to the whole person, with a renewed emphasis on soul healing. Although soul or mental/emotional healing is not something talked about much in the church or in Christian colleges, it has always been part of divine healing, because Christ continues to make whole the entire person-- to heal bodies, souls, and spirits.

We conclude the fourfold gospel with the fourth point: Second Coming. In our earlier discussion about radical holiness, we looked at the shift from "postmillennial" to "premillennial" views of Christ's Second Coming. Within radical holiness (and radical evangelicalism) in North America, that shift birthed a fervency in world mission. Indeed, the fourfold gospel allows us to look at the Second Coming from the Lord's perspective, hearing again his words in Matthew 24-25. By reminding ourselves of these words, we will become ready to make an important switch, to view the Second Coming as a matter of priority, as the first event that will lead to all events, rather than the last event that ends everything.[6] So, the question is then raised who first identified the Fourfold Gospel as a theological construct and promoted the concept.

That honor goes to A. B. Simpson—a man of vision and faith. A brief history of this man will be helpful for this study. Albert Benjamin Simpson was the founder of The Christian and Missionary Alliance and was born December 15, 1843, in Bayview, Prince Edward Island, Canada. At an early age, he felt the call of God on his life to preach and later experienced a dramatic conversion to faith in Jesus Christ. After discovering a line in Walter Marshall's Gospel Mystery of Sanctification, "The first good work you will ever perform is to believe in the Lord Jesus Christ," Simpson committed his life to "Jesus Only"- the anthem that also ignited an unquenchable passion in his heart to reach the lost.

Simpson was educated in Presbyterian schools and pastored Presbyterian churches in Hamilton, Ontario, the Chestnut Street Presbyterian Church in Louisville, Kentucky, and later the Thirteenth Street Presbyterian Church in New York City (NYC). His desire to minister to the flood of immigrants pouring into NYC met with great opposition from the leadership of his church. He resigned his prestigious pastorate in 1882 and set out to establish the Gospel Tabernacle, a church in the heart of the city, where all—the poor, homeless, sick, and displaced—would be welcome. By 1883, a formal program was in place and ministers and missionaries were being trained in a multi-cultural context. (This school was the beginning of Nyack College and Alliance

6 Transpacific Evangelicalism in the Twentieth Century: Revival and Evangelism in America and Korea by William T. Purinton © 2019 by William T. Purinton Published by OMS, 2020, 60-64.

Theological Seminary). In 1889, Simpson and his church family moved into their new home at the corner of 44th St. and 8th Av. called the New York Tabernacle. This became the base not only of his ministry of evangelism in the city but also of his growing work of worldwide missions.

Single-mindedly focused on this burden, Simpson began assembling like-minded people with a passion for taking the Gospel to the ends of the earth. He proceeded to hold evangelistic meetings on Sunday afternoons. These gatherings, which then grew to camp meetings and revivals in other locations along the East coast, were essentially the beginnings of The Christian and Missionary Alliance—a society fully devoted to experiencing the "deeper life" in Christ and completing the Great Commission (Matthew 28:18-20). In his 1890 book, *A Larger Christian Life*, Simpson discussed his vision for the church:

He is showing us the plan for a Christian church that is much more than an association of congenial friends to listen once a week to an intellectual discourse and musical entertainment and carry on by proxy a mechanism of Christian work; but rather a church that can be at once the mother and home of every form of help and blessing which Jesus came to give to lost and suffering men, the birthplace and the home of souls, the fountain of healing and cleansing, the sheltering home for the orphan and distressed, the school for the culture and training of God's children, the armory where they are equipped for the battle of the Lord and the army which fights those battles in His name. Such a center of population in this sad and sinful world![7]

Having also personally experienced miraculous physical healing, Simpson would go on to coin the foundation of the Alliance's doctrine. The Fourfold Gospel: Christ our Savior, Sanctifier, Healer, and Coming King. Although such teaching isolated him (and the C&MA) from the mainline churches that either did not emphasize or outright rejected healing, Simpson's uncompromising trust in the Word and power of God kept him steadily forging ahead of his times without criticism or rancor with those who disagreed. Simpson considered the expression "Fourfold Gospel a gift from God to him. He told his New York parishioners, "I know not why the term 'Fourfold Gospel' should have been suggested by the Holy Spirit, but it seems to have been taken up all over the land...". The *Fourfold Gospel* was originally a series of sermons preached in 1887 in New York, published as *The Fourfold Gospel* within *Tabernacle Sermons,* Volume 5. Simpson would later (1891) write an article titled "Fourfold Unity," where he compared the Fourfold Gospel to music sung in four parts: "[T]the title of a book written by A. B. Simpson in 1890. But he was the first to admit that he did not invent it. You could say that

---

7 *A Larger Christian Life*, Published by the Christian Alliance Publishing Co. 692 Eighth Avenue, New York 1890, by Rev. A. B. Simpson.

Simpson just wove the rich threads together into one beautiful tapestry, or he was like a collector who arranges multiple treasures together in a single room."

One of the reasons for its popularity was the book he wrote titled *The Fourfold Gospel*. Here, A. B. Simpson clearly explicated the Fourfold Gospel by following a careful outline of I. Christ Our Saviour II. Christ Our Sanctifier III. Christ Our Healer IV. Christ Our Coming Lord V. The Walk with God VI. Kept. For Simpson, the fourfold Gospel was to encourage the believer to engage in a daily walk with the Lord and then receiving the assurance of being kept. It is helpful to note the comments by Rev. Frederic Senft in his introduction to the 1890 volume.[8]

The title of this little volume, "The FourFold Gospel," has been a familiar phrase to thousands of God's children during the past forty years. Not that the truths contained in the statement were unknown before, but the grouping of them in this form was given to Dr. A. B. Simpson after he had happily experienced the fulness of the Gospel in his own life.

This does not mean that the blessings of the Gospel are limited exclusively to four-Christ our Saviour, Christ our Sanctifier, Christ our Healer, and Christ our Coming Lord. In one sense it is a manifold Gospel with countless blessings and ever deeper and richer experiences of God's grace and love. "But there are four messages in the Gospel," says the author, "which sum up in a very complete way the blessings which Christ has to offer us and which it is especially important that Christians should emphasize today." **These constitute four great pillars in the temple of truth**. (bolded by this writer)

Note the order of these great truths. First things first-Christ our Saviour. Rightly, the first has to do with the soul, lost through sin and estrangement from God, but "made nigh by the blood of Christ." It is no small thing to be saved-justified, forgiven, born again. This foundation truth needs to be reiterated in these days when sin is minimized or explained away, and the atonement of Jesus Christ is rejected by many. The same is true of Sanctification-a word and experience misunderstood and evaded by many believers. It marks a definite and distinct crisis in the history of a soul. The unfolding of these four phases of the Gospel will be made fascinatingly clear to the reader of this book. It is well worthy of thoughtful and prayerful study, and best of all of appropriating the full-orbed message-the all-sufficient Christ for spirit, soul, and body.

Addressing an audience in London many years ago, Dr. Simpson related the following experiences which marked three great epochs in his life: "Some twenty-seven years ago, I foundered for ten months. in the waters of despondency, and I got out of them just by believing in Jesus as my Saviour.

8 Rev. A. B. Simpson, D.D. With An Introduction By Rev. Frederic H. Senft, D.D. Christian Publications Inc. Third and Reily Streets, Harrisburg, Pa. 1890.

About twelve years ago I got into another deep experience of conviction, and I got out of that by believing in Jesus as my Sanctifier. After years of teaching and waiting on Him, the Lord Jesus Christ showed me four years ago that it was His blessed will to be my complete Saviour for body as well as soul."

One of our evangelists in the earlier years of the work used hundreds of them in that way with marked results.[9] The message is simple, Scriptural, and satisfying. The Church needs it as an antidote to error and apostasy, a sure remedy for failure, an answer to the cry of hungry hearts, a source of health for the body and an inspiration to complete the witness and bring back the King.[10]

This Fourfold Gospel had a tremendous influence on Charles Cowman and Juji Nakada and was the theological foundation of the Oriental Missionary Society. The Fourfold Gospel was actively taught during the first 40 years of the Society in Japan. China, Korea and still forms the foundation of the Statement of Faith of One Mission Society.[11]

Simpson's influence went on to move the hearts of missionaries, pastors, and people of all denominations towards spreading the gospel in all lands. Simpson actively pastored until 1918 and went to be with his Savior in October of 1919.

Simpson's distinctiveness on healing was mainly threefold. First, he stressed that healing was rooted in the atonement: Redemption finds its center in the cross of our Lord Jesus Christ. There we must look for the fundamental principle of divine healing, which rests on Jesus' atoning sacrifice. This necessarily follows from the first principle we have stated: If sickness is the result of the fall, it must be included in the atonement of Christ, which reaches as far as the curse is found. (qtd. in Graf 300).

---

9 Pastor Mar Ocampo, the President of Faith Evangelical Church of the Philippines (FECPI), in a personal interview on Saturday January 25, 2020 testified on how he was using the fourfold Gospel in local church revivals. He had learned about the Fourfold Gospel in the 2019 Wesleyan Holiness Summer Study Program at Seoul Theological University under the auspices of OMS-Korea, The Institute for the Study of Modern Christianity and the Missions Department of Korean Evangelical Holiness Church (KEHC). He noted the presentation of the fourfold gospel was easily understood by the people in the church. It enabled them to quickly comprehend and respond to these great truths and experience personal and societal transformation.

10 To meet the need of today's broken world, the WHCJ must renew its understandings and attitudes toward holistic healing by reconsidering the healing community, the means of healing grace, the causes of sins, and the fourfold gospel as a framework of the entire Christian life, Shinobu Yamazaki.

11 The omission of the Fourfold Gospel from OMS's foundational teaching requires more exploration. It was strongly presented by Cowman and Erny and their national partners in Japan, China (after the war this moved to Taiwan) and Korea. However, it was never presented in India or Indonesia or the Philippines. Unfortunately, this lack of knowledge and of promotion of the Fourfold Gospel is still true with many OMS missionaries.

Through an exegesis of Isaiah 53:5, he found four aspects in relation to atonement: Christ died (1) for human's transgressions or actual sins, (2) for human iniquities, (3) for the curse and consciousness of sin, and (4) for bodily healing through the agony on the cross (Hardesty 92). Second, Simpson maintained that "divine healing is not medical healing. It does not come to us through medicines, nor is it God's special blessing on remedies and means" (Gospel of Healing 47). Unlike Wesley, he believed that God did not use medicine to heal but gave people healing grace in the name of Jesus. He was sure that God has provided healing in the atonement (Graf 318). Third, Simpson stressed that a person should seek and receive the grace of sanctification before asking for healing; thus, he believed that Christians must receive the grace of the new birth before sanctification, and they must also receive the grace of sanctification before the grace of divine healing. He asserts, "Just as a person maintained a holy life by remaining entirely consecrated to God, so a person remained healthy by daily dependence on God's healing grace" (qtd. in Thompson 79).

For Simpson, divine healing was direct physical healing apart from medicine, but since he required the person to be sanctified or at least have a clear new birth experience before receiving healing grace, sanctification was a crucial element in healing. He did not describe sanctification as spiritual healing like Wesley, but he did sense that healing must be holistic.

In healing services, Simpson usually allowed others to pray for healing so that people would not assume healing was dependent on a particular act or a particular person (Hardesty 44). His healing ministry did not rely on anyone who had the gifts of healings; rather, anyone having faith in and a thirst for healing could pray for healing. A. J. Gordon, a close colleague of Simpson, shared the same teaching on divine healing. As Donald W. Dayton observes, "He clearly parallels sanctification and healing as the two-fold work of the Spirit whose benefits may be at least partially received in this life" (129).[12]

This brief look at A. B. Simpson's life provides some practical insight for understanding the application of the Fourfold Gospel. In his promotion and proclamation of Fourfold Gospel, he saw it as a providing a theological construct for training leaders for ministry in cross-cultural situation; as presenting a necessary foundation for accomplishing his vision for the lost that would lead to worldwide evangelism for all peoples; this was based on an uncompromising trust in the authority of God's word and an attitude of grace towards those who disagreed with his fourfold emphasis.

This Fourfold Gospel had a tremendous influence on Charles Cowman, Ernest A. Kilbourne, and Juji Nakada and was the theological foundation of the

12 Holistic Healing Ministry: The Current Understandings And Attitudes of Clergy And Laity of Wesleyan Holiness Churches of Japan, Shinobu Yamazaki, 2004 DMin Dissertation.

Oriental Missionary Society. The Fourfold Gospel was actively taught during the first 40 years of the Society in Japan. China, Korea and still forms the foundation of the Statement of Faith of One Mission Society.[13] This study will now turn its focus to the OMS founders and their background and utilization of the Fourfold Gospel.

Charles Cowman was born on March 13, 1868, in Illinois, and died on September 25, 1924, in California. During his 56 years of life, Charles was used by God to accomplish many amazing things for the Kingdom of God. How did God work? Let us see some of the processes and crises in his life. Charles was an intelligent hard working youth who at the age of 15, accepted a summer job working as a telegraph operator. He did so well that he chose not to return to school. With quick advancements, Charles was able to marry his childhood friend, Lettie Burd in 1889. When Lettie was very ill, Charles had prayed to God for her healing and had promised God that he would serve God. But when she became well, he forgot his vow to serve God, but God did not Charles' promise. In 1893 Lettie experienced conversion and one-month later Charles was profoundly converted. This conversion changed, transformed him into a vibrant witness for God and even a better worker. Serving Jesus was a first priority of his thoughts, words, and life. Within a short period of time, 75 people have come to Jesus in the Telegraph office. The first one was Ernest A. Kilbourne who was a co-founder of OMS. These converted co-workers formed The Telegraphers' Mission Band which sent letters explaining the Gospel to telegraphers all over the United States, Great Britain, and Australia.

In the late 1890s, Charles met and befriended Juji Nakaka at his church, Grace Methodist Episcopal Church. Charles and E. A. were students with Juji at Moody Bible Institute. While attending Moody Church, they heard A.B. Simpson preach. As he preached, his appeal moved them to give sacrificially for missions and awakened the concept of the Fourfold Gospel. On August 11, 1900, Charles received a distinct impression that he was called to work as a missionary in Japan.[14]

When Juji returned to Japan the Telegraphers' Mission Band financially supporting him. Charles experienced a clear call from God on August 11, 1900. So, Charles and Lettie left America on February 1, 1901, to serve as missionaries in Japan. They worked with Nakada and shared a mutual dream of starting a Bible training institute. "The aim of the institute would not be to produce classical scholars, but young men and women who could handle their

13 One Mission Society Articles of Faith.

14 Christian History Institute on Lettie Cowman.

mother tongue with effect, who were steeped in the Bible and who could so proclaim it as to arrest and influence all classes of people."[15]

Within a few months, God brought the dream to reality when they were able to open a mission hall where Nakada preached in the evening and leaders were trained in the daytime. This was the beginning of the Oriental Missionary Society. In 1902, E. A. Kilbourne joined Cowman and Nakada to assist in their growing ministry which witnessed moving into larger facilities in Tokyo in 1903.

No stranger to technology or the importance of communication, Charles quickly established a monthly periodical now called OMS Outreach. He had a vision to share Jesus with the unreached people of Japan; "whereby every person (58 million) in Japan might hear the Gospel in the next five years."[16] The Great Village Campaign started in 1913 and was completed in early 1918. Teams of missionaries visited every town, village, and home throughout Japan, proclaiming the Gospel and distributing Bibles (3 million bibles in Tokyo alone). This campaign took a toll on Charles' health and he and Lettie returned to the States in 1917.

Despite frequent heart attacks, Charles is described by Lettie as "Although broken in body, he kept an oversight of the home office and every department of work on the field, dictating letters by the hundreds."[17]

While Charles' burden for Japan was intense, God expanded his vision to include the whole orient. So, in 1910 OMS sent two missionaries from England, John, and Emily Thomas, to Korea to establish a Bible training institute. (the mother to STU). Even during his last days, Charles was planning for a bible institute in China. He never lost sight of his goal, "Train the sons and daughters of a nation, to reach the sons and daughters of a nation." In seeing missionaries as the scaffolding for the national churches, Charles Cowman like A. B. Simpson emphasized the holiness of life as part of the Fourfold Gospel. Consequently, he committed himself and his all into God's hands and was both an advocate and an illustration of Holiness which was practical and demonstrable. Cowman believed and practiced that before the soul can be beautified with spiritual graces, it must first be stripped of worldly ornaments and trifling loves that leave the heart divided against itself. He desired to develop people who understood and proclaimed the Fourfold Gospel. As part of that, he exercised prayer as the main weapon in fighting Satan and his wiles.

Streams in the Desert authored by Lettie Cowman provides a devotional approach to the truths of The Fourfold Gospel without mentioned the term.

---

15 Page 52 Missionary Warrior: Charles E. Cowman, by Lettie B. Cowman, New Condensed Edition, OMS International, Inc., 1989.

16 Ibid., 125.

17 Ibid., 142.

It appears that her ministry after Charles' death did not develop or utilize the term Fourfold Gospel.

However, that was not true of *Ernest Albert Kilbourne*.[18] Born in Ontario, Canada where A. B Simpson had pastored and attended University Kilbourne's family relocated to Chicago, USA while he was still young, as far as we know, he retained his Canadian citizenship the remainder of his life.[19] He was a bright and energetic young man who kept up with technology and learned Morse code, which eventually helped him find work in a Western Union telegraph office in Chicago at the age of 14. Entering the workforce early and sailing the world at the young age of 21, God undoubtedly used these experiences to expand his vision. Like many in the late 19th century, he was no stranger to spiritual values, having been raised in a devout Methodist family. His marriage to Julia Pittinger, who was from a staunchly Roman Catholic family, reflected either a deep respect for his devout manner or unparalleled diplomacy in an era that looked down upon interfaith marriages. He was about 30 years old when his fellow telegrapher, Charles Cowman led him to a personal saving knowledge of the Lord Jesus Christ. From that day forward their hearts were knit together, and Charles Cowman and Ernest Kilbourne began a lifelong friendship and Christian partnership. Subsequently, "*Ernest was alone in prayer when he received a dramatic revelation. He saw a great highway bridge that spanned the distance from North America across the Pacific Ocean to Japan. From Japan, a span of bridge reached Korea, and from Korea, a third touched China. From China, the great highway seemed to extend directly to heaven. More symbolic, across that final span would march a throng of the redeemed of Asia to their eternal home*."[20]

Ernest recognized this as part of God's call on his life. However, before he launched out to fulfill this great vision, he worked an extra year in the Chicago telegraph office to repay a debt he felt he owed to the telegraph company. Soon afterwards he left for Japan in 1902 to join his former friend and coworker, Charles Cowman. Kilbourne was 38 when he first arrived in Japan. He fit in well with the Japanese culture, reputed to be a man of quiet, deep, and intense faith, with a reverent mood. Retiring, reserved, and self-disciplined as a leader, he worked tirelessly behind the scenes, but faithfully alongside the more fiery and flamboyant Juji Nakada and Cowman, lending his steady hand and heart. He served in a multifunctional capacity as communications director and editor,

18 Most the information used throughout this article is extracted from "The Oriental Missionary Society Holiness Church in Japan 1901-1983" by Dr. John Merwin, former OMS missionary to Japan, and "Bridge Across the Century: *Volume One: Japan-Korea-China*" by Dr. Edwin Kilbourne, grandson of E. A. Kilbourne.

19 According to personal conversation with Dr. Ed Kilbourne, grandson of E. A. Kibourne, January 2014.

20 Quoted from the page facing the table of contents in "Bridge Across The Century."

public relations and fundraiser, and chief financial officer. The depth and sincerity of his commitment and his passionate pursuit for the fulfillment of the Great Commission can easily be seen in the early publications of the *Electric Messages* and subsequently, the *Oriental Missionary Standard*, forerunner of today's ***OMS OUTREACH*** magazine. His mind's eye was drawn to depict the vast orient and its, even then, millions of unreached and unengaged peoples of other faiths. Following the death of his life-long friend and colleague, Charles Cowman, Kilbourne naturally became the second OMS President, but only served another four years before he died of a cerebral hemorrhage on April 13, 1928, at age 63.

OMS Co-founder, Ernest. A. Kilbourne's commitment and convictions as a pioneer of today's OMS continue to be characterized in his work *The Great Commission*. He wrote with passion: Each generation of (Jesus' disciples) has a debt to pay to its generation of unsaved people of whatever nation or color; and while failure to accomplish its mission has marked each successive generation since the days of the early church, our individual responsibility has not lessened in the slightest degree, for the Great Commission has not been withdrawn or cancelled, but comes thundering down the corridors of time to this enlightened age and generation. Yes, it is human to shrink and shirk and shift, and to manufacture excuses, but this yoke is upon every child of God; and our efforts to throw it off only increase the condemnation which will fall upon all who fail to multiply the talent which God has given.[21] There's something about the spiritual tone and tenor, commitment and dedication of our spiritual forefathers that drive us to our knees in recognition of our weaknesses, frailties, and foibles. Our motivation and drive is brought into clear contrast and dark definition. We ask ourselves, what have I done with my life and calling? Have I spent myself in complete abandonment compared to those upon whose shoulders we stand? Have I used my time and talents wisely and without reserve? Or is it time to repent and renew our commitment and dedication, asking God to fill us anew with His Spirit and passion that characterized those who went before us. What will our spiritual legacy be? One can easily see that such comments reflect well the effects of practicing and proclaiming the Fourfold Gospel.

To show that the One Mission Society (at that time Oriental Missionary Society) held to the fourfold gospel, affirming each and every point of the four, we will time study an essay published in *Electric Messages* with the aim of bringing about theological clarity for the public who questioned OMS's stance on holiness and other evangelical doctrines.

The title of the article is "What We Teach at the Central Gospel Mission and Bible Training Home: Tokyo, Japan," published after a mere two years on

21 Bridge Across The Century, xii.

the mission field in Japan. Let us read first the part about holiness, noting that this article affirms the Wesleyan view of entire sanctification.

We believe that the Blood of Jesus cleanseth from all sin and not simply represses or covers up sin. We have heard some say that you were Keswick in your doctrine and so kindly ask you to tell us concerning your views on that subject. I do not know as I make it clear what I mean, but will you tell us what you think entire sanctification does for one. Please write me a little note explaining.

We are rejoiced to be able to answer this question. We *do not* hold the Keswick doctrine, but rather the John Wesley doctrine, or better still the *Bible* doctrine of heart *purity,* not merely *imputed* but *imparted.* The following statement we trust will help this sister and any others who are unacquainted with our teaching to know us better.

First—We believe and teach the *birth* of the Spirit is an absolute necessary qualification for *entering* the Kingdom of God. "Jesus answered, Verily, verily, I say unto thee, except a man be born of water and of the Spirit, he cannot *enter* into the Kingdom of God" (John 3:5).

We believe and teach that this "new birth" is not "baptism," but that it is a *radical* change of heart and *life,* according to the Scriptures: "Therefore if any man be *in* Christ, he is a new creature: (or, new creation) old things are passed away; behold, all things are become new" (2 Cor. 5:17).

Second—We believe that the *"root"* of sin, "*carnal* mind," "Old man" or, the "flesh" ("Sarx") which remains in the heart of every believer at and after conversion until he or she is sanctified wholly in a second definite work of grace, is removed, eradicated, burnt out by the "Baptism with the Holy Ghost and fire."

Our Japanese translation brings this out much stronger than the English, and this enables us in the Japanese language to preach it much stronger, leaving no room for our "suppression theory," or, "Jack in the box" friends to *guess* at what we mean. . . .

Third—We believe and teach, and all our students are so full of it that it crops out in almost every sermon and many testimonies: "The imminent pre-millennial return of our Lord." "Even so, come Lord Jesus"

Fourth—Divine healing as purchased in the atonement. "Himself took our infirmities, and bare our sicknesses." Mat. 8.17

There can be no doubt that this text refers directly to physical healing.... We would not stop with merely a *fourfold* Gospel, but we believe the Bible as a whole from Genesis to Revelations [sic] to be God's inspired record of His dealings with man. There are many important subjects:

For example: *Conversion* does so much for a man that his heart *burns* to tell others, while Sanctification or the Baptism with the Holy Ghost and fire, blows *every thing* [sic] else out of him and so *constrains* him that it is "Woe is me if I *preach* not the gospel." If he doesn't stand in the *pulpit* (they won't let you in many places except you have a *title*) he stands in the *streets:* If he don't [sic] *go* to foreign lands, he *sends.*

Salvation provides a pair of "field glasses" and says "Lift up your eyes and look on the *fields"* – note that word is in the plural—"fields" (John 4:35.) thus *forbidding* one to look merely on his county, state or country but emphatically states "Ye shall receive power after that the Holy Ghost is come upon you; and ye shall be witnesses unto me BOTH in Jerusalem, and in all Judaea, and in Samaria, *and unto the uttermost part of the earth*" (Acts 1:8).[22]

The Cowmans and Kilbournes affirm the fourfold gospel, noting that the order set by Simpson has been changed and that the fourfold has become flexible to include other doctrines from the Bible, especially world evangelism. The inclusion of Acts 1:8 at the end of this extended passage further clarifies that revival and evangelism are warp and woof of the fabric of evangelicalism within the Oriental Missionary Society at the beginning of the twentieth century.[23]

For Juji Nakada the emphasis on Healing and the Second coming of Christ took primary focus in his preaching and teaching. As an ardent preacher, he combined this with a strong view of sanctification which would signal that if one was ill, he/she was not sanctified. No medicine should be taken. Unfortunately, this led to a split with OMS and the denomination it founded The Japan Holiness Church.

Sensei Nakada[24] also brought the fourfold gospel which stressed the importance of holiness in the whole Ordo Salutis. He emphasized the primary

---

22 *Electric Messages from Japan: A Monthly Holiness Missionary Journal (Unsectarian)* C. E. Cowman and E. A. Kilbourne, Publishers Vol. 2 No. 1 (November 1903), 4.

23 Purinton, 65-66.

24 Nakada often quotes 1 Thessalonians 5:23 to support his teachings of healing. "May God himself, the God of peace, sanctify you through and through [completely]. May your whole spirit and soul and body be kept blameless at the coming of our Lord Jesus Christ." Nakada believes that believers must be sanctified both spiritually and physically in this life; therefore, for him, the full gospel means complete healing of the whole being in order to be ready for the second coming of Christ. The new birth and divine healing. Nakada describes his doctrine of healing in relation to other elements of the fourfold gospel. With regard to the new birth, Nakada believes that, in most cases, only human sin or Satan causes diseases (see Appendix A). Jesus heals a paralytic in Mark 2:5 saying, "Son, your sins are forgiven." Nakada asserts that the paralytic's sins or his parents' sins caused his diseases.

Another verse of the Bible that Nakada often quotes is 3 John verse 2: "I pray that you may enjoy good health and that all may go well with you, even as your soul is getting along well." Through this verse, Nakada connects sanctification to healing. John asks God that the recipients of his letter enjoy good physical health as well as spiritual health. Nakada believed that John's prayer is not based on hope, but on assurance (Yoneda, Nakada Jyuji Zenshu 1:299-301). Nakada believes that John was assuring believers that God would give Christians holistic health. With regard to the relationship between divine healing and role of the holy spirit in helping the believer to apprehend each aspect of the fourfold gospel. Juji Nakada or Nakada Jūji (1870-1939) was called the Dwight L Moody of Japan" because of his great revivalistic and holiness preaching. But it was not always so. When Juji started his pastoral ministry he felt an emptiness in his preaching and teaching. He believed God wanted him to attend Moody Bible Institute and his wife sold her dowry to provide the funds. While at Moody Juji was filled with the Spirit after hearing the Indian Evangelist VA David. Juji's preaching took on effective fervor and power. At Moody, he encountered Charles Cowman and E. A. Kilbourne whom Juji inspired with his vision of reaching the Japanese people with the message of holiness: the Fourfold Gospel: Jesus as Savior, Sanctifier, Healer, and coming King. With these men, Nakada established the Oriental Missionary Society (OMS) now called One Mission Society. He later served as the first bishop of the Japan Holiness Church (JHC). Unfortunately, in his later years, he became involved with the Japanese Israel movement which led to a schism in the church and Nakada being removed as Bishop of JHC.[25] Holiness unto the Lord should keep our focus on God first.

---

sanctification, Nakada asserts that "without holiness there is no divine healing" (qtd. in Yoneda, Nakada Jyuji Zenshu 1:316). He believes that complete elimination of sins is prerequisite for healing because he believes that in most cases, sin causes diseases. He asserts that through the grace of sanctification, a person must be filled with the Spirit who gives people life (zoe). He continues to say, once they are filled with zoe, they cannot have space for sicknesses; thus, he believes that once the souls are entirely sanctified by the Spirit, the whole body should remain physically healed, free from diseases. This teaching is similar to that of Carter who also stresses eradication of sin before physical healing. In short, Nakada strongly believes that God, who entirely sanctifies people, also heals all their sickness (299-319). Glorification and healing. With regard to the relationship between divine healing and glorification, Nakada says, "Divine healing is a prelude to our final resurrection" (qtd. in Yoneda, Nakada Jyuji Zenshu 5:459). He quotes 1 Thessalonians 5:23 to support his teaching on this matter and pays close attention to the phrase, "[m]ay your whole spirit, soul and body be kept blameless at the coming of our Lord Jesus Christ" (1 Thess. 5:23b). He believed that this text proves God makes people whole even before the second coming of Christ. He also encourages people to read Romans 12:1 carefully: "Therefore, I urge you, brothers, in view of God's mercy, to offer your bodies as living sacrifices, holy and pleasing to God–this is your spiritual act of worship." In this verse, the Greek word for living originally comes from zoe. Bodies here are obviously physical, not soul only; therefore, he asserts that the human body must be filled with zoe. The living sacrifice must be a flawless and perfect one; thus, he asserts that the living sacrifice is not a diseased body but a healthy body. He believes that if Christians want to see the coming Lord, their bodies must be sanctified along with their souls (Yoneda, Nakada Juyji Zenshu 1:320-34). Nakada connects healing grace with glorification because he believed that Christ would return soon. He believes God would heal all diseases to prepare for the second coming of Christ.

25 Based On No Guarantee But God_by Edward and Esther Erny, OMS, 1969 and Wheaton archival materials.

What lessons on the Fourfold Gospel, can we learn from Juji Nakada's life?

Juji used literature like Hono O No Shita (Tongues of Fire) to promote themes of heart purity, the filling of the Holy Spirit, the second coming of Christ, healing, and prayer. Shinobu Yamazaki states that for Nakada, the full gospel is the fourfold gospel. In other words, the fourfold gospel contains all aspects of salvation; thus, Nakada proclaims that, in order to receive the full gospel, no element of the fourfold Gospel can be deleted.

Christians walk through the order of salvation, new birth, sanctification, and glorification, but, if healing was not part of the order, salvation could not be presented in a full sense. Healing must always be interwoven with the other three–new birth, sanctification, and glorification. When the gospel of healing is always with the other three, salvation becomes holistic, including both soul and body, so salvation can be called "full salvation." Psalm 103:3 reads, "Who forgives all your sins and heals all diseases." Nakada uses this verse to explain the indivisible relationship between divine healing and full salvation (Yoneda, Nakada Jyuji Zenshu 1: 275-84).

In summary, Nakada believes God heals human bodies in this life. He uses three key verses to support his assertions: 1 Thessalonians 5:23, Romans 12:1, and 3 John 2. Nakada is convinced that God not only sanctifies human souls completely but also sanctifies their bodies in this life. By the work of God, both soul and body are completely healed. He believes that Christians must present their healthy bodies as living sacrifices in their daily lives. To this point, I have discussed Nakada and his theology of healing based mainly on his sermons, which were edited by others. Now, I will look at the outline of his lectures at Tokyo Bible Seminary for a summary of his teaching on divine healing. His teaching on divine healing is, therefore, interwoven with glorification. The more he stresses glorification, the more radical his teaching on divine healing becomes. His preaching becomes more extreme, and he begins to put too much stress on the sanctification of bodies. He originally stresses the sanctification of souls, but he gradually begins to believe that sanctification must extend to bodies to prepare for the second coming of the Lord Jesus Christ.[26]

Summary

The Fourfold Gospel provides a simple but comprehensive summary of major biblical doctrine. The Fourfold Gospel presents a consistent Christology that exalts Christ and His role in the life of the believer. When we are energized

26 "Holistic Healing Ministry: The Current Understandings and Attitudes of Clergy and Laity of Wesleyan Holiness Churches of Japan" by Shinobu Yamazaki, 2004 DMin Dissertation.

by the second coming of Jesus and not wanting any to perish, it inspires strong missiology which includes regeneration, sanctification and divine healing. This is in keeping with our Wesleyan heritage where we believe in the transformation of a person. Thus, we proclaim with Wesley: "We are people of the Book, one book, the Bible. We hold with that tradition which says there is a universal norm that **Christ is the central message of the Bible.** As such the **Gospel of Jesus Christ** Saves, Sanctifies, Heals and Promises His second Coming. Consequently, we do not hold that we interpret the Bible through the lens of the Fourfold Gospel but rather see that the Bible clearly presents these teachings as essential aspects of the Christian Faith. When asked what is the teaching of the scriptures on the Gospel or how the Gospel is defined, we readily answer: The Good News of Jesus Christ is: God saves and regenerates people. (born again). God enables them to be holy even as he is holy, sanctified, perfect in love of God and others. God heals the sins of the individual and society, to experience shalom, real rest and love. God is sending His Son, Jesus, back again. We can experience life with God, rest in His love, experience restoration of our soul and await the righteousness of the coming King! Soli Deo Gloria.

4

THE BIBLICAL PROCLAMATION OF CHRIST IN THE CONTEXT OF THEOLOGY IN ASIA

Jerin Reginald[1]

It is, undeniably, a great blessing for me to take part in the Festschrift written in honour of our respected Principal Rev. Dr. J. A. David Onesimu as I seldom forget to take boast of knowing him since my childhood. He is known for his kindness and he extends his mercy to anyone in need. He never stays idle which has been displayed all these years through various improvements in the seminary both academically and structurally. I believe that this article suits him very much as he always loves to grab any opportunity to proclaim the love of Christ who came down to earth as a Proclaimer of the Kingdom of God.

1. Introduction

It was Koyama who pointed out that "Asian theology should not, and cannot, merely be a counter-concept to theology in the West. Asian theology needs to be concerned with the biblical proclamation of Christ that is a God of Pathos and ethos, instead of a response to Western theology."[2] In the past,

1 *Rev. Jerin Reginald is an ordained priest from Evangelical Church of India (ECI), also teaching in the department of New Testament at the Madras Theological Seminary & College, Chennai. Currently, he is a doctoral candidate at Sam Higginbottom University of Agriculture, Technology & Sciences (SHUATS), Allahabad.*

2 "Asian Theology," in http://www.megaessays.com/viewpaper/86599.html, citing, Kosuke Koyama, *Your Kingdom Come: Mission Perspectives. Report on the World Conference on Mission and Evangelism* (Geneva: WCC, 1990).

the Asian churches were content with repeating the creedal formulas and the theological systems devised by the West. Furthermore, since the Christian mission in Asia was intimately bound with Western imperialism, the imported portrait of Jesus was what has been called the "colonial Christ," that is, Jesus as the white, male, all-powerful lord conquering souls and empires for God and implanting his Church. Since the 19th century, however, a distinctly Asian theology began to emerge as Asian theologians attempted to articulate their Christian faith in the context and terms of their own cultures and socio-political conditions.

2. The Present Nature of Asian Theology: A Counter Concept to the Theology of the West

When the missionaries came to Asian countries, although there were some who showed positive appreciation of indigenous culture and encouraged the indigenization of the Christian faith, the great majority of them were either indifferent or antagonistic toward the native religious traditions. Conversion rather than dialogue, confrontation rather than sympathetic understanding were the dominant way in which they presented the gospel. Needless to say, this uncompromising attitude caused a great deal of trouble and pain to the Christian converts who were simply unable to cut themselves off so abruptly from their cultural roots.

By and large, the churches from the developing world rarely have a creative theology that is unique to their own cultures and religiosity. The theological barrenness of churches from the developing world is partly as a result of the anti-intellectualist legacy of the past missions from the developed world. This legacy was fostered by the strong paternalism of these past missions on the one hand and the other, by their revivalist conversionism. The anti-intellectual legacy has brought two notable results to the missionised churches from the developing world: their profound dependency on theologies from the developed world and their resulting theological poverty, both interdependent elements.[3] This is also true of the Japanese Protestant churches, which have experienced the 'Germanic captivity of Japanese theology.'[4] It is also undeniable that the Korean Protestant churches, having more than 10 million adherents, have not yet produced official doctrinal statements that are distinctively different from

---

3 Jae-Buhm Hwang, "Theological poverty of the churches in the developing world: Its causes and effects," *HTS Theological Studies* 67(3): 5.

4 Jae-Buhm Hwang, "Theological poverty of the churches in the developing world...," 1, citing, Drummond, R.H., 1994, 'A New History of Japanese Theology,' *Mission Studies* XI– 2(22), 249.

the ones from the developed world.[5] This may also be the case for an African theology. Thus, Kofi Appiah- Kubi claims that:

> "...our question must not be what Karl Barth, Karl Rahner, or any other Karl has to say, but rather what God would have us do in our living concrete condition. For too long African Christian theologians and scholars have been preoccupied with what missionary A or theologian B or scholar C has told us about God and the Lord Jesus Christ."[6]

It is arguably Choan-Seng Song who has most deeply grieved over the captivity of Asian theologies by the developed world:

> "In short, Western mission agencies have not been satisfied with the role of planting and giving water to Christian communities in the non-Western lands. They have shaped these Christian communities, moulded them and forced them to grow into 'White' churches in 'Black' Africa or 'Yellow' Asia.'"[7]

What the native theologians have done instead of reflecting on and theologising about their cultures and religiosity is only idolising and imitating (and partly pirating) theology and culture from the developed world. As David Chellappa, a bishop of the Church of South India notes: 'Instead of struggling to find a theology that is at once Indian and Christian, the [Indian] theological students bury themselves in the writings of Western theologians.'[8]

3. Essential Nature of Asian Theology: Biblical Proclamation of Christ

Since the 1960s, the churches of the developing world have begun to think critically about their faith, which had been articulated predominantly in a way that speaks to the developed world. They then realised that having had little theological creativity, they had largely been held captive by theologies from the developed world. Acknowledging that Christian theology in India reflected 'an almost entirely Western type of thought and language', theologians in India lamented that 'they have not yet produced official doctrinal statements which

5 Jae-Buhm Hwang, "Theological poverty of the churches in the developing world...," 1.

6 Jae-Buhm Hwang, "Theological poverty of the churches in the developing world...," 1, citing, Aguilar, M.I., 'Postcolonial African Theology in Kabsele Lumbala', *Theological Studies* 63/2 (2002), 309.

7 C.S.Song, *Christian Mission in Reconstruction: An Asian Analysis*, (New York: Orbis Books, 1997), 7.

8 K. Bridston, 1965, *Mission Myth and Reality*, (New York: Friendship Press, 1965), 62.

express the Christian faith in a distinctively Indian way.'[9] Stephen B. Bevans rightly defines contextual theology as,

> "a way of doing theology in which one takes into account the spirit and message of the gospel; the tradition of the church; the culture in which one is theologizing; and social change within that culture, whether brought about by western technological process or the grass-roots struggle for equality, justice and liberation."[10]

It is an attempt at repentance. It proclaims the worthiness of Asian cultures as contexts where the gospel can be properly understood and lived out. It promotes the exploration of Asian cultural and moral resources rather than the continuing use of Western patterns and methods. In other words, contextual theologians attempt to de-homogenize Christianity by criticizing facile claims to universality and showing more appreciation for local cultures.[11] Michael Amaladoss suggests some of the ways in which Jesus could be proclaimed in Asia today in his article which would be very much helpful to give Christ in the cup of the target group.[12]

3.1. Understanding Christ and His Sacrifice

3.1.1. Jesus in History

Jesus as the Incarnate Word in history gives it a new importance. In Jesus, God has chosen to achieve his divine purpose with regard to the world and the humans in and through history, in a historical way, dependent, not only on time and space but also on the free interaction of the humans. This means that God is not adopting merely transcendent, transhistorical means to transform history and humans. God takes seriously the ongoing struggle between good and evil, justice and injustice in the world. God becomes human in Jesus and gets involved in that struggle, taking the side of the poor and the oppressed. He launches a new social movement with a group of his disciples, which becomes the Church. Such a mission has continued in history through charismatic figures in, and sometimes at the margins of, the Church. Gandhi is a good example. He traces his *satyagraha* or search for Truth to the Bhagavad Gita.

---

9 Robin Boyd, *An Introduction to Indian Christian Theology*, (Madras: The Christian Literature Society, 1969), 207.

10 Stephen B. Bevans, *Models of Contextual Theology* (New York: Orbis Books, 2002), 15.

11 Yahya Wijaya, "Economic Globalization and Asian Contextual Theology," *Theological Studies* 69 (2008), 309.

12 Michael Amaladoss, "Pluralism of Religions and the Proclamation of Jesus Christ in the Context of Asia," *CTSA Proceedings*, 56 (2001), 9-12.

But he would agree that it is the encounter with Jesus in the Sermon on the Mount and on the cross that sends him to rediscover his roots in the Gita.[13]

3.1.2. The Cross of Christ

Jesus Christ has been acclaimed as a great moral leader by many Asians. The Dalai Lama, Bhikku Buddhadasa of Thailand and Thich Nhat Hanh of Vietnam have all written books about Jesus to show that he was a perfect Bodhisattva.[14] Indian leaders like Keshub Chandra Sen, Swami Vivekananda, Mahatma Gandhi, and Radhakrishnan have acclaimed him not merely as a great moral leader, but as someone who had a special, intimate experience of God, experiencing the divinity in himself.[15] What most Asians find special about Christ, but difficult to accept, is the cross of Christ. People do seem to be drawn to Jesus suffering in solidarity with suffering humanity as a manifestation of his love and fellowship. Gandhi saw the sufferings of Christ as the height of his nonviolent love. The suffering Christ is the preferred image of many Hindu painters.[16] What seems to attract them is the vulnerability of a divine figure.[17] Suffering is a universal human experience. The affirmation that life is suffering is the first of the four truths of Buddhism. In Hinduism, suffering is seen as the fruit of one's actions - karma. The aim of sadhana or religious effort is to become free of suffering. Suffering is seen as an evil that one has to escape from. Even with the possibility of being born again, death is not a welcome experience. In such a situation, Jesus seems to give a positive meaning to suffering and death as an expression of love and self-gift Jesus does not seek to escape suffering, but welcomes it, not as a punishment, but as a sign of solidarity in the human struggle against injustice. Jesus on the cross was one of the favourite images of Gandhi. Suffering as a sign of kenosis or self-emptying also provokes echoes in some Buddhist traditions that speak of egolessness.[18] The cross of Jesus, therefore, may be a scandal at first sight. But looked at deeply it gives a positive meaning to suffering which remains an enigma to most people in or outside Asia... The image of Jesus in

---

13 Michael Amaladoss, "Pluralism of Religions…," 10.

14 Michael Amaladoss, "Pluralism of Religions…,"8, referring to, Buddhadasa, *Un bouddhiste dit le Christianisme aux bouddhists* (Paris: Desclée, 1990); Dalai Lama, *Le Dald-Lama parie de Jésus* (Paris: Brepols, 1996); Thich Nhat Hanh, *Living Buddha, Living Christ* (London: Rider, 1996).

15 S. J. Samartha, *The Hindu Response to the Unbound Christ* (Madras: Christian Literature Service, 1974), 6.

16 Richard W. Taylor, *Jesus in Indian Paintings* (Madras: Christian Literature Society, 1975), 4.

17 Richard W. Taylor, *Jesus in Indian Paintings* (Madras: Christian Literature Society, 1975), 6.

18 Michael Amaladoss, "Pluralism of Religions…," 9.

the multireligious context of Asia is not that of Jesus the king who comes to destroy the other religions and to impose his sacred power. He should not be identified with the victorious armies of the colonial empires. He does not come to dominate others with an exclusive claim to truth. He is rather the suffering servant who comes in humility to love and to serve and to give himself totally to promote the ongoing divine-human encounter.

3.2. Understanding the World and Humanity

Koyama suggests that the basic orientation for Asian theologians should be a responsible contextualization of theology. He feels that God calls Asians to a new understanding of the world and humanity.[19] Also, for Bevans, contextual theology is a way of understanding the Christian faith not only on the basis of Scripture and tradition – the two main theological sources of reflection of classical/traditional theology – but also on the basis of concrete culturally conditioned human experience. This is not to say that contextual theology is anti-Scripture. In fact, it has been said that Latin American liberation theology has been deeply rooted in, and nourished by, the underlined bibles of poor and marginalized peasants and urban dwellers. Neither is it anti-tradition but it appropriates the teachings of the church in a critical manner. Through concepts, symbols, stories and other forms of expression it has received from the church it reflects on the "raw experience" of people. Contextual theology differs from traditional/classical theology in two ways. First, it recognizes the signal importance of human experience as a source for reflection on Christian faith and morals. Second, since it is rooted in concrete human experience in a particular culture and society, it speaks primarily to that context. It is more apt, as Robert J. Schreiter puts it, to speak not of universal, permanent and unchanging theologies, but of "local theologies."[20]

For Choan-seng Song, the decentralization of God's power in history, seen in the prophets and the universalization of salvation in Jesus, require that the Semitic Christ be now incarnate in Asian flesh.[21] If Christology is an articulation of one's response or reaction to an encounter with God through Jesus the Christ, then Asian Christology has to start from the experiences of the Asian people, the majority of whom are poor and non-Christian. The Christologies of the missionaries, as well as those of inculturation and indigenization, ignored the Asian peoples' struggles for the fullness of life. They were so full of words that people could hardly hear the voice of or see

---

19 "Asian Theology," in http://www.megaessays.com/viewpaper/86599.html, citing, Kosuke Koyama, *Your Kingdom Come: Mission Perspectives* (Geneva: WCC, 1990).

20 Robert J. Schreiter, *Constructing Local Theologies*, (New York: Orbis Books, 1986), 55.

21 Choan-seng Song, *Third-Eye Theology: Theology in Formation in an Asian Setting* (New York: Orbis Books, 1979), 274

the face of Christ. Samartha's alternative, "bullock-cart Christology", may move slowly, but its wheels turn on Asian soil and it speaks to the daily life of the majority of the Asian people. The imagery of the bullock-cart graphically suggests the situation of the many Asians who continue to suffer exploitation and poverty.

Aloysius Pieris considers the Christologies of indigenization and contextualization inadequate because the former seemed to trick Asians to accept Christianity' and the latter did not take Asian culture seriously. What matters to him is not so much the Asianness of Christ but the "Christness of those categories of Asians who alone can reveal his Asian features". Thus, he appreciates Christologies that envision the Christ of Asia as Dalit, the *han*-ridden Christ, the breast-feeding *Christa*, and the third-world Christ of Asia who dwells among the humble of the earth as they strive for human liberation.[22]

3.3. A Direct Connection between Asian Thought and Jesus Christ

As an Asian theologian, Samartha formulated a Christology in India, a multi-religious society. He also attempted to contextualize Christian theology. He accomplished this by suggesting that a direct connection be formed between Indian thought and Jesus Christ. Samartha believes that for this connection to occur, Indians must accept the teachings and insights of their philosophers and use these to gain a better understanding of Jesus Christ. Samartha's theological focus is his concern to affirm that Jesus Christ is Lord and Saviour in India today. As he states, Indians do not have to become Jews to recognise the fullness of Christ, but instead should make use of their own, Indian philosophers, especially the Vedanta philosophers. A Vedanta philosopher, Sankara, believed in an Advaita view of the universe. Samartha used this perspective of Advaita, which is a Sanskrit word meaning "non-duality" or the eradication of duality, to explain his views and how this Indian philosophical insight can help Indians to read about Jesus Christ with the Indian eye.[23]

3.3.1. An Asian Jesus

In their search for a Christianity that makes sense in their contexts, Asian theologians began to take a look at Jesus the Christ through Asian eyes. Dialogue with Asian religions can also lead us to discover aspects of Jesus that have been obscured by the Western tradition. The post-synodal document *The Church in Asia* attributes to the Asian Bishops a desire to "rediscover the Asian

22 Muriel Orevillo-Montenegro, *The Jesus of Asian Women* (New York: Orbis Books, 2006), 45.

23 S. J. Samartha, *The Hindu Response to the Unbound Christ*, 23-25.

countenance of Jesus."[24] They can hardly do this without a dialogue with Asian cultural and religious traditions. The preferred image of Jesus in the West, at least as presented to the East, seems to have been that of Christ the King who seeks to extend his kingdom all over the world. In Asia, Jesus would be seen rather as a wandering Sage - a Sannyasi - who had no roots because he belongs to everyone everywhere. But he is a new kind of Sannyasi, who does not run away from the world but stands detached in the midst of it. He is witnessing to the forgiving and self-giving love of God, showing people by being the Way to liberation and wholeness. He loves others and gives himself to them totally, even unto death. He does not lead an armed struggle, but a movement of people with new values and perspectives that are seen as a threat to the established order. He does not need a powerful institution to back him up. He has a simple message - a new commandment: "Love one another as I have loved you!" He invites everyone to experience God, neither in an ascetical nor in a mystical way, but ordinary life in loving the other and in sharing, especially with those most in need. He empowers people and inspires them to act. He chooses followers who will walk along his path as itinerant prophets, with little baggage, staying where they feel welcome, ready to be persecuted for their convictions that upset established order, setting up open communities characterized by their fellowship and sharing (Matt. 10).

3.3.2. The Jesus Within

The incarnate Word leads us to experience the Word in us and the world. Western religious approaches are often characterized by a dichotomous attitude that separates God as a creator from the world that he has created. Indian religions speak rather about Advaita or nonduality. God and the world are not-two (separate beings). God is the deepest principle of ones being, the source of oneself.[25] What is important is the awareness that God is not apart from us in such a way that we need a bridge maker or pontifex to bring us together. God is within us as a source of life and communion. Sr. Sara Grant, reflecting on the implications of the Advaita to Indian Christianity, spoke about the challenge of "our manner of thinking of baptism and the gift of the Spirit as though God somehow 'came in from outside,' as it were, and were not already present 'in' us by the very fact of our being at all."[26] In the context of this Indian Advaitic tradition, Jesus is seen, first of all, as a human person who has experienced in himself God as the immanent transcendent in a special, personal way. As such a person, he is also a model to lead us to a similar experience of God

24 Michael Amaladoss, "Pluralism of Religions ...," 10.

25 Michael Amaladoss, "Pluralism of Religions...,"11.

26 Sara Grant, *Towards an Alternative Theology. Confessions of a Nondualist Christian* (Bangalore: Asian Trading Corporation, 1991), 56.

within us, empowering us. When Paul says: "It is no longer I who live, but it is Christ who lives in me" (Gal 2:20), he is not speaking in metaphor only. When John makes Jesus say: "That they may be one, as we are one, I in them and you in me, that they may become completely one" (John 17:22-23), he is not talking of high mysticism, but of a living experience. The traditional mission has emphasized sacramental and institutional Christianity. The contemporary emphasis on Jesus as liberator has opened up the social dimension.

3.4. Reimagining a Liberating Christ

Christology in Asia will have to rethink some themes that hinder, rather than foster, dialogue and block a liberationist direction. The theme of the uniqueness of Christ, for example, will not work as a starting point for dialogue among religions. In Christological articulation, Christians must view the uniqueness of the title Christ not in terms of Jesus as the "exclusive medium of salvation for all" but in light of the absoluteness that the word *Christ* conveys. The Christ may even take a non-Christian character because we need to remember that "Jesus is Christ, but not all of Christ is Jesus" (*Jesus est totus Christus, non totem Christi*).[27]

An Asian Christology can not proceed meaningfully if it takes the humanity of Jesus lightly. Only a historical Jesus, an embodied Christ, can show the love and compassion that can liberate the oppressed and suffering peoples of the world. Samartha notes that this step will lead to a Christology that is "spiritually satisfying, theologically credible, and ethically helpful to people in the religiously plural world."[28] The Gospels are clear about Jesus' preferential option for the poor and the marginalized, and they challenge the privileged to walk the Christic path with Jesus.

3.5. The Emergence of Asian Women's Voices

Asian women theologians affirmed much of what the Asian men said in their efforts to indigenize and contextualize Jesus. Yet, Asian women found the Christologies of their male colleagues inadequate. These Christologies did not address the multiplicity of women's oppression and suffering. Very few Asian male theologians addressed gender issues or wrote extensively about them. Exceptions are Aloysius Pieris, Tissa Balasuriya, C. S. Song, Stanley J. Samartha, Suh David Kwang-sun, Sebastian Kappen, and Michael Amaladoss. Some acknowledged their inadequacy to address gender issues. Most of the Asian male theologians, however, chose to ignore the realities of patriarchy, sexism, and androcentrism embedded in Christianity as well as in Asian

27 Muriel Orevillo-Montenegro, *The Jesus of Asian Women*, 47.

28 Stanley J. Samartha, "The Cross and the Rainbow – Christ in a Multi-Religious Culture," in *The Myth of Christian Uniqueness – Towards a Pluralistic Theology of Religions*, edited by John Hick and Paul Knitter (New York: Orbis Books, 1987), 84.

cultures and religions. This awareness has led to the emergence of women's voices in the Asian theological world.

Asian women have heard the voices of women from other continents. They have listened to the women among other minority groups in the United States, the Latinas in South America, and African women in protest over the totalizing claims of the male theologians. On the one hand, Asian women resonate with these women as they point out the inadequacy of Christologies that did not take into account their experiences of oppression because of their gender, class, race, ethnicity, and culture. On the other hand, Asian women also criticized their white sisters, whose claims on women's experience seemed to have a tendency to erase the identities of women of colour.

Perhaps the seeds of Asian feminist theologies were so long ago by Asia's brave but unknown Christian women. But beginning in the latter part of the twentieth-century Asian women have made substantial contributions to the understanding of Christology. Asian women's Christologies are marked by their unique contexts and experiences within the vast continent of Asia. By embracing the reality of their differences and celebrating their commonalities, Asian women have forged solidarity in their common experience of suffering. By virtue of their locations, Asian women's christological approaches are diverse. However, they recognize that there are threads that connect Asian women's common dreams and vision; their liberation from patriarchy is intertwined with their vision of the ultimate liberation of the marginalized and oppressed, and fullness of life for all.[29]

4. Conclusion

Nowhere else than in India, perhaps, is the importance of the aesthetic more manifest, for here we find that the distinctiveness of Jesus Christ is expressed through art by persons who do not necessarily belong to the visible Christian community. India might well be the only place where persons of other faiths have related themselves to Jesus Christ through art, thus breaking down the walls of exclusiveness. These artists, standing outside the confines of institutional Christianity, make evident that it is not the dogmas and doctrines about Christ or the institutions of the church that have touched the heart and mind of India, but the life and teachings of Jesus of Nazareth, his death and resurrection. There seems to be an "unbaptized *koinonia*"[30] outside the gates, which the church is most reluctant to recognize or even talk about it.

Over the centuries there have been many examples of this influence of Christ beyond the confines of the church. A noted Hindu poet Manjeshwar

29 Muriel Orevillo-Montenegro, *The Jesus of Asian Women*, 50.

30 Stanley J. Samartha, "The Cross and the Rainbow – Christ in a Multi-Religious Culture," 74.

Govinda Pai,'s lengthy poem *Golgotha* is marked by literary beauty, depth of religious perception, and a sensitive understanding of the crucifixion of Jesus Christ. A Hindu lawyer Muliya Keshavayya's drama *Maha Chetana* ("Great Energy"), brought out the compassion of Christ toward the poor and the power of his cross and resurrection. Gopal Singh, a well-known Sikh scholar, and diplomat wrote a poem entitled *The Man Who Never Died.* According to Jyoti Sahi, a noted Christian artist, Indian Christian art was initiated not by Christian, but by Hindu artists. For example, there is the well-known painting of the Last Supper by Jamini Roy of Calcutta.[31] This might well be regarded as "signs" of the increasing "traffic across the borders," helping to develop new relationships between persons of different religious communities and bringing out new meanings in Christology.

Theologians from the developing world might stop only imitating the theologies of the developed world, whilst sincerely studying their theological thoughts and thinking patterns. Creativity requires self-knowledge. For a theologian from the developing world, however, self-knowledge means a double reflection: on their own cultures, on the one hand, and Christian tradition of two thousand years, on the other. As Asian Christians, we should readily answer Jesus Christ who will surely ask us "Who do you say that I am?"

31 Stanley J. Samartha, "The Cross and the Rainbow – Christ in a Multi-Religious Culture," 88, referring to, Manjeshwar Govinda Pai, *Golgotha* (Mangalore: Baliga and Sons, 1948), Muliya Keshavayya, *Maha Chetana: A Drama on the Life of Christ* (Mangalore: Kodialbail Press, 1976), Gopal Singh, *The Man Who Never Died* (London: Macmillan, 1969), Jyoti Sahi, "Trends of Indigenisation and Social Justice in Indian Christian Art," *Indian Journal of Theology*, 31 (1982), 89.

5

CHALLENGES AND CHANCES OF URBAN EVANGELISM IN THE ULTRAMODERN SOCIETY

T. Aaron Martin[1]

1. Introduction

Evangelism should be like the blood which runs in the veins of all Christians. Proclaiming the message of Jesus Christ could be a passionate responsibility. The gospel is preached since the time of the first century and people were discipled in the Christian faith. This research paper focuses on challenges and chances of urban evangelism in ultramodern society. Urban evangelism has its roots since the time of Jonah in Nineveh and Paul in Corinth, and it has extended to the present days. Pagitt calls the present era as the inventive age where knowledge is no more a goal, but just a means to achieve the unimagined goals.[2]

Coping up with the present reality is the need of the hour even in urban evangelism. This research paper is an attempt to analyze existing challenges and possible solutions in urban evangelism. It is an undeniable

---

1 *Rev. Thomas Aaron Martin is an ordained priest from Evangelical Church of India (ECI). Currently he is a doctoral candidate at Asian Centre for Theological Studies & Missions (ACTS), South Korea. This research paper is drafted by T. Aaron Martin for the compendium of essays titled as Reconstructing Theology: Essays in honor of Rev. Dr. J. A. David Onesimu's 65*[th] *Birthday. The writer of this paper had a wonderful opportunity to serve with Dr. Onesimu in the ministries of Madras Theological Seminary & College and Evangelical Church of India.*

2 Doug Pagitt, *Church in the Inventive Age* (Minneapolis: Sparkhouse Press, 2010), 5ff.

fact that booming up of present-day advanced technologies could be used as an opportunity and tool for urban evangelism. [3] There has been importance paid for reaching the Generation Z people in the process of urban evangelism and how to use communication as an instrument in reaching the unreached people in the urban vicinity. This paper follows the structure of focusing on the meaning of evangelism, urban area, literature review, information about ultramodern society, challenges such as secularization, pluralization, persecutions, LGBTIQ, heretic and cultic movements, followed by changes in urban evangelism with an alternative paradigm and also reaching out Generation Z using communicative media in addition with cyber church.

2. Evangelism

The term evangelism comes from the Greek word *euangelizo* (εὐαγγελίζω) which means "to announce glad tidings," "to proclaim/declare good news". It is a combination of two words *Eu* – good and *angelos* (ἄγγελος) - angel or messenger. Therefore, to evangelize is to share the good news with others. What is the good news? – The good news is that Jesus has conquered sin, death, and the grave. Jesus has died on the Cross to grant salvation.[4] The noun form of *euangelion* has occurred seventy-six times in the NT which is translated as "gospel," "good news," or "evangel." Evangelism does not stop with preaching the gospel, but it includes several other aspects such as bearing witness, making disciples, being witnesses, and so on.[5] Evangelism is not an NT concept, but it runs all through the Bible. Redemption is the theme which is sung as a melody from Genesis to Revelation. Beginning from Gen 3:9, scripture shows a redeeming God who seeks his estranged creation. In continuation, the theme of atonement and the grace of God is also indirectly visible in Gen 6. Even though there are continuous scenes of murder, conspiracy, idolatry, wicked behavior, and God's judgment since Gen 12 God's unfolding plan of redeeming humanity is an indisputable fact. Similarly, the exodus event reveals the great salvific movement in the OT. Even the image of bronze serpent (Num 21) is being used as imagery that foreshadows the work of redemption of Jesus

3 William Carey who is the father of modern mission was also very innovative and truly creative in utilizing technology of his days to advance the gospel. Establishing printing press was one of his achievement using which Bibles were printed into many of the Indian languages. See, Andrew B. Spurgeon, "Integration of Technology and Theological Assignments," *Journal of Asian Evangelical Theology* 23, No. 1 (March 2019), 71-84.

4 There are so many misconceptions about evangelism such as mute approach, scalp hunting approach, professional fisherman approach, Cop-out approach, and so on. See, Alvin Reid, *Introduction to Evangelism* (Nashville, Tennessee: Broadman & Holman Publishers, 1998), 4-9.

5 Church growth movement has defined evangelism as 3ps – presence, proclamation and persuasion. See, Elmer Towns, ed. "Evangelism: P-1, P-2, P-3," *Evangelism and Church Growth* (Ventura, Calif: Regal Books, 1995), 212-216.

Christ on the cross. There are also prophetical writings that focus on the suffering servant, Messiah, new covenant, a prophetical declaration about the birth of Jesus.[6] The redemptive act of God is progressively revealed in NT as well which could be viewed in the gospels and epistles. There are also proofs about mass evangelism and the way to get saved which is clearly depicted in the Bible. Even at the great commission,[7] Jesus commands to involve in doing evangelism without any compromise.

3. Urban

At the outset, it is essential to describe the term "urban" while dealing with urban evangelism. Joel Garreau lists that the functions of an urban society include industry, commerce, safety, culture, religion, companionship.[8] Whereas Jane Jacobs has given a simple definition that urban locality is one that has a consistent generation of economic growth from a local economy.[9] But this definition is more from an economic perspective. But Kostoff proposes that urban locality contains energized crowding of people who are specialized in different works with a source of income, territory which feeds and fulfills their needs.[10] This definition has a little extended boundary in giving some details about people and their lifestyles. A city could be called as a "city" not just based on the number of people residing. Population is not becoming the indicator to decide a place as a city, rather it includes several other aspects such as culture, heritage, civic life, arts, architecture, buildings, facilities, employment opportunities, availability of resources and so on. Urban evangelism is inevitable in reaching the people in this postmodern era. When God could save bloody Nineveh city through Jonah's preaching, the same God is still at work. The concept of *missio Dei* must be in obedience with *missio Christi* (the mission of Christ).[11] Because Christ invites all the followers to be witnesses to the world. Through the urban evangelism, present ultramodern urban localities could be reached with the saving knowledge of Jesus Christ. It should be moved forward with the realization that every Christian has a mission from

6 There could be a criticism that this sort of reading the OT is through the lense of NT. But the writer of this paper here is not focusing on the division of the Bible. Hence, focus is given to look at the concept of evangelism from a wider perspective from a Christian understanding.

7 Cf. Matt 28:19-20; Mark 16:15; Luke 24:47-48; John 20:21; Acts 1:8.

8 Joel Garreau, *Edge City* (New York: Anchor Doubleday, 1991), 26.

9 Jane Jacobs, *Cities and the Wealth of Nations* (Harmondsworth: Penguin, 1986), 39.

10 Spiro Kostoff, *The City Shaped* (London: Thames & Hudson, 1991), 38-40.

11 Andrew J. Kirk, *What is Mission? Theological Explorations* (Augsburg: Fortress Press, 2000), 38.

everywhere to everywhere.[12] Because urban locality includes different sorts of people such as poor, wealthy, marginalized, powerful, ignored, living with differently-abled and so on.

4. Literature Review

Some of the previous researches which have a close connection to the theme of this paper is reviewed for better analysis. Stephen Hunt made an analysis of evangelism from a social and anthropological perspective.[13] But most of the analysis is from a western point of view and particularly paying attention to Holy Trinity Church in Brompton, London. There has been also some importance paid towards the concept of "spiritual marketplace". Hunt has also proposed that consumeristic attitude and postmodernity in the present era influences the religious absolutes. He has also critiqued about the mushrooming of classical/neo-Pentecostalism and doctrinal differences.

Writings of Doug Pagitt is also a major contribution relevant to the issue of urban evangelism. *Evangelism in the Inventive Age* and *Church in the Inventive Age* are two writings where some of the pertinent issues related to consumeristic society and the postmodern era is highlighted. Pagitt is suggesting practical application to those who are facing a struggle in converting other people or who are finding difficult to share faith endeavors with others. He also offers an essential framework to partake in God's mission in this inventive age.[14]

Emilio Castro began with defining the term mission, followed by evangelism from a Biblical perspective and moved to explain regarding the urban-rural mission. One of the main concerns in Castro's writing is that there are many poor and alienated people groups in urban and rural areas. Through the gospel of Jesus Christ, they could be liberated from specific difficult situations. Castro also quoted the recommendation made by the World Council of Churches regarding the need for "network" in working for the gospel proclamation. He has also attempted to speak about the dangers of proselytism

---

12 Mission from everywhere to everywhere is borrowed from Edinburgh 2010 Common Call. Similar to this phrase was stated by Kwok Keung Chan. Chan's statement is "Mission is from anywhere to anywhere". See, Kirsteen Kim and Andrew Anderson, ed., Edinburgh 2010, "Edinburgh 2010 Common Call," *Edinburgh 2010: Mission Today and Tomorrow* (Oxford: Regnum, 2011), 2; Kwok Keung Chan, "The First Mark of Mission: To Proclaim the Good News of the Kingdom of God," *Life-Widening Mission: Global Anglican Perspectives,* ed. Cathy Ross (Oxford: Regnum Books, 2012), 19.

13 Hunt has been working under this theme and contributing his research work since 2001. He contributions includes, *Decade of Evangelism* (1990) and also usage of mass media for mission and evangelism. The book, *The Alpha Enterprise: Evangelism in a Post-Christian Era* contains fourteen chapters which are academically focused and balanced with missional perspectives. See, Stephen J. Hunt, *The Alpha Enterprise: Evangelism in a Post-Christian Era* (Thames: Routledge, 2004), 12ff.

14 Doug Pagitt, *Church in the Inventive Age* (Minneapolis: Sparkhouse Press, 2010), 2.

and manipulation present in spreading evangelism. He challenged the readers to be motivated by remembering the roots and identity in entering human struggles to portray the love of Jesus. Castro has also encouraged the readers to defend human rights and build a community through the work of evangelism. He also affirmed that the evangelistic work needs to be done in a dynamic way without having any hatred attitude. He also emphasized that justice should not be denied to the poor people while presenting the right knowledge about Jesus Christ.[15]

Binu Varghese has written an article entitled as "Urban Evangelism in the Modern Age: Challenges and Opportunities." In this article, Varghese has paid attention to the sociological foundations of the inventive age and theological foundations of evangelism in the inventive age. In the theological foundations, Varghese focused on the steps of evangelism from the book of Acts which is to release, invite, include, embrace, welcome, listen, proclaim and create. He also slightly highlighted the importance of urban evangelism for a local church to involve in. Even though the title of Varghese's article is about challenges and opportunities, but in reality, he did not directly deal with any issues of urban evangelism.

William Wade has written an article entitled "Evangelism in a Post-Christian age: Bridging the Evangelical/Emerging church tension." Wade is primarily tackling the issue of the gap which is present between evangelical and non-evangelical circles. He comments that the emerging churches are sometimes compromising their evangelical thrusts due to the influence of postmodernism. He feels that due to overemphasize using the technology of music and media in the emerging churches, the sound sermon based on scripture is paid less attention. Wade has also put forward several points of potential difficulties related to evangelism. This includes the whole process of approaching the non-Christian and guiding him all through the process of conversion. This includes how the earlier preaching related to "Hell" is no more paid attention. Rather, it has become a gospel-centered approach that pays attention to time, energy, creativity, and cultural engagement.[16]

Alvin Reid has identified some of the common challenges present in evangelism. He has made a comparison of the challenges with the early church and the present days. There are two categories such as internal and external challenges. In the internal challenge, Reid has incorporated hypocrisy,

15 Emilio Castro, "Mission and Evangelism in Urban Rural Mission," *International Review of Mission* 1 76, (July 1987), 137-152.

16 Wade has quoted J. Webb Kline who wrote "From the heart of a missional evangelist". Kline is also in agreement in his thought pattern regarding using of technology as like Wade. https://www.academia.edu/5179607/Evangelism_in_a_Post-Christian_Age_Bridging_the_Evangelical_Emerging_Church_Tension accessed on Dec. 16, 2019.

unending needs, and theological convictions, whereas, in external challenge, religious persecutions such as threats, burnings, physical abuse are included.[17]

David S. Dockery edited thirteen articles that pay attention to the evangelical standpoints in the midst of several challenges that are being faced in the present society.[18] Suggestions to overcome the challenges from an evangelical perspective are also provided in the area of theology, hermeneutics, religious pluralism, apologetics, evangelism, proclamation and so on. The literature review work shows how the previous researchers have approached this issue and given some practical applications which could be implemented. Of course, some of their works are not directly related to urban evangelism. But some aspects of their works could relate to urban evangelism.

5. Ultramodern Society

Arthurs' comment, "truth is a non-issue to most, the story is preferred over information, video is accepted more readily than manuscript and religion is relegated to opinion-driven relativity." There is a danger of driving away from the sense of personal relationship with God, instead, the color of external deity is attached for religious beliefs in the postmodern arena.[19] Wade has given a suggestion that if the respective message in evangelism and method of theo-praxis is balanced, then the ultramodern generation could be reached.[20] If specific cultural practice that does not lose the spiritual message in having a relationship with God is adapted, then it could become a grand theodrama in reaching the people with the seed of the gospel.[21] Some of the challenging issues present in the ultramodern society could not be ignored while involving in urban evangelism. Globalization,[22] materialism, elitism, neo-capitalism,

17 Reid has identified that in the midst of obstacles, early Christians shared about Christ. Those obstacles are present even in this postmodern era in either similar or different form. The same sort of obstacles could be witnessed in the lives of church fathers time. There were many early saints who worked for evangelism such as, Polycarp, Bishop of Smyrna, Blandina's martyrdom, Justin Martyr, and the unending list of martyrs. Alvin Reid, *Introduction to Evangelism,* 50-52.

18 David S. Dockery, ed., *The Challenge of Postmodernism: An Evangelical Engagement* (Grand Rapids, MI: Baker Books, 2001), 5-9.

19 J. D. Arthurs, "The Challenge of Postmodernism" *The Challenge of Postmodernism: An Evangelical Engagement,* ed. David S. Dockery (Grand Rapids, MI: Baker Books, 2001), 9ff.

20 https://www.academia.edu/5179607/Evangelism_in_a_Post-Christian_Age_Bridging_the_Evangelical_Emerging_Church_Tension accessed on Dec 20, 2019.

21 J. D. Arthurs, "The Postmodern Mind and Preaching" in *Preaching to a Shifting Culture,* ed. S. M. Gibson (Grand Rapids, MI: Baker Books, 2004), 177ff.

22 Some of the challenging issues could be broadly classified under the umbrella of "Globalization". Defining the term Globalization itself need skill. In a simple term, it can be called of "compression of the world" or "growth of supraterritorial relations." In

neo-imperialism, neo-colonialism, racism, gender exploitation, sexual liberation, environmental degradation, assisted reproductive technology, stem cell, and human replication are some of the threatening issues which are present vibrantly in the urban region and has substantial effects. While dealing with urban evangelism, one cannot avoid or ignore dealing with such issues which are hampering the faith of the people.

6. Challenges[23]

6.1. Secularization

According to Berger, secularization is a process by which "sectors of society and culture are removed from the domination of religious institutions and symbols."[24] Emery White commented that due to secularization, the church is losing its influence as a shaper of life and thought from the perspective of wider social order.[25] The explanation given by Prof. Chong Hung Ho is very simple and clear. He said secularization is a worldview centered around human beings. Reason and rationality are the two axes that are paid attention to solve all the human problems. As per the secularistic attitude, the divine realm becomes a mystery and superstition. This sort of worldview results in agnosticism and atheism.[26] The idea of secularization which makes the Christian faith less real

---

brief, world is becoming a smaller place in which structures of social relationships are not restricted to any physical geographical boundaries. Globalization has affected the Christian and social values, culture has become multilayered and so on. Ormerod and Clifton has done an extensive work regarding the mission of the church in the context of Globalization. See, Neil J. Ormerod and Shane Clifton, *Globalization and the Mission of the Church: Ecclesiological Investigations* (New York: T & T Clark, 2009), 76ff.

23 Even though many of the challenging issues are listed above, all cannot be dealt in a detailed manner in this article. Therefore, some of the pertinent issues are alone dealt and solutions for such challenges are given.

24 Peter L. Berger, *Sacred Canopy: Elements of a Sociological Theory of Religion* (Garden City, NY: Doubleday, 1967), 107. The thought drafted by Berger has been also accepted and referred by Marty and David Martin in the later days. David Martin has opined that church has gone away from its religious thrusts due to Secularization. Whereas Marty was focusing on the urban areas of France and Germany and commented that there are different levels of secularization such as utter secularity, mere secularity and controlled secularity. Cf. Martin E. Marty, *The Modern Schism* (London: SCM, 1969), 18ff; David Martin, *A General Theory of Secularization* (Oxford: Blackwell, 1978), 12.

25 James Emery White, "Evangelism in a Postmodern World," *The Challenge of Postmodernism: An Evangelical Engagement,* ed. David S. Dockery (Grand Rapids, MI: Baker Books, 1995), 360.

26 Chong Hung Ho and Yoon Ki Chul, "A Study on John Wesley's Living faith to overcome Secularization from Mission Theological Perspective," *South Korea Evangelical Theological Society Mission* 39, (2017). http://www.riss.kr/search/detail/DetailView.do?p_mat_type=1a0202e37d52c72d&control_no=530c7222599e9b30b7998d826d417196#redirect, accessed on Dec 28, 2019.

than other concerns is one of the dominating challenges in urban evangelism. To overcome this challenge, "Living Faith" teachings from John Wesley could be given as a suggestion. True living faith is purified in the furnace of affliction and it is referred to as "true holiness".[27] Holiness is not merely attributed to physical external behavior, but it is related to the actions that are concerned with the psychological, emotional, cultural, social, economic, and political aspects of life.

6.2. Pluralization

Pluralization is the process by which the number of options in the cloistered sphere of postmodern society is rapidly mushrooming at all levels about world views, faith, and ideologies.[28] Even though this interpretation made by Guinness is clear, it is not hitting the exact exposition. Because Landon Gilkey's observation is more appropriate towards the explanation of pluralism. Gilkey spots that there were religions that always existed, but in this postmodern arena, there is a realization of "new consciousness" which entails a feeling of rough parity, as well as diversity among religion.[29] This new consciousness propagates that all the different religious values are in equal validity. The result of this new consciousness is a devaluation of the eternal truth. It is a big challenge in evangelism because of the attitude of the new consciousness portrays Christianity is one of the competing world views. It is more of a syncretistic attitude. Emery White calls it a "mix and match" mentality.[30] Because individual put together different ideologies from various religions and make their value system which suits their taste. To address this challenge, the pattern from the early church could be applied. The early church had a pluralistic culture where Jesus is portrayed as a singular person who is the remedy of salvation.[31] This could be the evangelical stand in the midst

27 This suggestion has been given by Prof. Chong Hung Ho and Yoon Ki Chul. Because the teachings related to "living faith" seems to be strong to tackle the issue of secularization. Dreyer has done an exposition work on the contributions made by John Wesley. Dreyer has also explained the importance of faith and experience from Wesley's sermon. Cf. Frederick Dreyer, "Faith and Experience in the Thought of John Wesley, *JSTOR* 88, No. 1 (Feb 1983), 12-30; Chong Hung Ho and Yoon Ki Chul, "A Study on John Wesley's: Living faith" to overcome Secularization from Mission Theological Perspective," *South Korea Evangelical Theological Society Mission* 39 (2017), 193ff.

28 Os Guinness, *The Gravedigger File: Papers on the Subversion of the Modern Church* (Downers Grove, IL: InterVarsity Press, 1983), 93.

29 Langdon Gilkey, *Through the Tempest: Theological Voyages in a Pluralistic Culture* (Minneapolis: Fortress, 1991), 21.

30 James Emery White, "Evangelism in a Postmodern World," 362.

31 Robert H. Gundry has quoted C. H. Dood who has pointed out that the early church had a noticeable six patterns in doing evangelism. The pattern includes, 1. Jesus inaugurated the fulfillment of messianic prophecy, 2. He went about doing good and performing miracles,

of challenging new consciousness which is related to religious pluralism. To compromise this pluralistic issue, some have developed *functional substitutes* adapting some of the belief systems and ritual practices from other religions.[32] So that religious harmony could be maintained. But there is also a danger which makes the real identity to be diluted from its original thrust. Therefore, careful attention needs to be paid while adapting functional substitutes as part of urban evangelism.

6.3. Persecutions

Persecutions are unending stories that are happening in most parts of the globe. There are occurrences of institutional persecution where governments and organizations align themselves against Christians. Cochran groups persecutions into six categories such as bias, slander, discrimination, incarceration, violence, and oppression.[33] Even the cross-cultural missionaries who are serving in different nations are being chased away.[34] ISIS terrorist attacks are also increasing in different parts of the world where many churches are destroyed, Christians are burnt alive. Even though there are several persecutions outside of Christianity, there are also persecutions increasing within the church which is the body of Christ. Because of denominational differences, there are also constant verbal persecutions that are going on as an accusation against Christian leaders and followers. In the process of urban evangelism in this post-Christian era, there is no escape from these sorts of denominational (internal) persecutions and the external persecutions.

6.4. LGBTIQ

Moral relativistic thoughts and autonomous individualism are highly broadcasted by the members of LGBTIQ. There is a breakdown of morals in the present reality which functions as a big challenge. "What is true for me

---

3. He was crucified according to God's plan, 4. He was raised and exalted to heaven, 5. He will return in judgment, 6. Therefore, repent, believe and be baptized. Of course, even though scholars like Martin Dibelius, A. M. Hunter, and C. T. Craig agreed to this, there were some differences of opinion about the application of this pattern. Robert H. Gundry, *A Survey of the New Testament* (Grand Rapids: Zondervan, 1981), 75ff.

32 Some people call it as "symbolism". See, Alan Richard Tippett, *Introduction to Missiology* (California: William Carey Library, 1987), 190ff.

33 Gregory C. Cochran, *Christians in the Crosshairs: Persecution in the Bible and Around the World Today* (Wooster, Ohio: Weaver, 2016), 17; Grant Zweigle has included martyrdom which has become part of Christian mission. See, Grant Zweigle, *Sorrow & Blood: Christian Mission in Contexts of Suffering, Persecution, and Martyrdom* (Pasadena, California: William Carey Library, 2012), 38ff.

34 As per the mission report, there are 150 Korean missionary families who were sent out from India within the years 2017-18 alone (Reference: Class lecture of Prof. Chong Hung Ho during October 2018 at ACTS University, South Korea).

is true for me and what is true for you is true for you." – this is the attitude that is broadcasted through moral relativism. In the same fashion, autonomous individualism portrays that the value of individual person is autonomous in terms of their decision and accountability. Their decisions or choices are determined by their personal pleasures and not by moral authority.[35] This issue is yet another big challenge that is put forward in the context of urban evangelism. There are various theological and ethical responses that emerged to address this issue in the form of rejective-punitive position, rejective-Non-punitive position, qualified acceptance of homosexuality, full acceptance position.[36] To approach this challenge in the urban setting, Jesus' model of witness could be applied. Jesus emphasized on a higher ethical standard during His earthly ministry. At the same time, He had great compassion in the search for the lost. Jesus did not wait for the lost to come to Him. He invited them to participate in God's gracious kingdom, extended to them His powers of healing. He did not approach sinners with hatred attitude or arrogant behavior. When sinners responded favorably to the message of Jesus, they were not treated as second-class members of God's people but welcomed without reservation.[37] Jesus was not condemning the sinners, but He was loving them and extended His care towards them. That's the approach that could be set as a model while approaching the LGBTIQ community in urban evangelism.

6.5. Mushrooming of Heretic and Cultic movements

The emergence of heretic movements and cultic groups are rapidly growing in the ultramodern society. These groups deviate their teachings from the original essence of the true evangelical gospel. This has also become a challenging factor in urban evangelism. Because most of the heretic groups have the major agenda of reaching the people. They function in a strategic way to persuade the listeners to their own doctrines. They mesmerize and brainwash their followers to prove that their teachings are the real gospel. In some cases, they don't reveal their self-identity. They hide their identity and portray as if they are part of the mainline churches. They change their doctrinal teachings basing on the audience in a different setting. Misinterpretations are provided about new heaven, new earth, sanctification, hyper-grace, righteousness, the concept

35 James Emery White, "Evangelism in a Postmodern World," 362-3.

36 For detailed explanation about various theological and ethical responses related to this issue, refer, James B. Nelson, "Homosexuality: An Issue for the Church," *Readings in Christian Ethics: Issues and Applications*, vol. 2 eds. David K. Clark and Robert V. Rakestraw (Grand Rapids: Baker Books, 1996), 183-93; Aaron Martin and Chong Hung Ho, "Utilization of Cross Cultural Communication as a Tool to Reach out LGBT Community," *ACTS Theological Journal* 33 (2017), 85-113.

37 Robert A. J. Gagnon, *The Bible and Homosexual Practice: Texts and Hermeneutics* (Nashville: Abingdon Press, 2001), 212-213.

of sin, salvation, good news and so on.[38] They make sure that their teachings are very people friendly so that they can attract huge followers. If in case, the cultic movements' local country does not recognize them, they move on the third world countries where the gospel is preached among unreached people groups and proclaim that their preaching is the right gospel.

7. Chances in Urban Evangelism

As per the great commission given by Jesus Christ, reaching out to the unreached is an untiring task for all Christians. Reaching out to the diverse groups of people irrespective of regional boundaries, race, caste, religious background is possible through the urban evangelism.[39]

In urban evangelism, there is also a chance to focus on different groups according to their age group and based on their diverse occupation. There are various groups such as diverse age group of children, youths, young couples, parents of small children, childless couples, retired people, single people, flat dwellers, sheltered housing people, land workers, industrial workers, professionals, and self-employed, service personnel, office and shop workers, hospitalized people, fellowship clubs, holiday clubs, international students and so on.[40] If the churches could join hands to venture into co-operative evangelism, then there could be a celebration of reaching out to many responsive individuals. Some of the strategic tools in evangelizing the urban people could be Personal Evangelism, Parenthood Evangelism,[41] Servanthood Evangelism, Love for God, and Love in Action.[42] There could be the training

38 David M. Litwa, *Refutations of All Heresies* (Atlanta: SBL Press, 2016), 18ff.

39 Because the job opportunities and educational facilities are at higher frequency in urban area, most of the people migrate or wish to migrate to urban area. Therefore, the usual population in the urban area is not limited to one particular people group. It will usually mixed people group.

40 Clive Calver, Derek Copley, Bob Moffett and Jim Smith, eds., *A Guide to Evangelism* (Basingstoke: Marshall Morgan & Scott, 1984), 130ff.

41 In an urban setting, when some well-established churches extend their support towards the developing and newly emerged pastors/missionaries/ministers with a parenthood heart, then parenthood evangelism could happen well through which the recipients of the gospel could be reached at a significant level. Mission has attained a paradigm shift where churches has started to focus on mission beyond their boundaries.

42 In the third world countries, slums are increasing rapidly in the urban areas. Showing Christ through living could be a tool to reach people for Christ. Sidney Rooy exegete the Greek word *Dikaioma* as the righteous deed or doing of justice and name it as "Love in action". To love one's neighbor means to do justice to the neighbor. Biblical teaching to Israelites was to love the resident alien by giving food and clothing (Deut 10:18-19). Abraham and the descendants were chosen to be a blessing for nations. It is being elected to be a blessing for all other people who were not part of the elect group. When Christians show their mercy acts towards the needy, this could be also a way to show Christ's love. See, Sidney Rooy, "Righteousness and Justice: Reflections on Revelation 22:11c and Amos 5:24,"

of church members at a different level for involvement in urban evangelism at different capacities. This could be the men's team, women's group, youths, and also potential children in the church.

7.1. Alternative Paradigm of Urban Evangelism in the Ultramodern Society

7.1.1. Culturally Conducible

The method of urban evangelism should adhere to the local cultural setting. For instance, Jesus' style of dealing with different people varied by entering their worldview.[43] In the same pattern, while presenting the gospel to different people in the urban setting, entering their own cultural world is inevitable for better communication. This does not mean to go to the extreme of going away from the original thrusts of the gospel but being inclusive to accommodate for the reason of evangelism. Emery White has also suggested that the approach, method, and style should be culturally relevant.[44] In other words, preaching of the gospel in an urban setting should be conducive to contemporary culture.

7.1.2. Dynamically Witnessing

Living a life that portrays Christ through one's own character, actions and behavior could be one of the dynamic ways of witnessing while involving in urban evangelism. Traditional way of visiting door to door to pronounce "Jesus Loves You" and calling for repentance in bus stops and train stations does not work at a large level in the urban setting.[45] But it seems people are busy in their world and they do not give importance to what is transpiring around them. So, living an exemplary life could contribute to better reach the people for Christ.

Theological Fraternity Bulletin, no. 4 (1978): 7; Harvie M. Conn, *Evangelism: Doing Justice and Preaching Grace* (Michigan: Zondervan Publishing House, 1982), 42; Joel S. Kaminsky, *Yet Jacob I loved: Reclaiming the Biblical Concept of Election* (Nashville: Abingdon, 2007), 80ff; Nathan MacDonald, "Did God Choose the Patriarchs? Reading for Election in the Book of Genesis," *Genesis and Christian Theology*, eds., Nathan MacDonald, Mark W. Elliott and Grant Macaskill (Grand Rapids: Eerdmans Publishing Company, 2012), 245-66.

43 When He was dealing with fishermen, he talked about fishing. Whereas when He spoke to the woman at the well, He talked about water. While conversing with tax collectors, he spoke about money.

44 James Emery White, "Evangelism in a Postmodern World," 366.

45 The write of the paper does not undermine the traditional methods, but it is to say that in an urban setting it does not function very effectively. This thought is borrowed from Emery White. See, James Emery White, "Evangelism in a Postmodern World," 367.

7.1.3. Intentionally Building Relationship

Building intentional relationships with non-Christians could be one way using which gospel presentation could be made possible. In the long run of the continued relationship, there could be building up of good rapport and credibility in exchanging constant communication. There could be developed a chance to share a personal testimony. The inductive method of sharing the gospel works well in this setting.[46] Listeners can see the truth in such a way that they are ready to accept, agree with, and respond to that gospel truth.[47] This can contribute to the building up of strong faith in the lives of new believers.

7.2. Reaching out Generation Z in an Urban Setting[48]

They are hypercognitive generation who always look for cross-references through various sources of information. The context of Generation Z is having easy mobility and access to social networks and digital natives. Experts have coined the term communaholic for the behavior which connects to different truths.[49] This group of people doesn't even distinguish between the friends whom they meet online and the friends in the physical world. Generation Z gives more importance to online communities. Sometimes, they even live in an imaginary world by being connected with the people around the globe. Using technology as a tool, they need to be also reached with the gospel of Jesus Christ.

7.3. Communicating Through Video Sharing Sites

Using video technology could be one of the tools in reaching Generation Z in the urban setting. Neil Postman comprehends, "Pictures present the world as objects, language presents the world as ideas."[50] If this technology could be used in urban evangelism, it can easily reach the Generation Z community. The truths of the gospel could be presented in the form of pictures with audio

---

46 Inductive method begins with particular life experiences and point towards principles or truths. Inductive preaching is "a quest for discovery." Cf. Rick Gosnell, "Proclamation and the Postmodernist" in *The Challenge of Postmodernism: An Evangelical Engagement*, ed. David S. Dockery (Grand Rapids, MI: Baker Books, 2001), 382-3.

47 Ralph L. Lewis and Gregg Lewis, *Inductive Preaching: Helping People Listen* (Westchester, Illinois: Crossway, 1983), 81.

48 People who were born between 1995-2010 falls under the category of Generation Z. Previous generation is Generation Y is entitled as "millennials" – people who were born between 1980-94. The context of Generation Y is globalization, economic stability and emergence of internet. Refer, https://www.pewresearch.org/fact-tank/2019/01/17/where-millennials-end-and-generation-z-begins/ accessed on Dec 26, 2019.

49 Generation Z is also commented as highly misunderstood generation. They are more depressed without paying the attention to the reality of this world.

50 Neil Postman, *Amusing Ourselves to Death* (New York: Penguin Press, 1985), 72.

and video. Video sharing sites allow people to upload and share their video clips with the public at large or to invited guests. YouTube became a popular video sharing site on the web since Google acquired it in 2006.[51] These sites permit anyone with a web camera to post any sort of video and make it available to users globally. It allows personal tones towards the content and sharing of ideas about faith in creative ways. Readers have the provision to post comments in reaction to the posts about content on their own blog using a trackback. These sites allow people to embed audio/video hosted remotely onto their blog or website. Christian-specific sites have also recently sprung up to provide faith-based video sharing services. Such technological provisions develop communities through interconnectedness.[52] Occasionally, these online communities lead to meeting people in person and can extend to other forms of Christian community and fellowship.

7.4 Usage of Blogs

Principally, blogging dominates an individual's faith expression in the urban context. Articles concerning God, Jesus, church, faith, and so on are published in the blogs. As part of urban evangelism, Christian bloggers can use multimedia to create audio and video blogs that offer one's own experiences, views, discussions, stories, and teachings. Many prominent Christian thinkers, authors, and leaders have blogs with a podcast or streaming audio speeches, lectures, or sermons as part of their evangelistic work.

7.5. Cyber Church

Since the awareness about the cyber world is more vibrant in the urban area, there are more chances for the development of cyber church which could be used as a tool for urban evangelism. Cyber church is the extension of the universal church into cyberspace. It is an institution that teaches and practices its religious beliefs entirely or primarily through online methods. The presence of Christian community online is often viewed as the emerging church attempting to express faith within the given cultural change. Cyber church is a venture which can nourish and strengthen the spiritual and psychological sphere of the people. Members of the cyber churches meet, connect or congregate through the internet. A wide variety of ways hundreds of churches use the Internet to facilitate their religious activities. The people are not bound to space or location. Cyber church provides the space for people to participate, share and interact with one another.[53] The cyber church engages through websites, audio/

---

51 http://encyclopedia2.thefreedictionary.com/Video+sharing accessed on Dec 27, 2019.

52 http://revivemegod.org/?p=318 accessed on Dec 27, 2019.

53 John Joshva Raja and Samson Prabhakar, ed., *Introduction to Communication and Media Studies* (Bangalore: BTESSC/SATHRI, 2008), 170.

video podcasts and blogs, social networking sites and other electronic online provisions that act as interactive means within cyberspace. Thousands of audio/video sermons, recordings of conferences and seminars, documentaries, faith-themed films, and more are accessible online. These tools could be applied for an effective urban evangelism.

7.6. Utilizing Present-day Innovative Technology

Since the use of the internet and mobile phones and electronic gadgets are at a peak in these present days, there is a provision to use this technology for urban evangelism. There are already some mobile applications that are developed by some Christian organizations to propagate the scripture and gospel songs 24x7. Additionally, Bible stories with cartoon imageries could be added to it to reach out to the Generation Z group of people. There could be also Christian movies and short films which could be broadcasted through social media such as youtube. It is important to update these technological techniques as per the necessity of the modern usage while using it as a tool for urban evangelism.

8. Importance of Communication in Urban Evangelism

Christianity has its roots from the Jewish origins, where God intervenes to the people through various methods of communication like oral communication such as oracles, prophecies, dreams, and teachings.[54] God also uses human beings for communication purposes. Prophets, Priests, Counsellors, and Judges became the mouthpiece of God and they became the representatives of God, transmitting God's message to the people. Bible stories emerged from the oral traditions that were handed down from generation to generation. The communication process denotes two dimensions: one is vertical, and the other is horizontal. Horizontal communication incorporates communication with the whole creation, and it is the basis of all social interaction.[55] The aim and work of Christianity have to communicate with people in all its fullness, and people also express themselves to God. God by nature is a communicator.[56] Christ communicated with the apostles and then commissioned them as communicators (Matthew 28:18-20). As an ambassador of Christ (2 Corinthians 5:20), we are called to communicate the message of Christ.

54 John Joshuva Raja and Samson Prabhakar, ed., *Introduction to Communication and Media Studies,* 36.

55 Cited by C.R.W. David, ed., *Communication in Theological Education: A Curriculum* (Bangalore: BTESSC, 1986), 8.

56 God "expressed" himself at the time of creation. He had company with Adam, Abraham, Moses and David. He allowed His son to take a human form and lead a life in a social context. He lived among the people and communicated the values of life. Cf. Viggo Sogaard, *Media in Church and Mission: Communicating the Gospel* (California: William Carey Library, 1993), 12-5.

9. Conclusion

Even though there are various challenges present in urban evangelism, the still mission is not impossible. Because the mission belongs to God. There is a mission because God loves people.[57] Since, God is the fountain of sending love, God's love towards people which is exhibited through the mission is possible without resistance. In the ultramodern society, there is a need for a global fraternity to work against all sorts of injustices as a living witness for Christ. There should be a strategic planning and prayerful attempt for the propagation of the gospel in the present days. Utilizing all the present-day modern technology for the sake of urban evangelism is something that is inevitable. There are lots of biased opinions present among Christians with regard to the usage of present technologies. But this research is an attempt to prove that being culturally conducible, dynamically witnessing, intentionally building relationships, utilizing cyberspace and internet-related electronic gadgets as a communicative device, one could advance the urban evangelistic work at a higher level.

57 David J. Bosch, *Transforming Mission: Paradigm Shifts in Theology of Mission,* 14th ed. (Maryknoll, NY: Orbis Books, 1999), 390.

PART II

THEOLOGICAL

6

RETHINKING THE CALLING OF DOCTRINAL THEOLOGIAN IN LIGHT OF CALVIN'S CONCEPT OF *DOCTRINA* FROM A KOREAN EVANGELICAL THEOLOGICAL PERSPECTIVE

Sang Hwa Han[1]

First of all, I convey my sincere congratulations to Dr. David Onesimu as I remember him very well with loving memories. I would like to express my prayerful heart of God's abundant blessings for him as celebrating his life on the occasion of the 65th Birthday.

---

1 *Prof. Rev. Dr. Sang Hwa Han is currently the Dean of the graduate school of Asia United Theological University (AUTU). She graduated from Sung Jun University in Korea in 1984, BA in Western Philosophy and earned M.div degree in AUTU aka ACTS (Asian Center for Theological Studies and Mission) in 1988. She also studied theology in Cambridge, Uk from 1984-87. She obtained her Ph.D. degree in the field of historical and theological field in 1996 at Westminster Theological Seminary in Philadelphia, USA. The title of her doctoral dissertation is "The Debate between Gadamer and Habermas Revisited from a Reformed Epistemological Perspective: Towards a Christian Theistic Hermeneutics" She has been serving as a professor of systematic Theology in ACTS since 1996. She was formerly the president of the Systematic Theology Division of Korean Evangelical Theological Society. She published Postmodernism and Evangelical Theology (CLC, 2008), Introducing Theocentric Theology (CLC, 2010) and Theology For the love of the Gospel (ACTS, 2019). She also translated into Korean, Introducing Radical Orthodoxy (2011) and Christianity and the Postmodern Turn (2013). She has written numerous academic articles in the fields of hermeneutics, Christian Philosophy, and theology.*

Introduction

This paper is addressed to Asian evangelical theological educators on the topic of "The Calling of an Asian Biblical Scholar/Theologian: Challenges Facing Asian Evangelicals Today." Being a doctrinal theologian, the writer has narrowed down the topic to the calling of a doctrinal theologian. However, "Why should we only focus on Calvin?" "Does the reformer of the 16th century still have relevance to the 21st century Asian Christian context?" An affirmative answer is possible in view of the fact that Presbyterianism covers the majority of Korean Christianity and that Calvinism particularly dominates the conservative Presbyterian churches and seminaries. Especially in this year, 2017, the year of quincentennial of the Reformation, numerous seminars, forums, and consultations are being held by various churches and Christian institutions in commemoration of it. In this context, studying Calvin is very much relevant and timely, and all the more important is the proper implementation of the Reformer's theology into contemporary contexts. One danger of Korean Calvinism is the tendency towards the strict orthodox Reformed Traditionalism backed up by authoritarian doctrinalism which refuses to respond to the demand of the contemporary world.[2] In order not to fall prey to barren doctrinalism, a theologian should always not only interact with theologians of other traditions but also be open to the current cultural changes to which Christian churches should successfully respond. Here successful response implies both maintaining biblical (doctrinal) identity and cultural relevancy.[3]

It is common to think that the main task of a doctrinal theologian leans more towards the former, namely keeping doctrinal purity, so as to maintain Christian identity including a certain denominational identity. This common understanding may be superficially true. Nevertheless, if we consider the

---

2 One example is that some Reformed theologians and pastors reject all contemporary Christian music and want to revive the 16th century Genevan Psaltery in the worship with neglecting different sensibilities of young Christians. Another example is that within the largest conservative Presbyterian denomination, a stronger opposition against woman-ordination is declared recently by passing a more specifically stated law against it than the past. There is a stronger tendency of distancing away from so-called evangelicalism than before with a stronger "Reformed" consciousness.

3 Daniel L. Migliore also argues that the balance between the doctrinal concern and the cultural concern should be maintained in his article entitled, "Christology in Context: The Doctrinal and Contextual Tasks of Christology Today," *Interpretation* 49/3 (July 1995), 242-56. In relation to it, Christine Helmer, *Theology and the End of Doctrine* (Louisville, KY: John Knox Press, 2014) seems to argue for the reconnection between doctrines and reality in a fresh way by linking George Lindbeck's cultural-linguistic approach to transcendence. The discussion on the nature of doctrine is another crucially important area to investigate. See Alister McGrath, *The Genesis of Doctrine: A Study in the Foundation of Doctrinal Criticism* (Grand Rapids, MI: Eerdmans, 1990).

matter more deeply, there are other dimensions within the task of a doctrinal theologian, namely implementing the doctrine within the pastoral context. It is precisely because of neglecting this pastoral dimension that a dogmatic theologian falls into the barren doctrinalism. Here doctrinalism can be defined to be "strict adherence to a particular set of doctrines," undermining other areas of religious life. It is different from "dogmatism," which signifies more of an opinionated attitude. This paper concerns the way of "use" or "treatment" of doctrines, rather than the personality or character problems of arrogant, authoritarian or less scholarly attitudes. The purpose of this study is to highlight that the calling of the doctrinal theologian is not limited to keeping "*sana doctrina* (sound doctrine)" in line with the Gospel and the Scriptures, but extends to embrace the broad horizons of applying them to various contexts of ecclesiastical and social life. Most of all, doctrinal theologians must always be sensitive to the spiritual dimension of doctrines that are directly related to salvation and judgment (1 Tim 4:16; 2 Tim 4:1-5).

This paper begins by stating the problems found in the theological academia in general, and particularly in Korea, and then examines Calvin's usage of the word, *doctrina* in a limited extent. With some insights gleaned from the study, this paper stresses the spiritual nature of the doctrine, which leads to a reconsideration of the calling off the doctrinal theologian. The attempt of this paper is especially significant not only in responding to the challenges of the secular academism, commonly found in current theological scholarship globally but also to those from the strict doctrinalism within the conservative Reformed circles in general.

1. The Problems Stated: Dangers of Secular Academism and Barren Doctrinalism in Theological Academia

A book entitled *Christian theology in Asia,* edited by Sebastian C. H. Kim (2008) starts with an interesting introduction written by David M. Thompson subtitled, "Introduction: mapping Asian Christianity in the context of world Christianity."[4] Here, Thompson significantly describes the process of the separation between academic and ecclesiastical theology.[5] There was a time

4 Sebastian C. H. Kim, ed., *Christian Theology in Asia* (Cambridge, UK: Cambridge University Press, 2008), 3-21.

5 Kim, ed., *Christian Theology in Asia,* 4-5. The separation between the ecclesial theology and the social theology went on together with the bifurcation between the conservative theology and liberal theology. The former stressed the salvation of individual soul whereas the latter the social justice. Now in the 21st century fortunately the awareness of the integrative nature of the gospel became more and more prevalent among the theologians of both camps. The Christian message of the Bible originally not only directs towards individual changes but also with its emphasis on the coming of the kingdom of God points to the total change of the old eon.

when these two theologies were the same. After the Enlightenment and with the result of biblical criticism, the gap between academia and the church grew causing the agenda of academic theology to become different from that of the church. This process also changed the authority and the role of the Scripture in doing theology. Most of the 19th and 20th-century modern Protestant theologies were done in the department of religious studies at Western universities.[6] Due to the separation from the church theological academia globally finds the common challenge of secular academism. Secular academism is secular in the sense that studies are not directed to serve the church but directed towards a secular society. Also, it is academic in the sense that studies are often carried out to solve the problems of academic scholars' own creation, and their contributions remain within the academic circles. Theological academia, in general, has the pressure to push towards a more societally-oriented, universal theology rather than an ecclesiastically-oriented theology that directly addresses the agenda of the regional churches. Even though, as a historical theologian, Thompson does not directly give any evaluative judgment on the separation between academia and the church, this situation is one of the challenges that an Asian evangelical theologian needs to consider deeply.

He then goes on to say about the western dominancy on theological agenda as follows:

> Very often when people refer to a western-dominated theological agenda, they are referring to the agenda of the western universities, … Furthermore the sense that others, whoever the others may be, are determining the agenda is not unique to Asia, Africa, or Latin America; sometimes in Britain it is felt that the theological agenda is determined by Germany, France or USA.[7]

Asian theological academia gets more complicated with the problem of heavy dependency on western scholarship. This problem has been recited by many for quite some time, and yet there has not been any sign of the change (including this paper).

Another factor that characterizes Asian theology is that it is considered to be "contextual theology." After introducing liberation theology in Latin America as a new style of theology, Thompson discusses Minjung theology in Korea, the Three-Self movement in China, Water Buffalo Theology of Koyama in Japan and Dalit theology of India.[8] Despite the importance of the contextual issues in theology, these theologies do not represent the evangelical

---

6 See James C. Livingston, *Modern Christian Thought Vol. 1: The Enlightenment and the Nineteenth Century*, Second Edition (Minneapolis, MN: Fortress Press, 2006).

7 Kim, ed., *Christian Theology in Asia*, 5-6.

8 Kim, ed., *Christian Theology in Asia*, 10-17.

faith of the Church. Certainly, Minjung theology in Korea does not express the faith of the majority of the Korean Church now or even then when its fame was at its pinnacle during the 1970s. It is one of the best examples of socially-oriented academic theology which might have contributed to the democratization of Korean society but not the growth of the Christian church. With the enunciation of the social, cultural and contextual elements of theology as well as the contributions that the above social theologies have made in many ways, biblical, evangelical and ecclesiastical elements should be stressed for a balanced Asian Evangelical theology. The missiological concerns should go hand in hand with the doctrinal concern without one overriding the other.

In the case of the Korean Presbyterian Church, the liberal faction faces more dangers from secular academism than the conservative faction. However, the conservative Presbyterian Church finds another danger, namely, that of the strict traditional, authoritarian and barren doctrinalism. In order to understand the current situations of Korean Presbyterianism, it is necessary to know its division history. Korean Presbyterian Church went through three historically significant divisions. The first one was the separation of the Goryeo group from the General Assembly of the Presbyterian Church of Korea in 1952 based on differing views of Shinto Shrine worship. The second division occurred in 1953 between the Presbyterian Church of the Republic of Korea (Kijang) and the Presbyterian Church of Korea (Yejang) concerning the view of the Scriptures. The former formed a liberal view that accepted the biblical criticism upon the Bible, while the latter rejected a conservative view that regards the Bible as the inerrant word of God. The third large division was made in 1959 within Yejang splitting it into two parties: the Presbyterian Church *of* Korea (Yejang Tonghap) and the Presbyterian Church *in* Korea (Yejang Hapdong) concerning the matter of joining the World Council of Churches. There are many complex issues in the history of the division of the Korean Presbyterian Church, which goes beyond the purview of this study.[9] Nevertheless, it is generally accepted that within the conservative Korean Presbyterian Church which consists of quite large numbers, there is a strong sense of doctrinalism that exists.

The more alarming tendency found in the current development of the Korean Reformed Theological circle is that the increased distancing away from Evangelicalism, partly due to the latter's theological laxity and doctrinal looseness. Without getting into the complex issues of the relationship between the Reformed theology and the evangelicalism, the assertion of this paper is that the Reformed theology must be wary of the tendency towards the

9 S. Kim and K. Kim, *A History of Korean Christianity*, 197-206. For the early period of the history of Korean Protestant Christianity see Sung-Deuk Oak, *The Making of Korean Christianity: Protestant Encounters with Korean Religions, 1876-1915* (Waco, TX: Baylor University Press, 2013).

doctrinalism that has a strong emphasis on the doctrine of the sovereignty of God, predestination and covenant theology. The best remedy for the danger of doctrinalism is self-consciously embracing the evangelical emphasis on the personal conversion experience by the saving grace of Christ through the work of the Holy Spirit. Korean Reformed Christianity should not forfeit its own evangelical and revivalistic root.[10] Despite some drawbacks of the past Korean revivalism, we should not throw away the baby with the bathwater.

2. Calvin's Dynamic Use of the Term, 'doctrina.'

A good way to check the current dangers of a tradition is to go back to the very root, namely, "back to the sources, *ad fontes*." One of the grounding figures, before any divisions within the Reformed theological tradition, is John Calvin (1509-1564). The purpose of this section is to highlight Calvin's unique understanding of *doctrina* based on some Calvin scholars' studies. This discussion will serve to bring out some ideas for rethinking the calling of the doctrinal theologian.

Victor E. d'Assonville, Jr., a South African Reformed scholar, wrote his doctoral dissertation entitled, "Der Begriff 'doctrina' bei Calvin: eine theologische Analyse" (2000),[11] and from it he published two shorter English articles later.[12] In his first article, "The ministry of the Word – the concept of doctrina as used by Calvin in his first Institutes (1536)," he focuses on analyzing the various usages of the term, *doctrina* and presents Calvin's Word-of-God theology in the pastoral context.[13] Here, the bond between the Scripture and the *doctrina* as a proclamation is particularly accentuated. The second article deals with Calvin's Word-of-God theology in the exegetical context, with the special emphasis on the close relationship between doctrina

10 Robert E. Buswell, Jr. and Timothy S. Lee, *Christianity in Korea* (Honolulu, HI: Hawaii University Press, 2006), 331-408. For the evangelicalism, together with revivalism in Korea see Timothy S. Lee, *Born Again: Evangelicalism in Korea* (Honolulu, HI: University of Hawaii Press, 2010).

11 Victor E. d'Assonville, Jr., "Der Begriff 'doctrina' bei Johannes Calvin - eine theologische Analyse," (Rostocker Theologische Studien, Bd. 6, zugleich: Rostock, Univ., Diss., 2000), Münster: LIT, 2001.

12 Victor E. d'Assonville, Jr., "The ministry of the Word – the concept of *doctrina* as used by Calvin in his first Institutes (1536)," *Koers* 66 (1 & 2) 2001:71-86 and "Calvin as an exegete of Scripture: a few remarks with reference to Calvin research in general," *In die Skriflig* 44, Supplement 3 2010:129-143. The original form of the latter appears in *The Calvin Handbook*, edited by Herman J. Selderhuis (Grand Rapids, MI: Eerdmans, 2008) 378-384, under the title of "Exegesis and Doctrina."

13 D'Assonville, "The ministry of the Word – the concept of doctrina as used by Calvin in his first Institutes (1536)."

and exegesis of the Scripture.[14] For Calvin, not only is the principle of "sola Scriptura" important but so is the principle of "tota Scriptura," i.e., to take the whole of Scripture into account when expositing a certain biblical text. Here doctrina is used as the teaching of "tota Scriptura," therefore, it is one *doctrina*. As the Word of God, the one *doctrina* is one truth of God ("Una est Dei veritas").[15] With this unity of the Holy Scriptures, Calvin maintains the broad biblical-theological horizon of a particular text. Calvin regards the original intention of the writer of a particular biblical book as the most important and uses both a sound theological-methodological and historical-grammatical method.[16] From these two articles, he stresses the significance of the diverse usage of the term, doctrina. The contribution of d'Assonville not only analyzed the diverse usage of the term and showed its whole wide semantic range before other scholars did but also draws scholars' attention to its significance in Calvin studies as well as in the Reformed theologies in general. He maintains that it is of considerable importance to analyze the way Calvin used the concept of doctrina, not only in a dogmatic and historical sense but also within homiletics, catechetics, and pastoral care. Concerning the diverse meanings of *doctrina*, he states, "The scale ranges from summary or focus of Scripture, the gospel, contents of faith, exposition, the proclamation of salvation, via teaching or sermon to pastoral care, confession, doctrine, canon, dogma or doctrinal system."[17] The wide range of usage goes far beyond the usual semantic parameters of the term, which seems to be one prominent characteristic of the rhetorical style of Calvin. D'Assonville argues that the diverse and dynamic usage of *doctrina* requires the sensitivity and flexibility in interpreting the Reformer's intention and meaning by various textual contexts. An interpreter needs carefully heeding to a particular context without generally applying the arbitrary lexicographical meaning.

Herman J. Selderhuis, the president of the International Calvin Congress, also acknowledges the practical nature of doctrine in Calvin and describes the theology of Calvin as *theologia practica* ("practical theology"[18]). He extends the study of *doctrina* from Calvin to Heinrich Bullinger, Heinrich Alting (1583-

14 D'Assonville, "Calvin as an exegete of Scripture: a few remarks with reference to Calvin research in general."

15 D'Assonville, "Calvin as an exegete of Scripture: a few remarks with reference to Calvin research in general," 381.

16 D'Assonville, "Calvin as an exegete of Scripture: a few remarks with reference to Calvin research in general."

17 D'Assonville, "Calvin as an exegete of Scripture: a few remarks with reference to Calvin research in general," 139.

18 It should be clarified that "practical theology" here means the practical nature of the whole theology which must not be confused with the sense of the current use of the term, a sub-discipline of theology which studies about homiletics, liturgics, church practices and so on.

1644) and David Pareus, and further still to its use in the confessions, church orders and catechisms of the 16th century Reformed tradition in his article, "Der Begriff, '*Doctrina,*' in der Reformierten Tradition des 16. Jahrhunderts."[19] Here, drawing from many of d'Assonville's discoveries, he also presents the diverse ways in which doctrina is used in Calvin. He starts with Wilhelm Niesel's critique against Emil Brunner's misjudgment that Calvin opposes doctrines applied to life and piety. Niesel criticizes that Brunner did not understand what *doctrina* is according to the Reformation when Brunner seemed to belittle the promise and the commission of doctrines valid for the church in preaching.[20] Selderhuis shows in his work that in the Reformed tradition, at least in its early period, *doctrina* was always situated within the context of the life and faith of the church.

He mentions that the term *doctrina*, appears in more than 9500 pages of Calvin's work, *Corpus Reformatorum*, and this frequent use of the term does not make Calvin a doctrinaire.[21] For Calvin's use of the term *doctrina*, it should not at all be equated with what its meaning in Englis 'doctrine' or in German 'Doktrine,' which usually signifies a systematic representation of the religious teaching. Referring to d'Assonville's doctoral dissertation, he also acknowledges the richness of the meanings of *doctrina* in Calvin.[22] He then explains the pastoral nature of the term as follows:

> Besides, it is striking that Calvin also connects pastoral care with *doctrina*. In their exercise, the mediation and the teaching of *doctrina*, as the content of the gospel, serves the believer to find consolation. *Doctrina* is thus not intended for the mind, but for the heart, which is also the purpose of the *doctrina* when it comes to preaching. In Calvin, "*doctrina*" and "preaching" are almost synonymous. *Doctrina* must be proclaimed, because only in this

---

19 Herman J. Selderhuis, "Der Begriff '*Doctrina*' in der Reformierten Tradition des 16. Jahrhunderts," in *Bewegung und Beharrung: Aspekte des reformierten Protestantismus, 1520-1650*, edited by Christian Moser & Peter Opitz (Leiden, The Netherlands: Brill, 2009), 413-432.

20 Selderhuis, "Der Begriff, '*Doctrina*' in der Reformierten Tradition des 16. Jahrhunderts," 413, footnote #1.

21 Selderhuis, "Der Begriff, '*Doctrina*' in der Reformierten Tradition des 16. Jahrhunderts," 415. In the footnote #7, he exemplifies Bouwsma who makes this error when he says that the way Calvin uses the terms, 'gospel' and '*doctrina*' led him to believe that faith is understood 'less as trust in God's promises than as intellectual assent to a body of propositions' in William Bouwsma, *John Calvin – A Sixteenth-Century Portrait*, New York 1989, 99. This same quotation of Bouwsma is in d'Assonville's article, "The ministry of the Word – the concept of *doctrina* as used by Calvin in his first Institutes (1536)," 73.

22 Selderhuis, "Der Begriff, '*Doctrina*' in der Reformierten Tradition des 16. Jahrhunderts," 415.

> way it is salvational, and thus the proclamation of this "*doctrina salutis*" must, therefore, be absolutely pure. The holy word is the spiritual *doctrina*, and the *doctrina* is like a door to the heavenly kingdom.[23]

From the above, we observe that *doctrina* is the content of the gospel and the Scriptures and that should be mediated through preaching for the salvation and consolation of the believer. Thus, *doctrina* is spiritual and heavenly in nature.

Another important element of *doctrina* manifests in the following subtitle of the first edition of *Institutes of Christian Religion* (1536): "Embracing almost the whole sum of piety, & whatever is necessary to know of the doctrine of salvation: A work most worthy to be read by all persons zealous for piety, and recently published." Here Calvin assumes that his work attempts to embrace the Summa (totality) of piety and the whole teaching of salvation, which refers to doctrina. This holistic perspective of Calvin is well expressed in his presentation of Christian doctrines in the form of "institutes" rather than "loci." Selderhuis compares Calvin's *Institutes* with Melanchthon's *Loci Communes* and says that the latter shows the more logical treatment of doctrines.[24] Moreover, the first edition of Calvin's *Institutes* was prepared as a catechetical handbook for the benefit of the faithful believers in France. It was presented as a summary of the Protestant doctrine. From this fact, we observe that the holistic and catechetical nature of *doctrina* in Calvin.

What is striking is Calvin changes *doctrina* in the *Institutes* first edition to *Sapientia* (wisdom) in the 1539 edition. The first sentence of chapter one of *Institutes* 1536 edition say,, "Sum of almost all *sacra doctrina* (sacred doctrines) consists of the two parts: the knowledge God and that of ourself...." The same sentence in the 1539 edition finds *sacra Sapientia* (sacred wisdom) instead of *sacra doctrina*.[25] It is not clear why Calvin makes this change, but *doctrina* as wisdom also fits well with the kind of the knowledge of God Calvin talks about in general. For Calvin, the knowledge of God is not an objective and neutral knowledge, but the pious and personal knowledge that implies trust and reverence.[26] *Doctrina* is always directed to a wider knowledge of

23 Selderhuis, "Der Begriff, '*Doctrina*' in der Reformierten Tradition des 16. Jahrhunderts," 416. The translation is mine. Here, in this quotation, Calvin's words in *the Sermon of 1 Sam* [CO 30, 299] and in *Catechism of the Church of Geneva* (OS 2, 128) is cited.

24 Selderhuis, "Der Begriff, '*Doctrina*' in der Reformierten Tradition des 16. Jahrhunderts," 415.

25 Selderhuis, "Der Begriff, '*Doctrina*' in der Reformierten Tradition des 16. Jahrhunderts," 416.

26 Calvin, *Institutes of Christian Religion* (1559), I.2.2.

God, and self-knowledge. According to Calvin, it is in this twofold knowledge that the totality of Christian doctrine lies.

Here, we should clarify the relationship between the totality of Christian doctrine and many doctrines. The totality (Summa*)* consists of many parts (pars). Perhaps the best place Calvin describes this relation is his following statement found in "To the Reader" of the last edition (1559) of *Institutes:*

> Moreover, it has been my purpose in this labor to prepare and instruct candidates in sacred theology for the reading of the divine Word, in order that they may be able both to have easy access to it and to advance in it without stumbling. For I believe I have so embraced the sum of religion in all its parts, and have arranged it in such an order, that if anyone rightly grasps it, it will not be difficult for him to determine what he ought especially seek in Scripture, and to what end he ought to relate its contents.[27]

First, Calvin makes clear the purpose of his writing to help the people for the reading of the divine Word and then he explains that he covers the whole of Christian teachings, *the Summa* in all its parts, *pars* in proper order and arrangement, which shows the systematic nature of doctrines. However, it is important to understand this systematic relation between the one *doctrina* and many *doctrinae*, so that doctrinal studies, not only be concerned with explicating one particular doctrine but always explicating doctrine within its organic and structural relation to the totality of doctrines. Here, when Calvin regards *doctrina* as that of "Christ and the Apostles," and "the Gospel," he means *the Summa.*

The teaching character of *doctrina* (docere) may be the background for Calvin's view of the Scriptures as the school in which people learn the knowledge of God. He says, "For Scripture is the school of the Holy Spirit, in which, as nothing is omitted that is both necessary and useful to know, so nothing is taught but what is expedient to know."[28] In addition to Scripture, Calvin also speaks of the church as the school.[29] However, in both cases, it is not an institution to expand intellectual knowledge, but a body in which people are shaped into the likeness of Christ through the Holy Spirit, the best teacher, (*Optimus Magister*). Thus, Calvin regards the disciples as the pupils of these schools when he states, "Now, in order that true religion may shine upon us, we ought to hold that it must take its beginning from heavenly doctrine and that no one can get even the slightest taste of right and sound doctrine unless

27 Calvin, *Institutes of Christian Religion* (1559), "John Calvin to the Reader," 4.

28 Calvin, *Institutes of Christian Religion* (1559), III.21.3.

29 Calvin, *Institutes of Christian Religion* (1559), IV.1.4.

he be a pupil of Scripture."[30] This quotation truly manifests that *doctrina* here, is not human doctrines of reason, but the teaching of God Himself through the Holy Scriptures, and that is why it is called "heavenly," and "sacred," and true religion (piety) comes from its teaching. It is interesting to notice that our learning is expressed as "taste." Wen finds an even more intriguing expression in the following quotation, namely *doctrina*, as the rule of God through his Word, the eternal truth. Calvin writes,

> Now he means by the word, "regnant" not the power with which he is endowed, and which he exercises in governing the whole of nature, but the *doctrina* by which he asserts his lawful sovereignty. For errors can never be uprooted from human hearts until true knowledge of God is planted therein.[31]

Here this quote seems to mean that *doctrina* is identified with the eternal truth of God, which appears in few sentences earlier in Calvin's text, through which God rules our hearts by eradicating errors from our hearts.

Lastly, Selderhuis points out that *doctrina* is a mirror in which we perceive the image of God and when we look into this mirror, we are formed in the image of God. By giving the *doctrina* this meaning, the concept is indeed equated with Christian Wisdom (*Sapientia Christiana*)[32] and, with this designation of *doctrina*, the practical focus of the term is underlined. This *doctrina* as formation and edification can be traced back to the humanist-rhetoric tradition of teaching, which aimed not the noetic knowledge, but the formation, the education, and the pedagogy of humankind.[33] However, the formation in the Christian sense is different from the humanist tradition in the sense that it is the work of the Holy Spirit through the Word of God for the purpose of forming the image of Christ in his people. For Calvin, *doctrina* and application are inseparable.[34] As Selderhuis says, we can summarize Calvin's theology as *theologica practica.* Calvin uses *doctrina* as what God teaches (theodidactos) in the Holy Scriptures and the Gospel. Therefore, it is called to be heavenly and sacred. It also can be identified with the doctrine of Salvation, through which our conscience finds rest in God's grace. It is even called the

30 "Sic autem habendum est, ut nobis fulgeat vera religio, exordium a caelesti doctrina fieri debere, nec quenquam posse vel minimum gustum rectae sanaeque doctrinae percipere, nisi qui Scripturae fuerit discipulus" Calvin, *Institutes of Christian Religion* (1559), I.6.2.

31 Calvin, Institutes (1559) I.6.3.

32 Calvin, Commentarius in epistolam ad Philippenses, in CO 52, 12.

33 Selderhuis, "Der Begriff 'Doctrina' in der Reformierten Tradition des 16. Jahrhunderts," 418

34 Selderhuis, "Der Begriff 'Doctrina' in der Reformierten Tradition des 16. Jahrhunderts," 418.

reign of God in our hearts by the truth for the purpose of being like Christ in the life of the believer.

In addition to the above discussion, we need to include d'Assonville's treatment of *doctrina* in relation to ecclesiology. For our topic, the calling of the doctrinal theologian is related to the offices of the church. Calvin defines the church as "the society of all the saints, a society which, spread over the whole world, and existing in all ages, yet bound together by the one *doctrina* of Christ, and the one Spirit, cultivates and observes unity of faith and brotherly concord" (OS I,466).[35] From this definition, we can know that *doctrina* is the center of the life of the church. By persevering in the sound faith, a faithful testimony to *sana doctrina* is rendered. *Sana doctrina*, as *doctrina* of Christ, is, however, not a rational, intellectual concept but refers directly to life (*vita*).[36] It implies that the church is, according to the Reformed view, a church of the Word – in contrast to the Roman view of the church as a sacramental church (according to which grace is received through the sacraments). Therefore, the preaching of the Gospel, together with the sacraments are the two marks of the churh. (*notae ecclesiae*).[37] Calvin's Word of God theology fits well with his view of the four offices in the church, doctors (teachers), pastors, elders, and deacons. All four offices agree in all respects with the indivisible, intrinsic relation of doctrina with their respective jobs, the exegesis of Scripture, the proclamation of the gospel, the exhortation of believers, and the works of mercy.[38] It is interesting to see the way that Calvin makes the distinction between teachers and pastors. He says, "teachers are not put in charge of discipline, or administering the sacraments, or warning and exhortations, but only of Scriptural interpretation - to keep doctrine whole and pure among believers. But the pastoral office includes all these functions within itself."[39] Pastors are bound to the church. Here the office of a doctor can be identified with the calling of theologian in general, the calling of the doctrinal theologian as a part of it.

---

35 D'Assonville, "Calvin as an exegete of Scripture: a few remarks with reference to Calvin research in general," 137.

36 D'Assonville, "Calvin as an exegete of Scripture: a few remarks with reference to Calvin research in general," 137.

37 Despite d'Assonville's claim of including discipline which makes three marks of the church, I go by Calvin's treatment in *Institutes* (1559), IV.1.9. According to footnote #18 by John. T. McNeill, "Important as discipline is for Calvin, he does not distinctly make it one of the *notae,* or marks, by which the church is recognized, as does Bucer, *Scripta Anglicana*, 36.

38 D'Assonville, "Calvin as an exegete of Scripture: a few remarks with reference to Calvin research in general," 139.

39 Calvin, *Institutes of Christian Religion* (1559), IV.3.4

I. John Hesselink's study on "Calvin's Use of *Doctrina* in his Catechisms"[40] is worthy of our attention. In this study, Hesselink's concern is not with the concept of *doctrina* itself but with the interrelationship among Calvin's catechisms of 1538-9 and 1542-4 (*the Catechism of the Church of Geneva*) and *Institutes* (1536 and 1539) in the development of the Reformer's thought. Nevertheless, his confirmation of Calvin's use of *doctrina* in catechisms is valuable to give our discussions more validity. He provides a concise and clear summary of d'Assonville's arguments on *doctrina* and introduces Reinhold Hedtke's threefold use of the term, namely *doctrina* as knowledge (*Erkentnisse*), *doctrina* as the Christian life, and *doctrina* as warnings or admonitions (*Mahnungen*) and progress (*Fortschreiten*).[41] He goes on saying, "In all its manifestations Calvin's goal is to build the church and edify its members through the *utilitas*, *usus,* and *fructus* of *doctrina*."[42] This comment brings to light the key features of the Reformer's dealing with doctrine, which prevents Calvin from falling into doctrinalism. When Calvin exposits a doctrine, he does not do it purely for the sake of argument but always for the good of the church. Calvin always includes the usefulness and fruits in his discussion of doctrine. A far better remedy for the problem of doctrinalism is provided by Hesselink through Calvin's word. "Finally it should be kept in mind that if the teaching or preaching of doctrine is to be beneficial, it must be blessed by God and accompanied by prayer 'For doctrine is cold unless it is given divine efficacy.'"[43] "Every doctrine is useless unless God engraves it as if with his finger on our hearts."[44] Hesselink highlights that *doctrina* becomes effective with human prayer and through divine blessings.

3. Rethinking the Calling of the Doctrinal Theologia

From the above discussion on *doctrina*, one may glean some insights for a remedy of the current problems of secular academism and barren doctrinalism in theological academia. This probably more easily done for the latter than for secular academism.

---

40 In *Calvinus sacrarum literarum interpres*, edited by Herman J. Selderhuis (Göttingen, Germany: Vandenhoeck & Luprecht, 2008), 70-87.

41 John I. Hesselink, "Calvin's Use of Doctrina in his Catechisms," 72. Reinhold Hedtke, *Erziehung durch die Kirche*, 45, recited in footnote #8.

42 Hesselink, "Calvin's Use of Doctrina in his Catechisms," 72.

43 Hesselink, "Calvin's Use of Doctrina in his Catechisms," 72. Here cited Calvin's Commentary on John 17:1 (CO 47, 374), "Friget enim doctrina, nisi divinitus efficax reddatur."

44 Recited in Hesselink, "Calvin's Use of Doctrina in his Catechisms," 87. Calvin's Commentary on 1 Thessalonians 5:223 (Co 52, 178): "inutilem esse omnem doctrinam, donec cordibus nostris eam Deus quasi digito suo insculpat."

Against secular academism, a theologian, most of all, should be a believer before a scholar. Abraham Kuyper talks about two kinds of people and two kinds of sciences after dealing with science in the chapter entitled "Science Impaired by Sin" in his *Encyclopedia of Sacred Theology*. He reminds us that "regeneration (palingenesis) breaks humanity in two, and repeals the unity of the human consciousness."[45] A Christian theologian should belong to the regenerated group and be guided by the Holy Spirit, the Spirit of truth (John 14:16-17). Secondly, a Christian scholar whether in the biblical or the doctrinal field should relate the faith to the academic research at every level, from the presuppositional level to the methodological level. The attempt might be a greater challenge to biblical scholars in view that they feel more pressure from secular methodologies. These topics of theology, faith, and methodology cover another huge area of study that we cannot go into here. Lastly, since the academic arena is the realm where a fallen human mind is prone to be self-serving and boasting, and hence easily becomes an idol, a Christian scholar must always be wary of "the spirit of world" and must keep a humble and learning spirit guided by the spirit of God (1 Cor 2:12).

In facing the challenge of doctrinalism in the conservative theological circles, the above discussion on *doctrina* provides much food for thought. Firstly, a doctrinal theologian should not yield the Scriptures to the biblical theologian, for doctrines are supposed to come from the Scriptures and thus need to be verified by the Scriptures. A dogmatic or systematic theologian should try to be immersed in biblical teaching (*doctrina*) thoroughly.[46] One such pursuit may be attempting to keep a close connection with biblical theology.[47] After all, one of the important tasks of Dogmatics is to maintain the holistic perspective of the *tota Scriptura* and not to forfeit the broad horizon of the Kingdom of God.

In this respect, the common understanding that a dogmatic theologian is a specialty more of one's own denominational tradition than an unbiased representative of the Bible should boldly be reconsidered, so that they may nurture the global perspective for the good of the universal church. A dogmatic theologian may start with a perspective of a particular ecclesiastical

---

45 Abraham Kuyper, *Encyclopedia of Sacred Theology: Its Principles* (1898) (Reforming Science, 2008), 170.

46 This does not mean that every theologian should be a biblical scholar, but that a Christian theologian must be well-acquainted with the biblical storyline as well as its total outlook. In a word, since all fields of theology have to do with the Bible in one way or another, a theologian should strive to read and study the Scriptures as much as possible.

47 Long time ago, I had written an article entitled, "The Mutually Indispensable Relationship between Biblical Theology and Systematic Theology from the Reformed Theological Perspective," *ACTS Theological Journal*, Vol. 8 (1999), 210-250, and the present study reminds me of this thesis and freshly challenges me again.

tradition, such as the Lutheran, the Reformed, the Methodist, the Baptist or the Pentecostal tradition and even the Asian context. Nevertheless, they should not let that particular perspective limit their vision of the Kingdom. Following the Apostle Peter's teaching, we must grow in the knowledge of our Lord and Savior Jesus Christ. (2 Pt 3:18) Hence, the true ecumenical spirit of the Christian church comes from its Christ-centered orientation.

Secondly, however, a doctrinal theologian should keep in close relation with a local church. For doctrine is neither meant for scholarly debate nor even for correct understanding per se, but the application to the life of the church. The best way is to actually teach the doctrine to the congregation in a concrete language of everyday life, whatever the settings may be. By doing this, the gap between academia and the church will be reduced. Doctrine becomes alive within the ecclesiastical context.[48] Serve the church with a humble spirit!

Finally, the view that doctrine is taught by God (theodidactos) through the Word and the Spirit challenges the current theological situation, where the church doctrines are too easily dismissed by the modern critical scholars in the name of new discoveries. Conservative doctrinal theologians can become so reactive and defensive that they might seem always condemning and critical, losing the sight of the sacredness of their office. It is certain that the primary call of theologians is to preserve the healthy and sound teachings in line with the Gospel and the Scriptures. However, we should not lose sight of the goal and the purpose of our job, namely "channeling of the saving grace of Christ through teaching."[49] All offices of the church are the means of the saving grace of Christ to the world, including the vocation of the doctrinal theologian. This spiritual dimension of doctrine, which is directly related to salvation and judgment, should be stressed (1 Tim 4:16; 2 Tim 4:1-5).

---

48 See John Piper and D. A. Carson, *The Pastor as Scholar and the Scholar as Pastor* (Wheaton, IL: Crossway, 2011).

49 One example of doing this salvation centered teaching and researching is the "ACTS Theological Synoptic Movement," proposed by Dr. Chul Ha Han, and faithfully carried out by the faculty members of ACTS. The gist of the movement is the following: the "ACTS Theological Synoptic Movement" is committed to emphasizing and propagating "the central truth of Christianity." "The central truth of Christianity" is the core truth proclaimed by Jesus Christ and his apostles, transmitted by the church fathers and teachers, and clearly stated in all historic confessions of faith. It can be summarized as the message of salvation which declares that one may receive forgiveness of sins and sanctification by faith in the one and only Savior Jesus Christ who died and was resurrected for our redemption, and finally enter the eternal kingdom of God. This central truth is a grand theme that runs throughout the entire Bible (Luke 24:25-27; 44-48; John 5:39; 20:31; 2 Timothy 3:15-17) and serves as the ultimate criterion by which biblical revelation can be correctly interpreted. ACTS will emphasize the preeminent importance of the central truth, the starting point and foundation of faith that leads to salvation. For the whole statement of the movement, access the following address of the homepage of ACTS Research center of Theology, *http://ti.acts.ac.kr/html/sub02_03_2.asp*.

7

POLITICAL THEOLOGY IN INDIA TOWARDS RECONSTRUCTING THEOLOGY

Moses Manohar[1]

I was indeed glad when Rev. Dr. Vijayan told me about the festschrift in honor of Rev. Prof. Dr. David Onesimu. My congratulations to Dr. Onesimu for completing forty years of ministry in various capacities with the ECI and for completing his 65th year of age. Over the last twenty years, we have been meeting at the Senate of Serampore College. I have also seen his leadership as the Principal of MTSC. I found him as a man of deep faith and as a scholar, linguist and a leader with a friendly disposition. I wish him good health and long years of service in the mission of God.

Theology is the articulation of faith in the context of new knowledge. Faith without knowledge is ritualism and knowledge without faith is dangerous. From speculative to sectarian we now talk about contextual theologies. The method of theologizing has shifted to contexts and the challenges that are posed by new situations. Understanding the contexts and relating the faith is the role of theology. Changes that are taking place in society are rapid and unpredictable. Theology has the important role of making faith relevant and inspiring. Theology examines the contexts and helps people to find meaning and hope through faith. Therefore, theologizing is dynamic and even disturbing. Reconsideration and reconstruction of theology must be an ongoing process.

---

1 *Dr. Moses Manohar is the Executive Director of Inter-Church Service Association, ICSA, Chennai, <www.icsa.org.in> Chairman of the Constitution Committee of NCCI; former Treasurer of the Senate of Serampore College, W.B.; and a Scholar in Political Theology.*

Context of Theologizing in India

We hear many slogans in the Indian political arena such as India is a superpower, India sends rockets and satellites to the space, has many weapons including nuclear weapons in its arsenal, India marching towards a five trillion-dollar economy, etc. While these are all interesting for theology to examine, we also have another side of India.

There is a group of *Dalit* families struggling with a dead body without having a burial ground. Another group of *Dalit* families carrying the dead body but struggling without having an approach pathway to the burial ground as someone blocked it. We hear about villages where walls are constructed to exclude and prevent Dalits from entering the main village. Even in Tamilnadu, such untouchability walls are still in existence. Recently, near Salem, one such wall collapsed and fell on the huts of the poor people who were living on the other side of the wall, killing a few of them.

We have stories like what happened in Unnao village in Uttar Pradesh in June 2017, where a 17-year-old girl was raped by an MLA. The Police would not register the case. The father of the victim went to the Police station to give a complaint but he died mysteriously. Finally, the girl was attacked and she also died. All happened when Mr. Yogi Adityanath, a Hindu Swami is in power as the Chief Minister. There are many such horrors happening throughout India.

Due to excessive debt burden and extreme poverty, families as husband, wife, and children commit suicide. There are honor killings where relatives go after and kill young couples as a punishment to violate caste rules. When ordinary people struggling in unemployment and sickness, gather for prayer in a neighbor's house, gangs go and attack them.

This is the context for theologizing in India. In this context, we have to ask what is the meaning of being a Christian? What is the message we carry to these people? What is the meaning of our faith? A new theology emerges out of these questions. If the political system in India could not address the scenarios presented above, we ask, what is politics? Our response to this question gives birth to Political Theology.

Political Theology

Political Theology is an attempt to see politics as a Christian and as a theologian. A theologian tries to understand the forces that perpetrate the conditions explained above.

In India, politics is still associated with crime, corruption, and caste. Therefore, political theology in India would mean many things. Some of them are as follows:

1. Political Theology defines politics as people's right to Life, Liberty and Property.

2. Political Theology is the realization that the political principles of Justice, Liberty, equality, fraternity, dignity, welfare and so on are the secularized version of theology. The Bible, the teachings of Jesus and the witness of the Church are the foundations of modern political principles.
3. Political Theology is to set a standard for Indian politics based on Christian principles.
4. Political Theology is to enable the Dalits, Adivasis, Bahujans and the Deprived Communities to obtain their right to politics. The caste system denied the right to politics for the above people over thousands of years. The Right to politics means the right to Life, Liberty, and Property. It also includes the articulation of ideas, discuss, debate, express, choose, contest and hold an office. All these rights were denied with force.
5. Political Theology is to study justice and truth not as theological postulates but as legal entitlements. They must be fitted within the framework of the law. Law produces rights. Thus, justice becomes a right.

Theology must not end with the study of 'image and likeness of God' in the creation account, or repeating with Amos, 'let justice flow like river water.' It must see whether equality and equal treatment are legally binding. Whether justice and fairness are legally guaranteed and enforced by law.

1. Political Theology is to encourage people to speak about their life, liberty, and property within the framework of the law. It encourages people to promote a rights-based politics.
2. Political Theology treats every Indian citizen as a product of law. Thus, it educates people about the legal bases on which they stand as citizens.
3. Indian democracy has given ample scope for people's participation in governance. The Panchayat Raj system, co-operatives, women's self-help groups are some of the avenues to participate. Political Theology in India aims to train people in the art of governance and encourage them to enter the seats of power, starting from Gram panchayats, local body units at the village level.
4. A habitual study of the Indian Constitution is a necessity. It tells them the rules of the game and the direction of the goalposts. The Indian Constitution is a noble document and the fundamental law of the nation yet it is quite plain. It doesn't require experts to understand. Many of the concepts we find in the Constitution such as justice, equality, liberty, and fraternity are theological concepts (Karl Schmitt). Thus, a Christian has the advantage to understand

the Constitution. Political theology urges every Indian to learn the Indian Constitution because knowledge of your rights helps you to claim it.

Christian Approach to Politics

A Christian approaches politics in many ways because we trust that all power and authority belong to God and we also know that God is active in history in order to save the fallen human race. We are called to participate in consummating God's kingdom on earth. Therefore, let us see how to approach politics.

i. Learning from Politics

A Christian must be a keen observer of politics and political institutions. One can learn a lot about the way political systems have emerged in history. Wherever there are better models, Christians can learn and adapt. For example, the early Christians formed the ecclesia, the Church, after the model of Greek ecclesia. In the city-states of Greece, freemen assembled in order to govern the state. That assembly was called ecclesia. The early Christians adopted that model and developed the Church accordingly. But the Christians improved the idea of the ecclesia. The Church being the Christian ecclesia was an open assembly that admitted not only the free-men but also the slaves, women, working-class people, strangers, sick and orphans. So, the Church became an open Ecclesia. But the ideas were brought from the Greek political system.

The Greeks considered the State as the sign of the cosmos. The Christians considered the Church as the sign of the Kingdom of God. The Greeks believed that civility was possible only within the State. The Christians believed that the Church was the repository of God's salvation. St. Paul's description of Christians as the aroma of Christ to God (II Cor. 2:14,15) is also taken from the Roman context where Rome was filled with the smoke of fragrance when the Military General paraded to inform the Emperor about the victory. Alexander the Great, was an exemplary man who, unlike other conquerors, made the conquered as his partners and reconstructed the conquered kingdoms to rise in glory. Therefore, Alexander the Great was considered as 'more than a conqueror'. This should have been in the mind of St. Paul when he says that we are "more than conquerors through Christ who loved us" (Romans 8:37). Later the Church imbibed many institutional models from the Greek and the Roman political system. Even the idea of the diocese was taken from the Roman administrative system.

Similarly, we have to see the good policies that are available in the Indian political system. For example, the Constitution that stands for socialistic and secular society has to be imbibed and appreciated. The legislations such as the Right to Information Act; Right to Education Act; Rural Employment

Guarantee Act; Food Security Act are to be appreciated. The exemplary leadership shown by many political leaders in the contemporary India such as the Kerala Chief Minister Pinarayi Vijayan, the Delhi Chief Minister Arvind Kejriwal, Y. S. Jaganmohan Reddy, the Chief Minister of Andhra Pradesh and many such leaders and their ability to directly serve the poor have to be identified and shared. The Andhra Chief Minister has introduced five deputy Chief Ministers thereby there are Deputy Chief Ministers from *Dalit* and *Adivasi* communities. His scheme of Village Secretariats is also to be studied with interest. Therefore, learning from politics, observing it with careful eyes will help us to share the stories of best practices with other leaders. This is the primary duty of Indian Christians.

ii. Guiding Politics

Christians must be continuous learners of politics but they must also be in a position to guide politics. Plato and Aristotle were tutors of rulers. When Plato stood for knowledge of the ruler, Aristotle stood for the virtue of the ruler. No doubt, Aristotle's student who became the Great Alexander was virtuous in his dealings. The early Christians were attracted by the 'Rule of Law' which was originally invented by Plato and later adopted by the Roman Empire. Rule of law assumes that the law is the ruler and therefore human prejudices can be removed. There is an established procedure to try and judge an accused. The procedure involved a complaint, enquiry, report, warrant of arrest by a magistrate, trial in a court of law, an opportunity for appeal, a pronouncement of judgment and punishment or acquittal. This idea of rule of law is prevalent all over the world even today.

But early Christians though they appreciated the rule of law, were convinced that law would not always protect a poor and the innocent person. Therefore, Christians promoted the Rule of Grace which approaches human beings with God's love. Thus, Christians have a role to guide political systems and political ideas. Loving your enemy, forgiving those who are unjust to you, praying for your tormentors and interceding with God for the public good as a whole Church, are some of the political virtues of Christianity.

In the Western history of politics, theologians and Christian scholars assumed the role of teaching and guiding the rulers, the Princess, and the Emperors. From the beginning of the 16th century, the Christians in Europe produced a wealth of literature about the office of the king and prince. In France, Josse Clichtove wrote a tract on 'The Office of the King' in 1519. In the same year, Guillaume Bude wrote 'Education of the Prince' and presented it to Francis I. In Spain and Portugal, Jeronimo Osorio wrote 'Education and Training of a King' in 1540. Felipe de la Torre wrote a note on 'Education of a Christian King' and dedicated it to Philip II in 1556. In fact, Niccolo Machiavelli wrote 'The Prince' in 1513 and Ribadeneyta published his anti-

Machiavellian Tract on 'Religion and the Virtues of the Christian Prince' in 1595. Juan de Mariana issued a treatise on the 'King and the Education of the King' in 1599.

While in Germany Erasmus wrote, the 'Education of a Christian Prince' and presented it to the future emperor Charles V in 1516. He emphasized that the aim of the Government must be to achieve the highest degree of virtue. Jacob Wimpfeling (1450-1528) published his book, the 'Epitome of a Good Prince' during the reign of Maximilian. Antonio de Guevara's book 'Dial of Princes' published in 1529 was considered the most widely read book apart from the Bible in the whole of 16th century Europe. In England, Scholars concentrated more on Common Wealth rather than the Princes. Sir Thomas More (1478-1535) wrote the 'Utopia' in 1516. He alerted the people about the conspiracy of the rich who are aiming at their own interests under the name and title of the commonwealth (Quentin Skinner, Foundations of Modern Political Thought, Vol I: The Renaissance, Cambridge University Press 1978).

In India, theologians must raise to the level of guiding the State. If politics is a contract to have the right to life, liberty, and property for all, Christian theologians must guide the citizens, policymakers and those in authority about it. For this, we need to reconstruct our theologies.

iii. Setting the Agenda of Politics

Christians and theologians must help Indian politics to set a new agenda. In order to do this, we must not only observe the dominant practices and the models in India but also the legal basis such as the Constitution of India. The Constitution of India in its Preamble makes four promises such as Justice, Liberty, Equality, and Fraternity. In fact, these are all theological concepts. Bible, from the creation account until the last book is talking about these concepts. Therefore, it is not difficult for Christians to understand, interpret and bring out contextual meanings. The Constitution says that all power and authority is drawn from "We, the People of India". Therefore, it is necessary to make people of India as proud citizens. We must see the gap between the Constitutional affirmation and the realities of Dalit, Adivasis, and Bahujans in this country. We must compel the governments and the political leaders to set a new agenda that makes the citizens proud.

The Constitution says that we are a sovereign republic. These two words are extremely important. If sovereignty is derived from the people of India, every citizen is a sovereign. Moreover, India is a republic and not a kingdom. This means that every adult citizen is a king or queen and our children are princes and princesses. King David, the founder of Jerusalem city prayed "May our sons in their youth be like plants full grown, our daughters like corner pillars cut for the structure of the palace" (Psalm 144:12). If that is the vision of a King, many a thousand years ago, Christians also must have visions and dreams about our compatriots and the children of this nation. This is all the more necessary because the Constitution treats people as sovereign and rulers. Quite often we misunderstand our representatives who form the government and occupy the position in the council of Ministers as our rulers. Minister etymologically means a servant and the people are the masters. Law is the ruler in a democracy. Therefore, Christians have to infuse this Constitutional dream into the minds of the people of India.

We have defined politics as a contract among people to ensure their right to life, liberty, and property. The Constitution of India guarantees these rights for all. We have a chapter on Fundamental Rights which guarantees the Right to Liberty of all citizens and a Right against exploitation and discrimination, Abolition of untouchability, Equality before Law, Freedom of Expression and Freedom of Religion, etc. Article 21 of the Constitution guarantees Right to Life which is in fact drawn from the assertion of Jesus that he came to this world that we may have life and life in abundance (John 10:10). As Christians, we have the responsibility to interpret whether Article 21 which talks about Right to Life, guarantees fullness of life. Many of the Indians survive without dignity and personal protection. This cannot be called as life. So, the meaning of the fullness of life has to be interpreted by Christians as we have got the mandate from Jesus.

Similarly, the Constitution also talks about justice. Justice is a biblical concept. In simple terms, Justice means living without fear. The fear of survival, hunger, diseases, caste and gender oppression and violence are haunting most of our people in India. So, politics must create an atmosphere where people can live without fear. This is the minimum standard that has to be set to Indian Politics. Further, the Constitution has given a three-tier administrative model. Union Government, State Governments and Local Governments. Article 243 A of the Constitution provides power to ordinary citizens directly. It introduces Gram Sabha, Village Assembly where citizens of that respective village are the members. The Constitution says a "Gram Sabha may exercise such powers and perform such functions at the village level as a legislature of a State may, by law, provide." This gives political opportunity to ordinary citizens of India and enables them to participate in the village government and decide as per their priorities. The Gram Sabha could be a wonderful college of citizens. Political Theology helps people to set the political manifestoes and the agenda on life, liberty, and property of people.

iv. Knowing the Limits of Politics

Politics is dangerous and risky, yet it is attractive. Men and women seek power due to scarcity, diffident and for felicity. (Thomas Hobbes, Leviathan P 184). This is a never-ending desire. In India, politics is still crude and crime-ridden. Yet people rush to it, in order to amass power and wealth unlawfully. But a new politics is possible. Christians must get involved in politics, even in party politics. In a democracy, every political party is a ruler in waiting. But Christian presence in politics and political parties is for cleaning the political space. Make politics transparent and honorable. Politics for Christians is not to amass wealth and power for us but to promote the rights of people to life, liberty, and livelihood (property).

Theologically, Christians do not venerate or glorify politics. We know the limit of politics. We believe that the purpose of human life is to serve God. Political power is only instrumental to serve God. If politics is a worship of mammon, Christians are called to transform politics. Jesus when tempted, rejected the glamour of authority and glory and said, that worshipping the Lord God and serving him are the two duties (Lk 4:8). Christians are in the world but not of the world (Jn17:16). Christianity provides a participant-observer role to every Christian as far as the world is concerned. We are here yet we don't belong here. We have to live like aliens and strangers in this world (I Pet 1:11). Though we live happily in earthly tents, we have a building from God, an eternal house in heaven (II Cor. 5:1).

This world is not our permanent home, we are looking forward to a home yet to come (Heb 13:14). The Bible teaches that as Christians we are not here to eat and drink but to strive for God's Kingdom where there is justice, peace, and joy (Rom 14:17). We will be fools if we amass wealth so as to take life easy; eat, drink and be merry (Lk 12:19). Since the world, wealth and its glory are not the primary concerns, Christianity teaches a sober approach to politics. Politics is to serve God's people and to bring glory to our father in heaven.

We know the limit of politics. St. Augustine studying Cain and Abel, he concludes that Cain created a city (Gen 4:17) and became a citizen of the Earthly Kingdom. But Abel was a pilgrim in this world, as he belonged to the City of God (St. Augustine, City of God, Book XV). He reminds the Christians that we must go beyond politics. According to St. Augustine, Politics on earth is made of self-love and the city of God is made of the love of God. This is the basic message of the Gospel and the scriptures. As Indian Christians, we must participate in politics in order to serve God's mission.

Christian involvement in politics transformed politics itself. Christianity had seen many empires and principalities. But Christian gospel transformed them. The Church accompanied the State and as a result, absolute States were replaced by the Welfare States. This is a direct contribution of Christianity to the world of politics. The Constitution of India through the Directive Principle of State Policy presents a welfare state to Indian citizens. The idea of Welfare State was modelled by the Church in history.

The idea of modern nations where people of racial and cultural differences can live together as equals is a sure contribution of Christianity. Generally, a race became a nation and, in that nation, other races had no place. Jesus taught that a Samaritan could be a relative of a Jew (Lk 10:25-37). The Church became the first multi-cultural and multi-racial community with equal respect for all. St. Paul calls it as a 'mystery of Christ' where Gentiles are fellow heirs, members of the same body and partakers of the promise in Christ Jesus (Eph 3:4-6). On seeing the Church, human races and tribes believed that it is possible for people of different backgrounds to own a common nation and have a common identity. This is an important contribution of Christianity to politics.

Christian Politics

Christianity is the greatest blessing to India. It is a religion that preaches to love each other. It teaches that love is the basis of a nation. It proved in history that nations and kingdoms can be built not by weapon, battles, hatred, and money but by love and care. Jesus asserted that this secrete is hidden from the wise and revealed to the babes (Lk 10:1-24). Montesquieu, a great intellectual whose writings inspired the French Revolution and the profounder of the idea of separation of power, writes that Christian Religion, which ordains that men should love each other would, without doubt, is a blessing for every nation (Charles de Montesquieu, The Spirit of the Laws, Vol I, P 345, Digireads.com). He also feels that being a religion of love, Christianity has produced the best civil and political laws that no nation can hinder its entry.

Christian political theology in India is not about looking for power but about the sowing of love. Indians suffer from caste oppression. Caste is behaving like a nation and divides people. Caste oppression justifies other forms of oppression. Even intellectuals don't understand caste-oppression. Indian democracy, through the constitution, has given some space for equality and recognition of human dignity. Christian theology must strengthen and enlarge this space. This is very difficult yet it is inevitable. The success of Christian faith is not how many years you spent in solitude and jungles in meditation. But it is about serving the poor. In the final analysis, a successful Christian is one who responded to hunger, thirst, nakedness, sickness, a stranger and a prisoner (Mt. 25). The challenge of Christian theology is to guide Indian politics with the power of love, that we saw in Jesus.

8

INDIAN PHILOSOPHY AND THEOLOGICAL METHODS IN INDIAN CHRISTIAN THEOLOGY AN OVERVIEW

Arpit Simon Mathews[1]

As Christianity spread to the non-Jewish context in the first century, Christian thought and practices relied upon philosophies of particular contexts for its development. In India, the 'traditional' Indian Christian Theology depended upon Indian 'Brahmanical' Philosophy in its quest to seek indigenous expression of Christianity. As the movement of liberation theologies post 1960s spread across the world, in India, we witnessed the rise and development of 'theologies from the margins' such as Dalit Theology, Tribal theology, and Adivasi Theology. Rev. Dr. J. A. David Onesimu, as a theologian, has contributed numerous works in the area of Dalit theology, particularly from the perspective of the Ambedkar Movement. As a Pastor and an evangelist, God has enabled him to plant scores of churches, while giving long years of service to Madras Theological Seminary and College as an able Principal. This article on Indian Christian Theology and its theological methods is a tribute to Dr. Onesimu's exemplary services to the Seminary.

Introduction

Philosophy has always been an influential factor in Christian theology. Methodological concerns and frameworks in theology involve a philosophical

1 *Pastor Arpit Simon Mathews serves as an Assistant Professor in the Department of Christian Theology at Madras Theological Seminary and College, Chennai, India.*

outlook. When it comes to the Asian context, particularly South Asia, Samuel Rayan sees no division between the two. He says, "there is no clear division between philosophy and theology, or theology and spirituality and spirituality and mysticism. They feed into each other and may never be separated. Spirituality, theology, mysticism philosophy – all are interrelated."[2] This paper seeks to explore the Indian Christian Theology in relation to Indian Philosophy. The six schools of Hindu philosophy have been studied briefly, based on which Indian theology and its concern with Indian philosophy has been studied.

1. The Six Schools of Hindu Philosophy

Hindu philosophy is marked by the systematic philosophies of six Hindu schools: *Nyaya*, *Vaisesika*, *Samkhya*, *Yoga*, *Mimamsa,* and *Vedanta*. These philosophical systems are known as *sad-darsanas* (six insights or vision).[3] These six schools are grouped into three pairs: the *Nyaya* and the *Vaisesika*, the *Sankhya* and the *Yoga*, the *Mimamsa* and the *Vedanta*.

1.1. Nyaya

Nyaya school was founded by sage Gautama in the second century CE. This school of philosophy is a realistic philosophy based primarily on logic grounds, concerned with the means of acquiring the right knowledge.[4] On the questions of epistemology, it admits four sources of knowledge: perception (*pratyaksa*), inference (*anumana*), analogy (*upamana*), and verbal testimony (*sabda*).[5] Perception is the direct knowledge of the objects which arises out of their relation to our senses and inference is a priori knowledge which we know through some other perceived event.[6] Analogy is that knowledge which comes from the similarity of a thing to another familiar thing and verbal testimony refers to the knowledge obtained from the statements of reliable and authoritative persons.[7] Using these sources of knowledge the *Nyaya* philosophers put forward a natural theology that is based on analogical reasoning. This natural theology brings about arguments for the existence of God, which according to *Nyaya* tradition is that – since "all created things resemble artifacts, and just as

2 Samuel Rayan, "Philosophy and Theology," in *Doing Theology: Indian Christian Reflections on Theologizing in India Today*, ed. Kurien Kunnumpuram, vol. 2, Collected Writings of Samuel Rayan, SJ (Delhi: ISPCK, 2013), 166.

3 Theos Bernard, *Hindu Philospohy* (Delhi: Motilal Banarsidass Publishers, 1947), 4.

4 Satischandra Chatterjee and Dhirendramohan Datta, *An Introduction to Indian Philosophy* (Calcutta: Calcutta University, 1939), 33.

5 Shyam Ranganathan, "Hindu Philosophy," ed. James Fieser and Bradley Dowden, *Internet Encyclopedia of Philosophy*, accessed January 25, 2016, http://www.iep.utm.edu/hindu-ph/#H3.

6 Theos Bernard, *Hindu Philospohy*, 25–26.

7 Theos Bernard, *Hindu Philospohy*, 26.

every artifact has a creator, so too must all of creation have a creator."[8] *Nyaya* tradition sees in the world flow of misapprehensions, faults, activity, birth, and pain. Only when this chain of consequences is broken one can be freed and so to break the chain one has to know and have a full understanding of the true nature of things.

1.2. Vaisesika

The *Vaisesika* school of philosophy's basic text is Kanada's *Vaiseseika-sutra*, which was composed earlier than *Nyaya-sutra. Vaisesika*, as T. M. P. Mahadevan describes it, "is an atomic pluralism, believing in a plurality of reals and regarding the physical world as consisting of things each of which is reducible to a number of atoms."[9] There are four kinds of atoms, – earth, eater, fire, and air – out of which things are formed when they enter into a combination.[10] *Vaisesika's* enquiry is more into metaphysical questions. One of the main features of *Vaisesika* is *padartha* or category. The universe is reduced to six *padarthas*, which means that all objects of knowledge or real come under *padartha*.[11] *Padarthas* are divided into two classes – *bhava* or being and *abhava* or non-being. Under *bhava* there are six *padarthas* namely substance (*dravya*), quality (*guna*), action (*karma*), generality (*samanya*), particularity (*vishesa*) and inherence (*samavaya*). A seventh *padartha* was added later as a *padartha* by later *Vaisesikas*, which is non-being (*abhava*), belonging to the second class of *padarthas*.[12] Therefore all that is real comes under object of knowledge as a *padartha. Vaisesika*, like *Nyaya*, also sees a chain of consequences in accordance with the past karma of the individuals. Dharma or good conduct and knowledge are means to liberate oneself from the *samsara*.[13] The knowledge here refers to that of the *padarthas* which comes through a virtuous life. To free oneself one must stop performing actions as they lead to chain of consequences and therefore, "liberation is cessation of all life, all consciousness, all bliss, together with all pain and all qualities."[14] The liberated soul has its own particularity and individuality which is devoid of all qualities.

8 Ranganathan, "Hindu Philosophy."

9 T. M. P. Mahadevan, *Outlines of Hinduism* (Bombay: Chetana Limited, 1956), 109.

10 Mahadevan, *Outlines of Hinduism*, 114.

11 Chandradhar Sharma, *A Critical Survey of Indian Philosophy* (Delhi: Motilal Banarsidass Publishers, 1987), 175–176.

12 Sharma, *A Critical Survey of Indian Philosophy*, 176.

13 Mahadevan, *Outlines of Hinduism*, 115.

14 Sharma, *A Critical Survey of Indian Philosophy*, 186.

1.3. Samkhya

Samkhya is a school of philosophy founded by Kanada, considered to be the oldest of the systematic schools of philosophy. It is a philosophy of dualistic realism as it involves two ultimate realities, *purusa* (person) and *prakrti* (nature), which are independent of each other in their existence.[15] *Purusa* and *prakrti* are opposite to each other. *Purusa* is pure consciousness, which sees the changes happening around it but it itself never changes.[16] Whereas *prakrti* is the ultimate cause of the world, which is always changing and its end is the satisfaction of itself.[17] Everything originates from a combination of the two. *Prakrti* constitutes of three *gunas* (elementary principles), which are *sattva*, *rajas*, and *tamas*.[18] These three are originally in equilibrium, but with the association of *purusa* with *prakrti* the evolution begins, and this equilibrium is disturbed. First, *Mahat* emerges also called *buddhi* and from *mahat*, *ahankara* which is the principle of individuation and egoity evolves.[19] Suffering, therefore, arises out of the *avidya* (ignorance) which brings *aviveka* (discrimination) between the self and the not-self.[20] The misery leads to a quest for liberation which can be achieved through a reversal of the evolutionary process which brings final separation of spirit from matter, a return of the *purusa* to its pure nature as consciousness.[21] *Samkhya* school differs from *Vaisesika* in its understanding of creation as it refutes the latter's theories of creation and argues that all things evolve out of pre-existing material.[22] Also, they argue that God cannot be the creator of the world because he is an eternal and unchanging spirit, but to produce an effect, that is the creation of the world, the cause must change.[23] Thus, this school does away with the theistic belief however those within them who believe in the existence of God seem him only as a witness and not as a creator.

1.4. Yoga

The yoga school of philosophy was founded by Patanjali and is closely related to the *Samkhya* tradition. It accepts the dualistic cosmology of the latter and also it does not derive its authority from the Vedas explicitly.[24] However, the

15 Chatterjee and Datta, *An Introduction to Indian Philosophy*, 39.

16 Mahadevan, *Outlines of Hinduism*, 118–119.

17 Mahadevan, *Outlines of Hinduism*, 119.

18 Chatterjee and Datta, *An Introduction to Indian Philosophy*, 40.

19 Mahadevan, *Outlines of Hinduism*, 120–121.

20 Chatterjee and Datta, *An Introduction to Indian Philosophy*, 41.

21 Sharma, *A Critical Survey of Indian Philosophy*, 164.

22 Theos Bernard, *Hindu Philosophy*, 6.

23 Chatterjee and Datta, *An Introduction to Indian Philosophy*, 42.

24 Ranganathan, "Hindu Philosophy."

difference between the two is firstly a cosmological difference, that is, the Yoga system does not consider *mahat* (intellect) to be the greatest creation of nature; and the second difference is concerned with the mode of liberation.[25] In *Samkhya*, *Purusa* is a mere spectator and liberation comes when nature enlightens it, whereas in Yoga tradition *Purusa* is an agent in which *Purusa* makes an effort to bring about liberation.[26] The main obstacle to liberation according to Yoga Sutra is the uneasiness of the *Cit* (mind), for which it lays down eight steps in the practice of yoga – *yama* (restraint), *niyama* (moral culture), asana (posture), *pranayama* (breath-control), *pratyahara* (withdrawal of the senses), *dharana* (attention), *dhyana* (meditation), and Samadhi (concentration).[27] The ultimate goal in liberation is, "being concentrated on the self, the mind vanishes; and the self or spirit is left alone to enjoy its *kaivalya*."[28] Yoga is considered to be theistic *Samkhya* because it holds that God is the highest object of contemplation for concentration and self-realization. For the issue of the existence of God, it employs the argument that whatever has degrees must have maximum and therefore there ought to be a thing as perfect knowledge or omniscience, which is God.[29] In the school of Yoga there is the emphasis given on individual capabilities through which one can have a direct experience of the Ultimate reality.

1.5. Mimamsa

The *Mimamsa*, also known as *Purva-Mimamsa*, one of the most orthodox schools, was founded by Jaimini and is primarily concerned with the defense, justification, and interpretation of Vedic rituals and texts.[30] The authority of Vedas is argued by this school through a philological theory in which the relation between the word and its meaning is natural and therefore eternal. However, it considers only Veda as eternal over other literary works because of the particular order (*anupurvi*) of words in Veda, which is permanent and not arranged by any agent, human or divine.[31] The *Mimamsa* recognizes that Veda teaches dharma (religious duty), doing what is right and desisting from forbidden acts.[32] To preserve the independent nature of the Veda, *Mimamsa* tradition gives no place to God in its system. It holds that the universe has no

25 Ranganathan, "Hindu Philosophy."

26 Ranganathan, "Hindu Philosophy."

27 Chatterjee and Datta, *An Introduction to Indian Philosophy*, 43.

28 Mahadevan, *Outlines of Hinduism*, 129.

29 Chatterjee and Datta, *An Introduction to Indian Philosophy*, 44.

30 Theos Bernard, *Hindu Philosophy*, 6.

31 Mahadevan, *Outlines of Hinduism*, 133.

32 Chatterjee and Datta, *An Introduction to Indian Philosophy*, 45.

beginning or end, there is no creation or dissolution and therefore there is no need to assume a God.[33] It's the law of karma that governs the world.

1.6. Vedanta

Vedanta, like *Mimamsa* is concerned with the authority of *Vedas*, however, the difference between the two is that the latter is concerned with the former portion of the *Vedas*, whose concern is the rituals and dharma, while the former is concerned with the end of the Vedas or *Upanishads*, which are the knowledge sections having their basis on the inquiry into the nature of the Ultimate, or *Brahman*.[34] Several commentarial traditions have emerged in Vedanta, who base their commentaries on Badarayana's *Brahma-Sutra*, the systematic writing on the teachings of Upanishads, which in themselves are not systematic treatises.[35] Theos Bernard writes, "The central theme of the *Vedantasutra* is the philosophical teachings of the *Upanisads* concerning the nature and relationship of the three principles, that is, God, the world, and the soul, this also including the relation between the Universal Soul and the individual soul."[36] Of the several commentaries, three works stand out in this school, that of *Sankara*, *Ramanuja,* and *Madhava*. *Vedanta* school of philosophy has been mostly used for Indian theology, which is addressed later in the paper.

1.6.1. Sankara's Advaita

Sankara interprets the Upanishads and *Brahma-Sutra* to show the monotheistic nature of God, who alone is the only Reality and there is no multiplicity within him and that there is nothing except him.[37] Mahadevan sees three main constituents of the teaching of *Advaita*, namely, "the non-duality of *Brahman*, the non-reality of the worlds, and the non-difference of the soul from *Brahman*."[38] There is only one reality, *Brahman* or *Atman*, which is pure consciousness and devoid of all attributes (*nirguna*) and this *Brahman* appears as the qualified *Brahman* or *Iswara* in its association with *maya*, as the cause of the world.[39] However, this understanding of *Iswara* is from our knowledge, which is an empirical and relative standpoint according to Sankara. This knowledge (empirical) is not strictly knowledge for Sankara

33 Mahadevan, *Outlines of Hinduism*, 48.

34 Ranganathan, "Hindu Philosophy."

35 Mahadevan, *Outlines of Hinduism*, 140.

36 Theos Bernard, *Hindu Philosophy*, 116.

37 Mahadevan, *Outlines of Hinduism*, 48.

38 Mahadevan, *Outlines of Hinduism*, 141.

39 Sharma, *A Critical Survey of Indian Philosophy*, 252.

and therefore its content, that is, the world is illusory.[40] And the principle for this relative understanding is *maya*. *Jiva* (the individual self), is, in essence, the same as *Brahman*, but because of *avidya*, it sees plurality in the world instead of one reality, *Brahman*. Liberation therefore in *Advaita* philosophy means the removal of avidya by knowledge. True knowledge is produced by *pramanas* and cannot be produced by numerous rituals and injunctions or prohibitions.[41] Sankara recognizes the six *pramanas* from the Bhatta school – *Pratyaksa*, *Anumana*, *Sabda*, *Upamana*, *Arthapatti*, and *Anupalabdi* – of which the testimony of Vedanta is most important.[42] When the *avidya* is removed, the knowledge of non-dualism dawns on the *jiva*. Sankara does not separate *jiva* and *Brahman*, rather he accords a metaphysical unity between both in the absence of *maya* or *avidya*. When *jiva* is liberated, he becomes one with Brahman in a metaphysical sense.

1.6.2. Ramanuja's Visistadvaita

One of the main issues in Sankara's *Advaita* was whether Brahman is *nirguna* or *saguna*. Ramanuja was a pioneer in accepting God as *saguna* and whose system is known as *Visistadvaita*. Reality, for him, is definitely non-dual *Brahman*, "but it is not a distinctionless, homogeneous identity; it should rather be conceived on the analogy of an organism involving internal differentiation."[43] There are three ultimate realities in this system – God (*Iswara*), soul (*cit*), and matter (*acit*). God is the only Reality but within him there exist the other two realities that are dependent on him.[44] The world (*acit*) is the dwelling place of soul and through it of God as well. Every soul is given a material body in accordance with its *karma* and this confinement of the soul to the body signifies its bondage.[45] *Moksa* or liberation comes through *karma*, *jnana,* and *bhakti*. *Bhakti* involves meditation as *jnana* but in it, "meditation is characterized by the soul's feeling of love for and dependence on God. When *bhakti* matures and becomes complete, the soul has a vision of God."[46] However, in *Visistadvaita*, the soul is released only when its physical body perishes, unlike *jivanmukti* in *Advaita*. So even after acquiring *jnana* and *bhakti* the *jiva* has to continue to perform karma till the very end, along with the prayer and worship found in Vedas.

---

40 Mahadevan, *Outlines of Hinduism*, 145–147.

41 Sharma, *A Critical Survey of Indian Philosophy*, 287.

42 Mahadevan, *Outlines of Hinduism*, 144.

43 Mahadevan, *Outlines of Hinduism*, 150.

44 Chatterjee and Datta, *An Introduction to Indian Philosophy*, 51.

45 Chatterjee and Datta, *An Introduction to Indian Philosophy*, 51.

46 Mahadevan, *Outlines of Hinduism*, 154.

2. Indian Philosophy and Indian Christian Theology

The Natural theology of the Middle Ages, attributed to Thomas Aquinas found its philosophical basis in the philosophy of Aristotle. Quite similar is the case in the study of Indian Christian Theology, in which we find the Indian philosophy used to a great extent. However, most of the theologians have made use of the Vedanta tradition in their theological quest.

2.1. Sankara's Advaita and Indian Christian Theology

Sankara's philosophy of *advaita* has been adopted and utilized by some Indian theologians for the understanding of God. Rayan describes the use of *Advaita* as one of the philosophies for theological formulations in India as, "*Advaita*... has been taken up as illuminating the unspeakable mystery of God – God as the *anirvacaniya*, the undefinable, ineffable, unspeakable mystery, God as the fullness of truth or reality, *Purnam*. Fullness of being. Fullness of *Satya*, reality, being or truth."[47] Brahmabandhav Upadhyay is regarded as one of the leading thinkers in using *advaita Vedanta* in Indian Christian theology. The reason for Upadyay to do so arises out of methodological concerns.

He was well trained in Thomistic theology, which makes extensive use of Aristotle's philosophy in its theological activity. In Indian context, he proposed that the Aristotelian philosophy could be replaced by the *Advaita* philosophy of Sankara.[48] The grounds for the choice of *Advaita* philosophy comes from his personal realization that Sankara's philosophy represented Hindu thought at its highest (like the Aristotelian philosophy in the West). Robin Boyd remarks, "Upadhyaya was determined if Hindu philosophy were to be used to 'hew wood and draw water' for Christian theology, then only the purest water and the strongest wood were good enough, and those, he was convinced, were to be found in Sankara rather than in any other system."[49] Therefore, he identified the Thomistic understanding of the Trinity with the Vedantic understanding, that of Sankara's, namely – God as *Sat* (the absolute or Brahman), Son as the *Chit* (Intelligence), and Holy Spirit as *Ananda* (Eternal Bliss).[50]

However, with Sankara's Vedanta, the obstacle for Upadyay was accepting Sankara's interpretation of *maya*. According to Sankara, God is related to the world through *maya*. God is *sat*, the necessary being and the creation is *asat*, the nothingness. To employ it in Christian understanding Upadyay interpreted

---

47 Rayan, "Philosophy and Theology," 166.

48 Russell J. Chandran, "Development of Christian Theology in India: A Critical Survey," in *Readings in Indian Christian Theology*, ed. R. S. Sugirtharajah and Cecil Hargreaves, vol. 1, SPCK International Study Guide 29 (London: SPCK, 1993), 8.

49 Robin H. S. Boyd, *An Introduction to Indian Christian Theology* (Madras: The Christian Literature Society, 1969), 75.

50 Chandran, "Development of Christian Theology in India: A Critical Survey," 8.

maya to mean "not illusion or unreal existence but a dependant existence – that all things created are depending on God."[51] Boyd sees this as an attempt to interpret the idea of *creation ex nihilo* so that this interpretation is consistent with both scholastic theology and to the *advaita Vedanta*.[52] *Maya*, as Boyd concludes, has two functions according to Upadyay – firstly it is the creative power of God, and secondly, it is also the grace of God which causes the desire for human beings to return to him.[53] P. D. Devanandan, like Upadyay, recognizes that *maya* cannot be thought of as a mere illusion since it is willed by God, therefore, it is real although the world is not with the same reality as God.[54] However, Devanandan differs from Upadyay's interpretation of *maya* as a contingent being. He shifts the realm of *maya* from being to that of purpose by relating it to secular history and salvation history. Where God's will is followed that is a reality and where it is opposed, that is *maya*.[55]

Raymond Pannikar's uses *Advaita* in relation to his postulation that in Christianity, Hinduism finds its true meaning in Christ. He recognizes, as Boyd notes, the problem that Hindu philosophy such as that of *Advaita* faces in establishing the relationship between Brahman and the world.[56] Since Brahman is *nirguna*, therefore, Sankara's followers ascribed the *Iswara* as the cause, who according to Pannikar becomes the link between Brahman and the creation. To clear the ambiguity Pannikar asserts that recognition of Christ as *Iswara* solves the problem of One Reality or plurality in Hinduism.[57]

Upadhyay rejects the use of *avatara* for incarnated Christ because incarnation, for him, is higher than the *avatara* of Hindus.[58] The *avatara* of Hindu deities is qualitatively different from the incarnation of Christ. He explains it further by arguing that according to Vedanta, "human is... composed of five sheaths – animate, vital, mental, intellectual to spiritual... controlled by personality *(aham)*, in the incarnate Son they are activated by the Logos or the *cit* of the Trinity."[59] The rejection of *avatara* by Upadhyay is in accordance with the *Advaita* philosophy.

51 Sunand Sumithra, *Christian Theologies from an Indian Perspective* (Bangalore: Theological Book Trust, 1995), 71.

52 Boyd, *An Introduction to Indian Christian Theology*, 75.

53 Boyd, *An Introduction to Indian Christian Theology*, 76.

54 Boyd, *An Introduction to Indian Christian Theology*, 195–196.

55 Boyd, *An Introduction to Indian Christian Theology*, 196–197.

56 Boyd, *An Introduction to Indian Christian Theology*, 222–223.

57 Boyd, *An Introduction to Indian Christian Theology*, 223.

58 Sumithra, *Christian Theologies from an Indian Perspective*, 74.

59 Sumithra, *Christian Theologies from an Indian Perspective*, 74.

2.2. Ramanuja's Visistadvaita and Indian Christian Theology

A. J. Appasamy made use of *Bhakti* tradition in Ramanuja's *Visistadvaita* in his theological formulations. He rejects the Chalcedonian definition that Christ is fully God, the metaphysical unity with the Father, which according to him has the *advaitic* tendency.[60] He differs from the Trinitarian understanding of Upadyay, who derives it from the *Satchitananda* concept. Rather, Appasamy, sees a difference of function and a difference of person between Christ and God, and this difference makes possible the moral union or communion and not metaphysical unity between the two, which is an important feature of the *Visistadvaita*.[61] Vengal Chakkariah and P. Chenchiah also take a similar position as Appasamy by arguing that the theology cannot begin with abstract or unmanifested *Brahman* rather it should begin with the manifested one, that is, Iswara, which means Jesus Christ and this can be regarded as Christology from below from an Indian perspective.[62]

Appasamy persists on the preservation of separate personalities in humans' experience of union with God, and this union is best maintained by the *bhakti marga* among the three *marga* for *moksa*. He also agrees with Ramanuja's acceptance of three *pramanas* – *sruti*, *yukti*, and *anubhava* – to which he adds a fourth one, *sabha* (church).[63] Appasamy's usage of the concept of *Avatara*, arises from his position in Bhakti tradition and Ramanuja's *Visistadvaita*. He differs from Sen and Upadyay in this approach, as he asserts that a careful usage of the term *avatara* can be applied to the incarnation of Christ.[64] Boyd carefully examines the differences that Appasamy brings out between the features of *avatars* in Hindu tradition and when the term is used for Christ, which he finds closely related to the personal theism and *bhakti* tradition of Ramanuja.[65] The influence of *bhakti* tradition can be seen in Appasamy's works clearly in the fact that he criticizes all the structures that could align with the monism of Sankara in Christian theology and rather tries to reformulate and relook at basic tenets of Christian theology from the perspective of the *Visistadvaita* philosophy.

Despite his rejection of God as *nirguna* Brahman, there is some sort of synthesis that Appasamy offers between *Advaita* and *Visistadvaita* concerning the personal and impersonal nature of God. He acknowledges the usage of impersonal terms for Christ in the Gospel of John and concludes, as quoted

60 Sumithra, *Christian Theologies from an Indian Perspective*, 107.

61 Boyd, *An Introduction to Indian Christian Theology*, 120–122.

62 Sumithra, *Christian Theologies from an Indian Perspective*, 116.

63 M. M. Thomas and P. T. Thomas, *Towards an Indian Christian Theology: Life and Thoughts of Some Pioneers* (Tiruvalla, India: The New Day Publications of India, 1992), 190.

64 Boyd, *An Introduction to Indian Christian Theology*, 127.

65 Boyd, *An Introduction to Indian Christian Theology*, 128–129.

by Boyd, "those aspects of Christ which transcend personality as against those aspects which are personal."[66] Appasamy could not escape the popularity of the conception of God as *nirguna Brahman* in the minds of Indian people and brings a vague synthesis in this regard. Appasamy also makes interesting use of Ramanuja's 'soul-body' doctrine of God's relation to the created world. Appasamy makes use of it as an analogy in four different contexts. Firstly, in God's relation to the creation, as used by Ramanuja himself, to show that creation is real unlike in Sankara's monism; secondly, for the purpose to show the union of divine and human in Christ in which Christ is a single personality with human body within which God dwells as *antaryamin*; thirdly to describe the nature of the presence of Christ in the Eucharist; and lastly, the relationship of Christ with the church, where Church is the body and God is present in it as *antaryamin*.[67]

3. Rejection of Indian Philosophy

Nehemiah Goreh stands out among Indian Christian theologians in his rejection of Hindu philosophy, primarily found in his work, *A Rational Refutation of the Hindu Philosophical Systems*. In this work, he does a critical evaluation of the six schools of Hindu philosophy. His evaluation of the six schools in regarding the relation between God, human soul, and the world is brought by M. M. Thomas as, "He (Goreh) finds *Nyaya* and *Vaiseshika* systems more reasonable since, unlike *Sankhya* and *Mimamsa*, they posit the reality of a God and, unlike the *Vedanta*, do not identify God with the soul or make the world illusory; but even they are inadequate to meet the problems of human existence or to lead human beings to the Real."[68] He uses logical arguments to refute, particularly the *Vedantic* tradition. He reduces *nirguna Brahman* to zero for the reason that he is void of qualities and that he is not related to the world and therefore Goreh questions his existence on such a basis.[69] And the *saguna Brahman*, being a part of the world of *maya*, is in any case no more than nothing but an illusion.[70] Goreh refutes *maya* as a false way of interpreting reality. Boyd deduces Goreh's conclusion in this regard, "that what depends on falseness must itself be false, and that so the whole *advaita* view of the nature of God, of creation, and of our knowledge of them both, proves unusable."[71] Goreh's approach can be seen as that of an apologetic, which places Christianity on

66 Boyd, *An Introduction to Indian Christian Theology*, 129.

67 Boyd, *An Introduction to Indian Christian Theology*, 140–142.

68 Thomas and Thomas, *Towards an Indian Christian Theology: Life and Thoughts of Some Pioneers*, 39.

69 Boyd, *An Introduction to Indian Christian Theology*, 49.

70 Sumithra, *Christian Theologies from an Indian Perspective*, 78.

71 Boyd, *An Introduction to Indian Christian Theology*, 50.

loftier places over the gaping holes that Hindu philosophy, according to him, bears.

Conclusion

Indian Christian theologians have constantly involved Indian Philosophy in their theological framework. However, the six schools of Indian philosophy, except the Vedanta, have not been explored extensively in Indian Christian theology. Most of the work in this regard has been confined to the *Advaita* philosophy of Sankara and *Visistadvaita* of Ramanuja. One of the primary reasons for Vedanta philosophy to have a major bearing on the Indian Christian theology in comparison to other schools lies in its main concern towards God, soul, and the world. These three constitute the base for any theological enquiry, particularly in systematic theology. However, the limitation of Indian Christian theology to Vedanta can limit the scope of the former. It has to be involved in a theological activity concerning other schools of Indian philosophy. For instance, John Vattanky does acknowledge the importance of Vedanta for Indian theology but points out that Vedanta adopts the argumentative styles, techniques, and terms of *Nyaya* school of philosophy.[72] Vattanky thus argues that a true Indian theology will be created by employing the *Nyaya* tradition. This paper has drawn out chiefly from the Vedantic tradition which has been the case with the Indian theologians too with regards to the Indian Philosophy. For the purpose an Indigenous theology, this approach has its advantages and relevance in the Indian context.

72 John Vattanky, "New Perspectives in Nyaya Researches," in *Christian Contribution to Indian Philosophy*, ed. Anand Amaladass (Madras: Christian Literature Society, 1995), 235–236.

PART III

HISTORICAL-MISSIOLOGICAL

9

UNDERSTANDING THE CONCEPT OF "SUBALTERN HISTORY/HISTORIOGRAPHY" FROM BIBLICAL PERSPECTIVE AND ITS RELEVANCE

A. Jayakumar[1]

Introduction

The majority of the Christians in India are the subalterns who are the Dalits, tribal, Adivasi, and women. The history of Indian Christianity has been subjected to Eurocentric historiography during the colonial and during the twentieth century, during the national movement, various streams of thoughts and reactions rose. The Indian Christians historians felt the need to do away with the colonial perspective as they identified the inadequacies of earlier resources and cultural bias of the European intellectual tradition and religious norms. The Indian Christian historians insisted that the indigenous Church must develop its own historiography with a focus on the socio-cultural, regional, national and ecumenical perspectives. Thus, CHAI came into existence, it came up with a historiography and in its statement, it provided its aims and objectives, that the history of Christianity in India should be viewed as an integral part of the socio-cultural history of the Indian people rather than as separate from

---

1 *Rev. A. Jayakumar is the Vice Principal of Madras Theological Seminary and College (MTSC), Chennai; and teaching in the department of History of Christianity. He is an ordained priest from the Evangelical Church of India (ECI). He was the former Principal of Calcutta Bible Seminary, Kolkata. Currently he is a doctoral candidate at Sam Higginbottom University of Agriculture, Technology & Sciences (SHUATS), Allahabad.*

it. The history should, therefore, focus attention upon the Christian people in India upon who they were and how they understood themselves; upon their social, religious, cultural and political encounters. Then in the last couple of decades, the subalterns began to feel that they have been neglected or ignored and history has not been written from their perspective so they developed subaltern historiography focusing on the Dalits, tribal, Adivasis, and women. In this paper, I have dealt with the subaltern historiography.

History

The word "history" means inquiry, research, exploration or information. History is the living memory of human beings.[2] History is the study of life in society in the past, in all its aspects, in relation to present developments and future hope.[3] According to E. H. Carr, "History is a continuous process of interaction between the historian and his facts. It is an unending dialogue between the present and the past." Here, Carr suggests the continuing relation of history from past and present.[4] Sheik Ali points out that history is related to something changing in nature, humanity, etc., either growth or decline and it repeats itself.[5] R. G. Collingwood explains history as- i) an inquiry; ii) a record of human actions; iii) based on the interpretation of the evidence and iv) its purpose is human self-knowledge. From Collingwood's understanding, the third classification is understood as historiography.[6]

Historiography

Historiography literally means the art of writing history. It is a development of ideas and techniques associated with the writing of history and the changing attitudes towards the nature of history. Historiography is the history of history; it is the history of historical thought. It is the history of ideas which prompted a historian to adopt a particular line of thought.[7] Historiography also refers to the methodology of historical research while analyzing historical writings. In simple words, historiography is a study of perspectives. Historiography helps us to understand and evaluate the historical consciousness of the historians as well as their techniques of writing history. Ancient, medieval and modern historiographies focused on economically, socially and politically powerful

---

2 E. Sreedharan, *A Textbook of Historiography-500 BC to AD 2000*, (New Delhi: Orient Blackswan Private Limited, 2009), 1.

3 M. Thongkhosei Haokip, *A Guide Book to History of Christianity from the First to the Eighteenth Centuries,* (Secunderabad: G. S. Media, 2017), 15.

4 E. H. Carr, *What is History?* (New York: Penquin Books, 1982), 30.

5 B. Sheik Ali, *History: Its Theory and Method,* (Delhi: Macmillan Publishers India Ltd, 2010), 8.

6 Haokip, *A Guide Book to History...,* 16.

7 Ali, *History: Its Theory...*, 179.

men and those who were authoritative but excluded the roles of women, children, minorities and less authoritative persons.[8] This notion has been changed by the evolution of new theologies and historiographies from below that are from the so-called less-known, less-privileged, less-acknowledged and so on.

A Paradigm Shift in Indian Christian Historiography

Unlike medieval India, modern thinkers show great interest in history. This interest might have arisen as a result of a political and social need, with the independence movement in India.[9] The other reason for this change was the Indian Christian historians identified the inadequacies of earlier resources and cultural biases of the European intellectual tradition and religious norms. Thus, Indian Christian historians urged that the indigenous church must built its own historiography. With the independent nation, Indian Christians also began to search for its own selfhood of writing, selfhood of the nation and to re-discover its methodological writings of Indian Christian historiography. Kaj Baago insisted that the History of Christianity in India should be studied from a new perspective which means an Indian perspective. The church history Association of India (CHAI) came forward to face the challenge and started a project to write a history of Christianity from an Indian perspective.[10] Thus, the focus shifted from western mission achievements in India to the Indian church achievements on its people with several historiographies like post-colonial, subaltern, Dalit, tribal, feminist and Adivasi perspectives.

In the words of Sugirtharajah, it is an active confrontation with the dominant system of through, its irregularities and inadequacies, and underlines its unsuitability for us. It is a process of cultural and discursive emancipation from all dominant structures whether they are political, linguistic, or ideological. The present post-colonial studies to a great extent decolonizes the categories created by the colonial West and even involved in liberating their imagination to create a vital autonomous space. The post-colonial historiography refers to the development of a new historiography that emerged as a protest against the colonial historiography which taking serious about people's way of telling and writing history especially as they experienced it in the past and as they experience that connection reality in the present. The outcome of post-colonial historiography is deconstructing what has been produced by the west. It urges historians to deconstruct and decolonize the

8 Haokip, *A Guide Book to History...*, 19.

9 A. Mathias Mundadan, "Rewriting History: Orientations," *Journal of Dharma*, Vol. XXVIII, No. 2 (April-June, 2003), 158.

10 V. V. Thomas, *Dalit and Tribal Christians of India Issues and Challenges*, (Kerala: Focus India Trust, 2014), 65.

structure of colonial minds to get autonomous space to the colonized minds. The post-colonial approach to history is different in its perspectives and it is the "history from below." This approach attempts to rewrite history from the perspective of the neglected people and communities. The secular historians, anthropologists, and sociologists already made attempts to re-read the colonial history. Christian historians also followed their track.

Subaltern Selective

According to the Oxford Advanced Learner's Dictionary, the term 'subaltern' means, any officer in the army who is lower in rank than a captain. In India, the term came to the center of critical scholarship in the early eighties through a group of thinkers who were called the Subaltern Studies Collective. This path-breaking historiographical movement of Subaltern Studies Collective took its root with its pioneering work, *Subaltern Studies. I: Writings on South Asian History and Society* (1982), and *Elementary Aspects of Peasant Insurgency in Colonial India* (1983) by Ranajit Guha. Since then eleven volumes and several other books have appeared representing this school of history. The founding scholars of Subaltern Studies like any other modern academics have been influenced by a diversity of intellectual concepts. The Subaltern Studies from 1982-1989, have been significantly influenced by Gramsci. It is acknowledged by Ranajit Guha in his Preface to the first volume (1982), that the term "subaltern" is drawn from Gramsci's analysis of Italian history in *Prison Notebooks* (1971). According to Gramsci, Subaltern groups are located within and are subject to the hegemonic rule of the ruling class. Their history is thus intertwined between civil society and state. Gramsci's perspective on the dynamic between state and civil society generates a subtle, multi-layered web of interrelationships between dominant and subordinate classes and groups in which culture, as an expression of civil society, permeates and influences the political behavior of both rulers and ruled.[11]

The Methodological Issues of Subaltern Studies

The term "subaltern," which Guha equates with "of inferior rank," is deployed as a terminology for the general attribute of subordination whether expressed in "terms of class, caste, age, gender, and office or in any other way." Hence, the term 'subaltern' refers to any group of people who constitute the lower and marginalized strata of the society like the untouchables, the outcaste, the Dalits, the tribal, and the women. Thus, Subaltern studies include the studies and issues of the above-mentioned groups of people. Subordination is viewed as a constitutive element in a binary relationship in which the other constitutive

---

11 Kate Currie, The challenge to orientalist, elitist, and western historiography: notes on the "subaltern project" 1982-1989, *Dialectical Anthropology* 20: 1995, 220.

element is dominance, hence, "subaltern groups are always subject to the activity of ruling groups, even when they rebel and rise up. The Subaltern Studies project was constituted as a challenge to elitist historiography. Guha's opening contribution ("On Some Aspects of the Historiography of Colonial India," 1982) pursues the critique of elitist historiography in both colonial and bourgeois nationalist variants. Both variants privilege the elite (British in one instance, Indian in the other) in the emergence of the Indian nation. From the neo-colonialist perspective, nationalism is the outcome of an Indian elite's response to the institutions and opportunities, generated by colonialism, through which this elite could attain a share in the wealth, power and prestige created by colonial rule. The second variant, in which the indigenous elite alone is assumed to have inspired and led the people to freedom is, in Guha's depiction, romanticist and idealist. While elitist historiography is useful in charting the contradictions between the two elites (colonial and national), and uncovering aspects of elite ideology as the dominant ideology, it fails either to acknowledge or interpret the contribution made directly by the people and independently of the elite. Within elite historiography, popular nationalist action is either assessed negatively, as a law and order problem or, positively, as a response to initiatives of charismatic leaders or the manipulation of factions.[12] What is absent or, if present, marginalized, in these narratives, is the "politics of the people" or any autonomous domain, or any analysis of the processes of horizontal mobilization which, in his view, was autonomous and existed parallel to the domain of elite politics throughout the colonial period. This was politics "in which the principal actors were not the dominant groups of the indigenous society or the colonial authorities but the subaltern classes and groups constituting the mass of the laboring population and the intermediate strata in town and country." To write history from the subaltern point of view, Guha makes it clear that "the dominant groups will receive in these volumes the consideration they deserve without, however, being endowed with that forged primacy assigned to them by the longstanding tradition of elitism in South Asian studies." Guha's characterization as "forged" of the primacy attached to dominant groups by traditional ruling class historiography is, of course, provocative, and intended to be so. As Edward Said observes in his foreword to Selected Subaltern Studies, "Theirs [the subaltern historians] is no history of ideas, no calmly Olympian narrative of events, no disengaged objective recital of facts. It is rather sharply contestary, an attempt to wrest control of the Indian past from its scribes and curators in the present, since ... much of the past continues in the present." One knew that history was biased, that there was no such thing as "value-free," "objective" history, but

12 Kate Currie, The challenge to orientalist, elitist, and western historiography: notes on the "subaltern project" 1982-1989, *Dialectical Anthropology* 20: 1995, 222.

the rules of the game, so far as one knew it, involved revealing the bias in other historians' work and hiding your own as cleverly as possible. To confess one's own bias? It was audacious and honest.[13] Due to the oppositional reading to the nationalistic, elitist approach of history of Christianity in India, a shift of writing history from the Christian elite and the dominant people to the masses and people from Dalit and Tribal background emerged.

The Subalterns in India

Indian society is divided into three categories. First, we have the caste community, which consists of four castes that are hierarchically ordered. The Brahmins (priests) are the preservers and protectors of the eternal laws of the Universe (Dharma); the Ksatriyas (rulers and warriors) are the defenders and the guarantors of the safety and security of the community; the Vaisyas (business persons) are the conservers and distributors of wealth, and the Sudras (the labourers) are the working majority involved in the production of essential commodities. Although, there is a clear separation between the first three castes, which are ritually pure and socio-economically dominant (referred to as the twice-born), and the fourth labouring caste, which is ritually suspect and socioeconomically dominated (referred to as the once-born), they together form the constituents of the Hindu human community. Second, related to, but outside of, these four segments of the Indian human society there exists a fifth outcaste community. Even though their population consists of about sixteen percent of the Indian community, it was thought of as being sub or nonhuman; thus, it was not included in its composition. This large group was ejected from the boundaries of Hindu society: it still lives outside the gates of the Hindu society with the labels "Outcaste," "Untouchable," "Exterior Caste," "Depressed Class," and "Dalit." The word "Dalit" is derived from a Semitic root word "dal" which means to crack, open, split, scatter, stretch out to be dissected, broken, torn, destroyed and trodden down.[14] Hence, the term Dalit is especially being used for those people who, based on caste distinction, have been considered outcaste. According to James Massey, these groups of people are outcaste because they were not according to the architect of the system fit

13 Darshan Perusek, NOVEL: A Forum on Fiction, Vol. 25, No. 3 (Spring, 1992), Subaltern Consciousness and the Historiography of the Indian Rebellion of 1857, Duke University Press, 286-287.

14 Other names of Dalits are, Dasa, Dasyu, Raksosa, Asura, Avarna, Nisada, Panchama, Mletcha, Svapaca, Chandala, Achuta, Exterior caste, depressed class, Schedule caste, Harijan, Untouchables etc. See, James Massey, *Indigenous People: Dalits,* Delhi: ISPCK, 1994, 6. (Hereafter cited as, Massey, *Indigenous People*). See also, A. P. Nirmal, "A Dialogue with Dalit Literature," in M. E. Prabhakar ed., *Towards A Dalit Theology,* Delhi" ISPCK, 1988, 66. James Massey, "The Role of the Churches in the Whole Dalit Issue," *NCCR,* vol. CXVI, No. 5 (May-June, 1996), 396-397. James Massey, "The Role of Partner Churches in the Whole Dalit Issue," *NCCR,* vol. CXII, No. 7 (September, 1992), 504-505.

to be included in the four-fold graded caste[15] structure of our society.[16] In this life setting, the Dalits went through economic, social, political oppressions for centuries where they reached a point of losing their total humanness. In today's context, Dalit is not a pejorative designation anymore but rather a positive symbol of identity for the depressed classes, which solves the position of origin, roots, and history of these people.[17] However, it doesn't mean that they are free from discriminations from their rights, oppressions in both religious and social setup. Their struggles are being ignored by the high caste society of India. Therefore, in relative terms, there have been some improvements, but in totality, they are still what they were.

In the Indian caste system, and yet marginalized by caste communities, are many distinct and diverse communities that have been grouped under the term Adivasis. The term Adivasis (the ancient or original dwellers of the land) is utilized here to retain their claim of being the original people of the land and to point to their cultural and religious relatedness to things of the earth. Further, according to a recent article entitled "Call us Adivasis, Please," Gail Omvedt suggests that this is the term with which they would want to be named. The numerous Adivasis of India, constitute about eight percent of its population. The Adivasis have lived through exploitative, oppressive and suppressive social and political structures in India. Mostly, they have been "alienated from their land both by 'greedy' caste communities and by overzealous governments, which takes away tribal land for mining and big industries. Thus, poverty and estrangement from the means of their livelihood (land) threaten Adivasi communities in India.

The tribal of Northeast India prefer to call themselves as tribal. According to them, term 'Adivasi' is used in North Bengal, Sikkim, Arunachal Pradesh, Assam, Meghalaya, Nagaland, and Tripura to refer to the tea plantation labourers like the tribes like Santhal, Munda, Oraon, and Ho who had migrated to the region during the British colonial period. The local tribes in these States find it humiliating to identify themselves as 'Adivasi.' So, it needs to be restated that it would be a gross mistake to consider the term 'Adivasi' to be equivalent to the term 'Tribe' in India. The term 'Tribe' or 'Tribal', according to Oxford Advanced Learner's Dictionary means "a group of people of the same race, or and with the same customs, or language, or religion"[18] etc. The term is popularly used in India to indicate those who live a relatively

15 The four-folded caste structure includes the Priestly (Brahmins), the Warrior (Kshatriyas), the Traders (Vaisyas), and the Serving (Sudras).

16 Massey, *Indigenous People*, 6.

17 Massey, "Christian Dalits in India: An Analysis," *RS*, vol. XXXVII, No. 3 (September, 1990), 40.

18 *Oxford Advanced Learner's Dictionary,* 1387.

isolated life and are technologically backward.[19] In the Indian context, this term suggests primitive people living in the hills and forests, the original but not highly developed inhabitants.[20] It is unfortunate that in the history of India, tribal have been discriminated against and reduced to the status of slaves. For centuries the Indian Government used the term 'tribal' in a derogatory sense. However, by using the 'tribal' or 'tribe' the tribal are reaffirming that they are primal people, who are not spoiled by modern development and its philosophy of individualism. The term 'tribal' is also an affirmation of their history of suffering from exploitations and discriminations received from the main-line society of India. The problem is not with the term tribal, but the attitude of the dominant people of India, which need to change.[21]

Then there are women who are subalterns. Indian society is very much unequal, stratified and hierarchical, where women were considered as less human than the menfolk and always dependent on men and suppressed under the pressures of socio-economic, political and religious restrictions. If we look back to traditions such as 'Smriti' and people like Manu have made so many taboos for the women especially in the context of marriage. The tragedy is that "a woman should marry a man only from her caste even though, he may be lame or blind, illiterate or poor."[22] Even she was restricted for learning and was forbidden for any sort of education. According to Manu, her main work was to "look after the husband, children, and household affairs."[23] Even today, Indian women, in general, are illiterate, and still victims of social discrimination. In India, the Dalits and the women both formed the neglected sections of the nation's society. They are considered men's property and have no independence whatsoever.[24]

Methodological issues in Dalit, Tribal and Feminist Historiography

While analyzing history, these people were ignored or considered as no people. These are the people who need to know their past, which alone will

---

19 K. Thanzauva, *Theology of Community: Tribal Theology in the Making* (Mizoram: MTCA, 1997), 1. (Herafter cited as Thanzauva, *Tribal Theology*).

20 L. P. Vidyarthi and B. K. Rai, *The Tribal Culture of India* (New Delhi: Concept Publishing Company, 1985), 25. Some of the names used for them are Vanjajati (forest caste), vanvasi (inhabitants of the forest), pahari (hill dwellers), adimjati (primitive people), janjati (folk people), anusuchitjanjati (scheduled tribes) and adivasi (first settlers).

21 Cf. Thanzauva, *Tribal Theology*, 7-9.

22 Kumud, Pawde, "The Position of Women in Indian Society," *Indigenous People: Dalits*, edited by James Massey (Delhi: ISPCK, 1994), 147 (Hereafter cited as Pawde*The Position of Women*).

23 Pawde, *The Position of Women*, 147.

24 Ruth Manorama, "Dalit Women: Downtrodden among the Downtrodden," in Massey, *Indigenous People*, 164.

reveal them that once they were also fully human beings, enjoying all benefits of a normal human being which includes land, property, human dignity, natural resources, human freedom, etc. A thorough analysis of the population of India shows that a majority of Christians in India are from subaltern, i.e., Dalit and tribal background. It is estimated that about 65 percent of all Christians in India are of subaltern origin. So, now the need of the hour of Dalit people could be understood and their history should be recorded. In this way, Dalit historians are on the process of reconstructing the history of Dalits. Hence, Dalit historiography has to be from their context and situation, and the Dalit's point of view. It should be based on their own experiences, their sufferings, their aspirations, and their hope. Webster's contributions towards Dalit historiography was remarkable with the agenda of bringing forward the Dalit communities which were in the peripheries of history into the focal point or the center stage like any other communities in India. This helped in crafting historical narratives with the development. This is possible only when their history is written from their point of view. So far, the view that exists is that, whether it is history or theology, they are written by the high caste. The Dalit historiography needs to be produced by the Dalits, based on their own experience, their sufferings, their aspirations, and their hopes.[25] It will anticipate history, which is meaningful to them. Indian history needs a new understanding and interpretation of ancient Indian literature from the perspectives of the Dalits in India.

For many centuries, tribal history has been ignored and neglected by the high caste society of India. They have been discriminated, rejected, exploited in every set up of their lives. They are culturally alienated, socially stigmatized, economically exploited, poor and politically powerless. The tribal history was written was from Colonial and the main-line society of Indian perspectives. The distorted imposed history and culture have become an accepted history among the dominant society of India. This false concept and wrong history must be done away with, for which the starting point is the search for common historiography for the tribal.[26] Therefore, all written religious traditions need to be re-read and re-interpreted from the tribal's life setting. Tribal need to have their historiography based on their own life experiences, produced by the tribal of India. Hence, the central focus and the goal of the tribal historians are, to produce and rewrite their history from their native perspectives.[27] The tribal are the most exploited and impoverished people in most parts of India.

25 A. P. Nirmal, "Towards a Christian Dalit Theology," in Massey *Indigenous People,* 218-219.

26 Nirmal Minz, "Dalit Tribals: A Search for Common Ideology," *Indigenous People: Dalit,* edited by James Massey (Delhi: ISPCK,1994), 134-141.

27 Cf. A.Wati Longchar, *An Emerging Asian Theology: Tribal Theology Issues, Methods and Perspectives* (Jorhat: CTC, 2000), 24-25.

The history of tribal is a history of suffering from genocide, exploitation, discrimination, displacement, and alienation.[28]

The attention of feminist critique and analysis evolved from the background of exclusion, experience, and invisibility of women in history. Feminist historiography has two main tasks. It criticizes and deconstructs the male cultural paradigms on the one hand and the other hand it formulates new perspectives in an attempt to transform traditional androcentric values. Feminist scholarship criticizes patriarchy for privileging, prioritizing men at the cost of dehumanizing women. It is also critical of the economic, racial, educational, social, cultural and ethnic discrimination. Feminist methodology takes women's experience very seriously and these experiences became the starting point of Feminist historiography. Many of the Feminist writers have shown the need to reappraise the Christian past, giving honor and recognition to an army of faithful women, whose practice, defense, and proclamation of their faith had hitherto passed unnoticed by much of the Christian church and its historians. Feminist methodology still suffers without unanimity. However, there is an agreed point on the basis for their critique and analysis of the exclusion, experience, and invisibility of women in the writing of history. This alienation became the starting point of their reconstruction of history.[29]

In the recent past women, historians have articulated the theoretical problem of how to move from androcentric text to historical context and how to write women into history. The task of feminist historical interpretation is the placing of women and their lives at the center of historical reconstructions. Feminist historians ask what it was like to be a woman at various times in history and are exploring women's subjective responses to their environment. In other words, new approaches are being used to attempt to integrate women into the mainstream of historical development rather than isolating women as a separate category.[30]

Subalterns from Biblical or Theological Perspective

The issue of common ground between the Biblical world and Dalit world is of paramount importance for any exploration of either of these areas and to see their integral interconnection. The biblical texts are perceived to be the written expressions of the impact made by the exodus event upon the subjugated people in their struggle for freedom from oppression and by the Jesus-event seeking solidarity with the outcast and confronting

28 Thanzauva, *Tribal Theology*, 11.

29 Oommen, *Historiography of Indian Christianity*, 217.

30 A. D. Gordon et al., "The problem of Women's History," in Bernice A. Carroll, ed., *Liberating Women's History: Theoretical and Critical Essays* (Urbana: University of Illinois Press, 1976), 75-92. (Hereafter cited as, Carroll, *Liberating Women's History*). Cf. Fiorenza, *In Memory of Hert*, 84.

the ruling establishment. The struggles of Dalits can easily find certain natural affinity towards the struggles and experiences of the marginalized communities of the Bible written down as the faith expressions in their various traditions. Secondly, the liberative hermeneutics is the common ground and concern in our quest to see inter-relatedness between Biblical and Dalit worlds. The important objective in the liberative praxis for Dalits is their liberation from the socio-cultural oppression. The Dalit liberative praxis-oriented hermeneutics is geared towards the liberation of Dalits from the psychological, cultural and social oppression and to empower them to get organized in their struggle for freedom. The biblical narratives with liberation potential are already processed and reprocessed accounts addressed in their original settings and they continue to negotiate and renegotiate in our context to make the liberation potential possible.[31] Dalit hermeneutics also share in common some of the relevant concerns on par with any liberation hermeneutics for contemporary exegesis and various processes related to it. Biblical hermeneutics is the source of interpreting the texts, especially of their past history, whose original meaning is no longer immediately available to present in the light of their present experience. Hence, hermeneutics has two eyes, one before and one behind. With the 'eye behind', it looks back to the experiences of God's people, Israel, their creedal confessions and even the retelling of their traditions. This process will help us to be clear about the historical biblical context. With the 'eye before' hermeneutics looks to the present. It discovers the challenges of current social and historical reality. It further tries to make an integral connection between faith and life, between the loving actions of God in the past in the realm of Israel's faith and the present socio-economic and cultural reality.[32]

Understanding that tribal theology is a contextual/people's theology, the hermeneutical task of interpreting the Scriptures should seriously take into consideration the context of the people. K. Thanzauva opines that "unless the tribals are allowed to be different in their interpretation of the Bible, the Bible will not only lose its significant, Christianity will remain superficial without really taking root into the tribal culture." Mathew G. Kariapuram, a professor of Contextual theology at Sacred Heart Theological College Shillong, states that tribal hermeneutics means "focusing attention on the existential and historical concerns of the present-day tribal population in India

---

31 Felix Wilfred, "Postmodernism and Critical Theory: Their Implication for third World Societies," Paper presented at the National Seminar on "Postmodernism and Critical Theory" held at the Radhakrishnan Institute of Advanced Study in Philosophy, University of Madras, August 18-20, 1997, ll.

32 Lenardo Boff. *Faith on Edge* (San Francisco: Harper & Row, 1989). 19, III: Also M. Gnanavaram. "Dalit Theology and the Parable of Good Samaritan", 60

and on interpreting these issues to which theology addresses itself, from the perspective of tribal worldview and value system so that theology becomes a people's theology." Further, he says that the thrust of tribal hermeneutics lies not in abstract theoretical-analytical philosophical tradition and text but concentrates on "oral traditions and events or experiential contents of life.[33] Dr. A. Wati Longchar states that as "we want theology to the culturally rooted, pastorally transforming, spiritually sustaining and contextually relevant" thus it is important that the resources should come from their experiences and context. Yangkahao Vashum in his article "Sources for Studying Tribal Theology" gives a number of raw materials or resources that are necessary for shaping a tribal theology, they are Tribal traditional, Tribal experiences, Tribal history, and Christian heritage.[34]

Biblical feminists, however, want to explore their convictions about equality of women based on biblical teachings, to implement their findings according to biblical guidelines, and to use biblical methods of conflict resolution. Therefore, it will be within scriptural parameters that biblical feminists promote a climate in which women are free to act as equal human beings – and where Christian women can enter into their full inheritance as equal children of God. Biblical feminists see feminism not only as a social-justice issue but also as an issue of religious freedom. To the goals of political, economic, and societal equality of the sexes, biblical feminists add religious equality. Thus, biblical feminists bring the whole scope of Scripture to bear upon discrimination against women; they submit sexist problems in society, church, and family (which we will examine in subsequent articles) first of all to the light of the Bible. Biblical feminists believe that Scripture affirms the worth and value of men and women equally – and that all who have accepted Christ's offer of new life should have equal opportunity to serve God. They take seriously Paul's statement that "there is neither male nor female, for we are all one in Christ Jesus" (Gal. 3:28). Biblical feminists advocate partnership, not competition; mutual submission, not dominion by one sex over the other; the priesthood of all believers, not a male hierarchy. or biblical feminists, Calvary is both the great leveling agent and the great unifying agent. We are all the same at the foot of the cross, all equally needy of the same gift of salvation equally offered to all who believe.[35]

---

33 Mathew G. Kariapuram, Tribal Hermeneutics for a Contextual Theology (Shillong: Don Bosco Centre for Indigenous Cultures, 1999), 70.

34 Yangkahao Vashum, "Sources for Studying Tribal Theology," Tribal Theology: A Reader, 67-76.

35 https://www.cbeinternational.org/resources/article/priscilla-papers/biblical-feminism.

Conclusion

The earlier notion of history as the story of only the 'learned' is giving way to the inclusion of the so 'silenced' people in society. There is a need to develop history in a holistic way. The task of making a new historiography is to find proper, relevant and sufficient sources for the reconstruction of such history that is more relevant and gives justice and equality to people, keeping in mind their language, culture, and ethnicity, making history more as an identity where one can relate with. History has to be deconstructed and re-constructed for us, to understand it in our nativity and rationale. The Indian Church History is an attempt undertaken by many western scholars in the past to bring out critical events and things that have changed the historiography but in doing so; the colonial overtones can still be read and seen. The attempt taken by CHAI is praiseworthy as they have given importance to the Post-Colonial. The changing perspective motivates Christian historians to understand Indian Christianity from Socio, Religious and cultural point of view. The subaltern perspective today questions the hegemonic reading of the given history of Christianity in India. It looks to re-reading and re-construction of the Indian Church History from a different perspective.

10

MISSIONAL CHURCH MOVEMENT WHAT IT IS?

***K. David Udayakumar*[1]**

It gives me immense pleasure to greet Rev. Dr. J. A. David Onesimu on his 65th Birthday. We thank God for His mercies and guidance in the life of Dr. David Onesimu during the past 65 years, and especially during his leadership at MTSC. One thing I noticed in him is 'being happy'. Being happy implies being blissful and content with life. One is happy means feeling satisfied with whatever one has. Being satisfied does not mean that one should not strive further to achieve more in life. This is what I found in Dr. Onesimu during my short association with him. 'Being yourself' is an aspect of our lives that is never easy to do at every instance. But in my observation Dr. Onesimu could do that. Being yourself is important because it not only builds your character and your strength, but also takes a lot of courage to execute day-in and day-out. Being yourself makes a person stand out in this world full of people who are only followers, and makes a person a pioneer and a leader. That is what you achieved in your life Dr. Onesimu. On your 65th Birthday this is my prayer and wish that continue 'being happy' and 'being yourself', because you are unique and no one can replace you. May God bless you.

---

1 *Rev. Dr. K. David Udayakumar is serving as the Principal of Master's College of Theology, Visakhapatnam.*

Introduction

Missional Church Movement is relatively a new concept and has become very popular in Europe and North America. After the International Missionary Council (IMC) at Willingen in 1952 discussion and reflection on how Church is functioning and ought to function in the world, changed the understanding of Christian mission.[2] The Cape Town Commitment (October 2010) of the Lausanne Movement proposed the need to linking '*belief*' with '*praxis*.'[3] Through the history of Christian missions, one could notice calls for a fundamental change (paradigm shift) in concept and practice with ministries employing measures that began to redefine Christianity in specific localities.[4]

In this paper, an attempt is made to understand the "missional church movement" with a brief origin and history of the movement. Among many an attempt has been made to understand the characteristics or marks of the missional church and how it functions. A brief study is made looking into the responses of different church groups to this movement and finally concluded with 'missional church: what it is?

1. What is the Missional Church Movement?

The term *missional* has been used to describe a range of ministry aspects and is applied to multiple contexts and settings by churches and various groups with a variety of motivations. It appears to be one of the catchy phrases of choice used from the last two decades of the 20th century. With its diverse usage, the term *missional* has become a broad description for many things. Constructing a working definition for missional is essential for understanding and identifying its use and for application among the churches world over.

---

2 Darrell L. Guder writes, "*Mission is... seen as a movement from God to the world: the church is viewed as an instrument for that mission... There is church because there is mission, not vice versa.*" Darrell L. Guder. *The Continuing Conversion of the Church* (Grand Rapids, MI: Eerdmans Publishing, 2000), 20.

3 "The Cape Town Commitment: A Confession of Faith and a Call to Action." *International Bulletin of Missionary Research* Vol. 35, no. 2 (04, 2011): 59-80, The Cape Town Commitment was produced following the Third Lausanne Conference held in Cape Town, South Africa in 2010.

4 David Bosch defines paradigm shift as, "...a time of deep uncertainty – and such uncertainty appears to be one of the few constants of the contemporary era and one of the factors that engender strong reactions in favour of hanging onto the enlightenment paradigm, in spite of signs from all quarters that it is breaking up." *Transforming Mission: Paradigm Shifts in Theology of Mission*, (Maryknoll, NY: Orbis Books, 1991), 349. Bosch also provides a detailed examination of major paradigms in the history of Christianity and identifies the emergence of a "Postmodern Paradigm" as necessary for the continued vitality of Christianity in the West.

1.1. History of the Word 'Missional'

Craig van Gelder states that the word 'missional' was first used by historian C. E. Bourne in his book, *The Heroes of African Discovery and Adventure from the Death of Livingstone to the Year 1882.*[5] Here Bourne notes that Bishop Tozar was referred to as '*The Missional Bishop of Central Africa.*'[6] The word was used as a synonym for *missionary.* Related to this Van Gelder says it was Francis DuBose who used this term for the first time with theological substance in his book, *God Who Sends* published in 1983.[7] DuBose, drawing on the works of Karl Barth, argues that proper biblical theology is missional theology in the sense that it derives from and serves the mission of God (*mission Dei*) who sends the church into the world.[8]

Thus, the word '*missionary*' is a portmanteau[9] adjective applying to the many and various aspects of the entire mission efforts or activities of the church and the word '*missional*' seeks to put the emphasis on the '*sentness*' of the church. Guder puts it like this: "*With the term missional we emphasize the essential nature and vocation of the church as 'God's called and sent people.*'[10] Guder and his team coupled the word 'missional' with the word 'church' and making clear an explicit connection between missiology and ecclesiology.

1.2. Understanding Missional Church

The discussion on "missional church" can be traced back to the writings of late Lesslie Newbigin,[11] who served in India as a missionary from 1936-1947 sent by the Foreign Mission Committee of the Church of Scotland, and later became the Bishop of Church of South India in 1947 and continued to serve in this capacity until 1959. When Newbigin first arrived in India,

5 Van Gelder and Zscheile, *The Missional Church in Perspective,* 42.

6 C. Bourne, *The Heroes of African Discovery and Adventure from the Death of Livingstone to the Year 1882* (London: W.S. Sonnenschein, 1983), 191

7 Van Gelder and Zscheile, *The Missional Church in Perspective,* 44-5

8 F. Dubose, *God Who Sends: A Fresh Quest for Biblical Mission* (Nashville, TN: Broadman, 1983), 148-149.

9 A word blending the sounds and combining the meanings of two others, for example motel or brunch. For example, 'podcast is a portmanteau, a made-up word coined from a combination of the words iPod and broadcast', 'a portmanteau word combining smoke and fog', etc.

10 Guder, *Missional Church,* 11.

11 Ruth Tucker calls Newbigin the premier missiologist of the late twentieth century. She credits the strength of his particular missiological understanding (in contrast to McGavran's homogenous unit principle) to his conviction about community. Newbigin taught that diverse communities displaying the supernatural headship of the risen Christ help people to "see" God. This understanding of unity amidst diversity plays a profound role in missional church ecclesiology (Ruth Tucker, *From Jerusalem to Irian Jaya: A Biographical History of Christian Missions* [Grand Rapids: Zondervan, 2004], 455-57).

he was firmly deep-rooted in the view that the missionary work involves a simultaneous introduction of Western civilization, values, and culture along with the gospel. But, as his ministry progressed, he recognized that this view was inadequate, and he adopted a model of engagement with the world based on Paul's example[12] of common ground without compromise. Once common ground was established and trust earned, Newbigin challenged the prevailing cultural assumptions and presenting a better way in Christ.[13]

Newbigin's missiology was largely formed by the mission theology that took shape within the International Missionary Council (IMC) conferences of the 1950s through the 1970s.[14] In 1952 at Willingen, the Conference recognized that the church could be neither the starting point nor the goal of the mission.

> God's salvific work precedes both the church and mission. We should not subordinate mission to the church nor the church to mission; both should, rather, be taken up into the *missio Dei*, which now became the overarching concept. The *missio Dei* institutes the *missiones ecclesiae.*[15]

Though the notion that 'mission' is 'mission of God' and not the church was first articulated by Karl Barth in 1932, and after twenty years it was in Willingen the idea that (not the exact term) *missio Dei was discussed in detail.* Describing the discussions that began at Willingen, David Bosch writes.[16]

> Mission was understood as being derived from the very nature of God. It was thus put in the context of the doctrine on the *missio Dei* as God the Father sending the Son, and God the Father and the Son sending the Spirit was expanded to include yet another

12 I Corinthians 9:19-23: [19] For though I am free with respect to all, I have made myself a slave to all, so that I might win more of them. [20] To the Jews I became as a Jew, in order to win Jews. To those under the law I became as one under the law (though I myself am not under the law) so that I might win those under the law. [21] To those outside the law I became as one outside the law (though I am not free from God's law but am under Christ's law) so that I might win those outside the law. [22] To the weak I became weak, so that I might win the weak. I have become all things to all people, that I might by all means save some. [23] I do it all for the sake of the gospel, so that I may share in its blessings. (I Corinthians 9:19-23).

13 Goheen, "*As the Father Has Sent Me, I Am Sending You*," 423-24.

14 In 1959 he became General Secretary of the International Missionary Council (IMC) and guided it in 1961 to integration with the World Council of Churches (WCC), which he served until 1965 as associate general secretary, with responsibility for the Commission on World Mission and Evangelism. He then returned to India as CSI bishop of Madras until 1974.

15 David Bosch, *Transforming Mission: Paradigm Shifts in Theology of Mission* (Maryknoll, N.Y.: Orbis, 1991), 370.

16 David Bosch, *Transforming Mission: Paradigm Shifts in Theology of Mission* (Maryknoll, N.Y.: Orbis, 1991), 390.

> "movement:" Father, Son, and Holy Spirit sending the church into the world. As far as missionary thinking was concerned, this linking with the doctrine of the Trinity constituted an important innovation. Willingen's image of mission was mission as participating in the sending of God.

In the mid-80s "The Gospel and Our Culture Network"[17] (GOCN) was founded largely in response to book by Newbigin - *The Other Side of 1984: Questions for the Churches.*[18] The founders claimed that "Bishop Newbigin and others have helped us to see that God's mission is calling and sending us, the church of Jesus Christ, to be a missionary church in our societies, in the cultures in which we find ourselves."[19] According to those involved in the GOCN, the term "Missional" points to a paradigm shift:

> The Church of Jesus Christ is not the purpose or goal of the gospel, but rather its instrument and witness. (…) It has taken us decades to realize that mission is not just a programme of the church. It defines the church as God's sent people. Either we are defined by mission, or we reduce the scope of the gospel and the mandate of the church. Thus our challenge today is to move from church with mission to missional church.[20]

While fresh works on missional themes began to appear in the 1980s and 1990s – most notably by DuBose and Van Engen[21] - the work of Darrell Guder "*Missional Church: A Vision for the Sending of the Church in North America*" in 1998 set the stage for the extensive interest in missional ecclesiology. Guder, then professor of evangelism and church growth at Columbia Theological Seminary, was convinced that a theological revolution was needed in the area of ecclesiology that answered the question, "What would the church look like if it were truly *missional* in design and definition?"[22]

---

17 "The Gospel and Our Culture Network" is a "network of Christian leaders from a wide array of churches and organizations, who are working together on the frontier of the missionary encounter of the gospel with North American assumptions, perspectives, preferences and practices" (see www.gocn.org [accessed July 23, 2018]).

18 Newbigin, L. *The Other Side of 1984: Questions for the Churches* (Geneva: World Council of Churches, 1983).

19 Gudur, Darrell L. (ed.), *Missional Church: A Vision for the Sending of the Church in North America*, Grand Rapids 1998:5f.

20 Gudur, Darrell L. (ed.), Missional Church: A Vision for the Sending of the Church in North America, Grand Rapids 1998:5f.

21 Francis DuBose, *God Who Sends: A Freeh Quest for Biblical Missson* (Nashvillee Broadman, 1983); and Charles Van Engen, *God's Missionary People: Rethinking the Purpose of the Local Church* (Grand Rapids: Baker, 1991).

22 Guder, *Missional Church,* 7.

'Missional' is basically a British term and later on taken over in the North American context and discussion about a "missional church" started within the *Gospel and Our Culture Network* (GOCN).

1.3. 'Missional Church' – An Interim Definition

Though GOCN did not offer any accurate definition for "missional church," it did provide some "indicators of a missional church."

Besides GOCN there are a number of others who have contributed significantly to the missional church discussions, notably Michael Frost and Alan Hirsch. Their first joint publication *The Shaping of Things to Come* came out in 2003 in which they talked about three principles[23] that provide an interesting direction for what it means for a church to be missional.

1. The missional church is *incarnational*, not attractional, in its ecclesiology. By incarnational they mean it does not create sanctified spaces into which unbelievers must come to encounter the gospel. Rather, the missional church disassembles itself and seeps into the cracks and crevices of a society in order to be Christ to those who don't yet know him.
2. The missional church is *messianic*, not dualistic, in its spirituality. That is, it adopts the worldview of Jesus, the Messiah, rather than that of the Greco-Roman empire. Instead of seeing the world as divided between the sacred (religious) and profane (nonreligious), like Christ it sees the world and God's place in it as more holistic and integrated.
3. The missional church adopts an *apostolic*, rather than a hierarchical, mode of leadership. It abandons the triangular hierarchies of the traditional church and embraces a biblical, flat-leadership community that unleashes the gifts of evangelism, apostleship, and prophecy, as well as pastoral and teaching gifts.

Lois Barrett gives a very good definition of a "missional church" when she states.[24]

> A missional church is a church that is shaped by participating in God's mission, which is to set things right in a broken, sinful world, to redeem it, and to restore it to what God has always intended

23 Michael Frost and Alan Hirsch, *The Shaping of Things to Come: Innovation and Mission for the 21st Century Church* (Peabody, MA: Hendrickson, 2003), 12.

24 Barrett, Lois Y. (Ed), *Treasure in Clay Jars: Patterns in Missional Faithfulness,* Grand Rapids 2004: X.

for the world. Missional churches see themselves not so much sending, as being sent. A missional congregation lets God's mission permeate everything that the congregation does – from worship to witness to training members for discipleship. It bridges the gap between outreach and congregational life, since, in its life together, the church is to embody God's mission.

1.4. A Comprehensive Definition

A missional church is a unified body of believers,[25] intent on being God's missionary presence[26] to the indigenous community that surrounds them,[27] recognizing that God is already at work.[28]

2. Marks of a Missional Church

Having attempted to define 'missional church' let us turn our attention to the marks or features of a missional church.

Craig Van Gelder and Dwight J. Zscheile in their book *The Missional Church in Perspective: Mapping Trends and Shaping the Conversation* published in 2010 suggested the following four theological distinctives that mark missional churches.[29]

---

25 The importance of unity, which shows up consistently in missional literature, is rooted in Trinitarian theology. The triune God is eternally unified in His mission, and believers under the headship of Christ must be unified in the accomplishment of His mission as well. See Alan Hirsch, *The Forgotten Ways: Reacttvattng the Missional Church* (Grand Rapids: Brazos, 2006), 217-41. This concept of unity was also championed by Lesslie Newbigin in a work based on his Kerr Lectures at the University of Glasgow called, *The Household of God: Lectures on the Nature of the Church* (New York: SCM, 1953; reprint, London: Paternoster, 1998). See also Allster E. McGrath, *Theology: The Basic Readings* (Oxford: Blackwell, 2008), 31. In his latter years Newbigin decried the privatization of the church in modernity and felt it was antithetical to the spread of the gospel. See Michael W. Goheen, "As the Father Has Sent Me, I Am Sending You: J. E. Lesslie Newbigin's Missionary Ecclesiol-ogy" (Ph.D. diss., University of Utrecht, 2000), 420.

26 This is based on Jesus' statement in John 20:21, "As the Father has sent me, I also send you." This was an important cornerstone to Newbigin's missional ecclesi-ology (Goheen, "As the Father Has Sent Me, I Am Sending You," 277).

27 The needs of the indigenous culture have always been taken seriously by biblical writers, as evidenced, for example, by Paul's message to the Athenian philosophers on Mars Hill in Acts 17:16-34. Rodney Stark asserts that Christianity was an urban movement in the first century, with Christians especially concerned about serving specific needs in their cities (*Cities of God: The Real Story of How Christianity Became an Urban Religion and Conquered Rome* [New York: Harper One, 2007], 30-31).

28 Wright, *The Mission of God,* 22-23.

29 Craig Van Gelder and Dwight J. Zscheile, *The Missional Church in Perspective: Mapping Trends and Shaping the Conversation* (Grand Rapids: Baker Academic, 2010).

i. *God is a missionary God who sends the church into the world.* This sending is rooted in the sending by the Father of the Son and the sending by the Father and the Son of the Spirit. This sending component is part of God's identity. The church is the people of God indwelt by the presence of God, and so this sending, the fundamental and distinctive characteristic of God is constitutive of the identity of the church. The church should not be seen as having a missions program or component. Instead, God's mission has a church. The church in its core identity is simultaneously sent and sending.

ii. *God's mission in the world is related to the Kingdom of God.* This Kingdom encompasses all that God has planned since the beginning for extending his rule through human beings to the entire earth.

iii. *The missional church is an incarnational (versus attractional) ministry sent to engage in a postmodern, post-Christendom, globalized context.* The missional church is not just a Western church. In its many global and glocal expressions, the church engages in its context incarnationally and contextually.

iv. *The internal life of the missional church focuses on every believer living as a disciple engaging in mission.* The church is not only the gathered church but is also the scattered church, infiltrating every sphere of society, every geographic and economic location in a community, and every node and network in an interconnected world.

3. Responses to Missional Church Movement

As a response to the missional church movement different ecclesiastical traditions are adapting missional-church ideas to their own traditions, creating a new synthesis that both reinforces their tradition and also expanding it in new directions. The more the traditions lean toward conservative and evangelical perspectives, the missional emphasis is on evangelism. The more the traditions lean toward mainline and liberal perspectives, the emphasis is on justice and the betterment of society. The following are some observations related to responses to the missional church movement.

- Many mainline churches and groups that emphasize compassion, relief and justice aspects of the mission are open to a strong focus on social activism. These traditions are being influenced by the missional conversation toward more intentional witness in the world, but maintain their social and universal focus.
- The conservative evangelicals emphasize attractional models for evangelism. Their focus is on how to expand evangelism through their members into the world as a result of the missional conversation.

Their focus remains firmly on the priority of evangelism in the mission of God.

- Church-growth-oriented evangelicals integrate their emphasis on church growth with an emphasis on every member being a missionary and every social and geographic location and network being a mission field. These groups, influenced by Alan Hirsch and Michael Frost (*co-authors of the influential book The Shaping of Things to Come*), are also doing more to come to terms with the increasing social marginalization and political pressures of the church is facing. They go beyond conservative evangelicals by emphasizing holistic ministry and impact, but they still maintain a very strong accent on church growth as a crucial result.
- Theological Academia presses the agenda of developing an adequate theology of the Trinity and the missio Dei as the root of any and every particular expression of missional ecclesiology and practice in the world. They also emphasize God's agency as primary and have worked to develop this idea in richly theological directions. They keep the activists in the broader missional conversation from becoming human-centered and exclusively pragmatic. At the same time, as the primary initiators of the missional conversation, they have needed to respond to the questions of practitioners, supplying models and principles of practice in order to be heard more broadly and to have an impact on how churches and Christians actually live.

4. Missional Church – What it is?

i. Missional Church is About the Missionary Nature of God and his Church

The Missional Church movement recognizes that both God and the church are intrinsically and principally *missionary* in nature. God is a missionary God who sends a missionary church. A survey of the term *sending* (*apostello* and *pempo*) in its various forms in the Bible, it reveals the missionary nature of the Triune God, as well as the very essence of the church. The redemptive activity of God, his relationship to the world, and his dealing with humankind is described in Scripture by the word "sending." God the Father sends the Son, and God the Father and the Son sends the Spirit, and God the Father and the Son and the Spirit sends the church. In the Gospel of John alone, nearly forty times we read about Jesus being sent. In the final sending passage in John's Gospel, Jesus sees himself not only as one being sent but also as one who is sending: "*As the Father has sent me, I am sending you*" (John 20:21). The word "sending" is the "sum and substance of God's creativity and activity."[30]

30 Georg F. Vicedom, *The Mission of God*, 9.

It is important to understand that the 'church' is a vital part of the missional discussions. While appreciating and admiring the churches that send and support missionaries and missionary activities, it is important to realize that the church should not be seen simply as an entity that sends missionaries. On the other hand, we must recognize that the purpose of the church is derived from the very nature of a sending, missionary God, which in turn compels it to be sent as a missionary people, both individually and collectively.

ii. Missional Church is About Incarnational Ministry (Versus Attractional)

Those with a missional perspective no longer see the church service as the primary connecting point for those outside the church. While there is nothing wrong with attracting people to participate in various meetings of the church, the missional church is more concerned about sending out people in the church to the people in the world, rather than getting the people of the world among the people of the church. In line with 'centripetal' and 'centrifugal' mission, some have described this missional-attractional distinction as a challenge to "go and be" as opposed to "come and see."

The attractional model, which has dominated the church in the West for the past two and a half centuries, seeks to reach out to the culture and draw people into the church. The missional churches see their primary function as one of actively moving into a community to embody and enflesh the word, deed, and life of Jesus into every nook and corner. Alan Hirsch speaks of the "missional-incarnational impulse," where the word "missional" expresses the sending nature of the church, while "incarnational" represents the "embedding" of the gospel into a local context. In other words, "missional" speaks to our direction – we are sent; while being "incarnational" is more about *how* we go, and *what* we do as we go.

iii. Missional Church is About Actively Participating in the *Missio Dei*

There is a strong notion among many of us that the primary activity of God is in the church, rather than recognizing that God's primary activity is in the world, and the church is God's instrument sent into the world to participate in His redemptive mission.

This key distinction clarifies the difference between a church with a missions program and a missional church. A church with a missions programme usually sees missions as one activity alongside many other equally important programmes of the church. A missional church, on the other hand, focuses all of its activities around its participation in God's agenda for the world.

As the sent, missionary people of God, the missional church understands its fundamental purpose as being rooted in God's mission to restore and heal creation and to call people into a reconciled relationship with Himself. We should not think that the church as the starting point when thinking about mission. Instead, the church must be seen as the result of God's mission. In the words of David Bosch: "*It is not the church which undertakes mission; it is the missio Dei which constitutes the church.*" Or stated in a slightly different manner; "*it is not so much that God has a mission for his church in the world, but that God has a church for his mission in the world.*"[31]

Final Remarks on Missional Church

- God's mission in the world is related to the reign (kingdom) of God.
- Missional churches see themselves not so much sending, as being sent.
- The missional church is not only the gathered church but is also the scattered church, penetrating into every area of society, every geographic and economic location in a community.
- A missional church is a church that is shaped by participating in God's mission, which is to set things right in a broken, sinful world, to redeem it, and to restore it to what God has always intended for the world.
- A missional congregation lets God's mission permeate everything that the congregation does – from worship to witness to training members for discipleship.
- The missional church is an incarnational ministry sent to engage a postmodern, post-Christendom, globalized context.
- To talk about the priesthood of all believers was to reintroduce the idea of every Christian having a calling and a responsibility to serve God, to be actively involved in God's work in the world, and thus to break with the concept of "ordinary" believers being mere 'minors' and immature 'objects' of the church's ministry.
- With Martin Luther's reformation came the realization that a mission field is any place where people are trusting "other" gospels, that is, gospels clearly different from the Christ-gospel proclaimed in the New Testament scriptures.

Conclusion

Advocates of the missional church view that the mission of the church is to represent the Kingdom of God in the world. As Guder states.[32]

> Therefore, the church's own mission must take its cues from the way God's mission unfolded in the sending of Jesus into the world for its salvation. In Jesus' way of carrying out God's mission, we discover

31 Christopher Wright 2006, 62.

32 Guder, Darrel L., ed., *The Missional Church: A Vision for the Sending of the Church in North America,* Grand Rapids, William B. Eerdmans Publishing Company, 1999, 102.

that the church is to represent God's reign as its community, its servant, and its messenger.

This understanding of the church as representing the Kingdom of God (*be careful, church is not the Kingdom of God but only points to or represents*) is helpful in that it sees mission in a holistic way. With regard to the church representing the reign of God as its servant, the COGN team writes.[33]

> Our responses of compassion and service, like our actions for peace and justice are deeds of authority and therefore signs that the reign of God is present now in our world and is on the way as its future... Whatever our responses may be, they bring wholeness and dignity to the world and thereby provide a taste of a future in the reign of God under the rule and authority of Christ's lordship. These are signs that invite people to enter and taste more, to eat and be full.

33 Guder, Darrel L., ed., *The Missional Church: A Vision for the Sending of the Church in North America,* Grand Rapids, William B. Eerdmans Publishing Company, 1999, 102.

11

CHRISTIANITY AND SECULARISM TOWARDS RECONSTRUCTING CHRISTIAN MISSION

K. Vijayan[*1]

As a mark of acknowledging Rev. Dr. David Onesimu's contribution in theological education as the Principal and the Professor of Christian Theology, it is right and appropriate for me to be part of this festschrift in celebrating his life and work in his 65th Birthday in the year 2020. Dr. Onesimu, the author of Constructing Dalit Theology for Dalit Liberation; Dr. Ambedkar's Critique Towards Christian Dalit Liberation; who also published a couple of books; and several articles and also the co-editor of several books. He was one of the Principals of the MTSC who served the Seminary as Principal for a long period of time since 2007. It was also a great privilege for me to work along with him since 2017. And I wish and pray for him in this auspicious occasion a long life and continue to serve God in this historical institution for many years.

Introduction

The word 'secular' comes from the Latin word *saeculum,* which means age, era, epoch etc., and indirectly means the world of change. According to

1 *Rev. Dr. K. Vijayan, hails from Trivandrum, Kerala, basically from the Church of South India (CSI), South Kerala Diocese; however, chose to work with the Evangelical Church of India (ECI) since 1997. He was formerly working as Lecturer at the Calcutta Bible Seminary (CBS). Currently he is teaching at the Madras Theological Seminary and College (MTSC), Chennai; & the Gurukul Lutheran Theological College and Research Institute (GLTCRI), Chennai as an Associate Professor in the Department of Missiology. He can be contacted in this E-mail: revvijayan@gmail.com*

the Random House Dictionary as quoted by Joseph, 'secular' is that which pertains 'to worldly things or to things that are not regarded as religious, spiritual or sacred.'[2] 'Secularization' can be defined as the experienced, gradual disintegration of all mythical and religious legitimizations of society. In the modern world, religion is relegated to the personal sphere whereas the public sphere is organized by the ideologies of secularization and pluralism. According to Joseph, the Reformation in its opposition to church authority advocated the separation of the Church and State. The French Revolution was an attack both on the political and ecclesiastical authorities.[3] The term secularization became real since the time of the Peace Treaty of Westphalia, in Germany in 1648, in which secularization was used to describe the transfer of territories previously under ecclesiastical control to the domination of lay political authorities. The ideology of Marxism supported secularization and tried to get rid of religion altogether.

The 'secularism' paved the way for religious tolerance in most of the western countries. At the same time, secularism replaced the religiously sanctioned value systems with secular value systems. For instance, as Joseph observes that in a secular state the person may be a good citizen before the State but maybe an evil person before his fellow humans. One remains a good citizen before the State provided the person commits crimes and evils in such a way that he or she is not caught. In such a situation, hypocrisy and duplicity would be the accepted norm in human relation.[4] However, the Indian/Asian secularism is different from Western secularism in which a sharp divide exists between the state and religion. Though religion is considered a private matter by the Indian state, the official policy of equal recognition of all religions (*sarva-dharma-samabhavana*) has only opened up more and more public space to all religions in the civil society. This article is an attempt to provide a descriptive analysis of Christianity and Secularism from a postmodern context, in order to see some of the issues in relation to Christianity and Secularism which will also ensure alternatives with the aim of reconstructing Christian mission in India.

I. An Overview of the Christianity and Secularism in the Postmodern Context of India

Christianity and Secularism in Asia, particularly in the Indian situation, it was not in the process of becoming secularized in the same way as Europe. They

2 Joseph Valiamangalam, "Challenges of Modernity and Postmodernity to Mission" Paul Vellarackal and Dasan Jayaraj (eds.), *Mission in Civil Society: Challenges and Responses*, (Anand: Gujarat Sahitya Prakash, 2015), 65.

3 Joseph Valiamangalam, "Challenges of Modernity and Postmodernity to Mission"..., 66.

4 Joseph Valiamangalam, "Challenges of Modernity and Postmodernity to Mission"..., 66.

become scientific and modern without becoming secular. The proponents of postmodernity like Carrier claim that the grand (meta) narratives have lost their significance in today's world and that modernity has exhausted its innovative dynamics.[5] The French Postmodernist Jean-Francois Lyotard (1924-1998), who is known as the father of postmodernism, proposed a philosophical basis for the concept of postmodern age by showing how the great or grand traditions have lost energy to construct the social life of the contemporary world. The grand narratives are the general and fundamental representations that give meaning and justification to men and women in everything that they undertake. Some of the grand narratives of the modern age are Capitalism, Humanism, Scientific technology, Democracy, as well as Religious ideologies of Hinduism, Islam and Christianity. These narratives are universal and are made to serve the universal ambitions of their proponents. They, therefore, attempt to assimilate alternative accounts into their own narratives and at the same time suppress the objections raised against their discourses.[6] But, the failures of such grand narratives to create a just and prosperous world, for the underprivileged, clearly showed the limits of grand ideologies. This new emerging consciousness was described as postmodernity. As opposed to the grant narratives, the postmodern era has given birth to little traditions/ small narratives that respond to the needs and aspirations of people who are preoccupied with constructing their own identities in their cultures.[7] While modernity stood for the grand narratives-the Enlightenment, the belief in the omnipotence of reason and adherence to the myth of scientific progress-the postmodernity stood for small narratives marked by the crisis of the self and reason, the decline of universalistic ideologies, the denial of institutional religions, the renewed interest for religiosity and the environmental issues.[8]

Modernity introduced the values of freedom of the individual, democracy, secularism, pluralism in religions and ideologies and human rights. But, postmodernity has expressed disillusionment with modernity and its promises of unlimited progress and happiness to men and women in the world of today. It has challenged the validity of meta or grand narratives with their dominant value systems of the world and the churches. Mission in postmodernism will reconstruct all the meta-narratives of the modernity and will encourage the

---

5 Herve Carrier, *Evangelizing the Culture of Modernity* (New York: Orbis Books, 1983), 51; cf. Joseph Valiamangalam, "Challenges of Modernity and Postmodernity to Mission"..., 67.

6 cf. Joseph Valiamangalam, "Challenges of Modernity and Postmodernity to Mission"..., 67.

7 These little traditions stress the singularity of each group and class of people. Each of them has its own specific set of values that are evolved from their own specific traditions and expressed through their own cultural way of life. Cf. Joseph Valiamangalam, "Challenges of Modernity and Postmodernity to Mission"..., 69.

8 Some examples of small narratives in India are the Feminist movement, the *Dalit-Tribal* movement and the Ecological movement.

small narratives with their traditions and the rise of new cultural, religious and secular movements, liberation movements of indigenous people for their rights. It will also provide alternatives for the mission of the churches to engage in dialogue and collaboration with the men and women of all cultures, ideologies and religious traditions, to promote peace and harmony by witnessing to the presence and growth of the kingdom of God in the world at large and Asia/ India today.

II. Some of the Issues in Relation to Christianity and Secularism

There is some uncertainty regarding the term 'secular' in the Indian constitution. As a matter of fact, in the early form of the Indian constitution, the term secular is not mentioned. It is substituted only 18th Nov. 1976, in the forty-second amendment came into force. In the preamble to Constitution: (a) for the words, 'sovereign democratic republic' the words 'sovereign socialist secular republic' shall be substituted; and (b) for the words 'unity of the nations', the words 'unity and integrity of the nation' shall be substituted. So, India continues to remain 'sovereign socialist secular republic.'[9] It seems that the essence of secularism rates on two basic principles: (i) Separation of religion from politics and (ii) Acceptance of religion as purely and strictly private affairs of individuals having nothing to do with the state.

1. Secularism and Religion

According to the leadership of the VHP, Christianity and Islam have "to make Hindus a minority in India in the next 30 years; and that they want to established their rule in India and completely destroy Hindu culture." Thus, efforts had to be made by the *Sangh Parivar* to check Christianity and Islam, and this had to be supplemented by taking up proselytization by Hindus themselves and shore up Hindu numbers. The fundamental right of freedom of religion has always been a source of political insecurity for the *Sangh Parivar*. This right is seen as a privilege granted by a "secular" constitution to minorities mainly, Muslims and Christians-to expand their ranks. That is why organizations such as the VHP demand that the freedom of religion granted by the constitution be amended by banning conversions.[10] Shri Guruji condemns that Christians claims that the constitution has conferred on them a right to propagate, which is as good as a right to convert. Neither the Hindu Society nor the law of the land accepts that the right to propagate means right to convert. Moreover,

9 A. P. Avasthi, *Indian Government and Politics* (Agra: Lakshmi Narain Agarwal Educational Publishers, 2001) 170-171; as quoted by Sam Varghese, "An Appraisal of Tussle Between Secularism and Hindu Fundamentalism in Today's Indian Scenario" *Conviction: Journal of Bethel Bible College*, 3/2 (July - Dec.2015), 44.

10 Manjari Katju, "The Politics of *Ghar Wapsi*..., 21.

it should be noted that the act of conversion to Christianity violates a basic feature of our Constitution i.e. of secularism.

M. K. Gandhi brought the idea of *Sarva Dharma Sama Bhava* (which means all the religions should be regarded and respected equality). This is in a broad sense the point where we reach very near to secularism in the Indian version of the term. About Secular thought in India, the Late President Maulana Abdul Kalam Azad wrote about the place of Islam in India "... Just as a Hindu can say with pride that we are Indians and follows Hinduism, so also Muslims can say with equal pride that we are Indians and follow Islam." In the same way, Christians can also say with pride that we are Indians and follow Christianity.[11] But, Shri Guruji accuses that the Christian Church has never made a secret of their conviction that theirs is the only true religion and as such superior to others. Conversion is the corollary of this conviction. The Christian Church will not hesitate to approve the secularist ideals. A Christian missionary talks in the loudest language about secularism because it helps his conversion and denationalization activities.[12] At the same time, there are some Hindu religious fundamentalist argues to remove the "secular" state from the constitution of India, in order to make the county a *Hindu Rashtra*. Is there any doubt that this kind of religious/political proselytization manipulate against the basic principle of secularism preserved in our Constitution?

2. Secularism and Religious Fundamentalism

The word 'fundamentalism' simply means "the adherence to fundamentalist" or in the Christian context, "the maintenance of traditional orthodox beliefs."[13] The "fundamentalist" movement originally was a reaction against the secularization of American society at the end of the 19th century among the pietistic immigrants from Germany. The term 'fundamentalism' is to refer the theological standpoint of some American Protestant churches at that time as they confronted by the three challenges: Darwin's evolution theory, biblical criticism and anti-supernaturalism.[14] The word seems to have been originally used by a group of American Conservative Evangelicals who branded themselves together to defend their faith against the liberal adaptation of the church doctrine, sought to go back to the biblical 'fundamentals' of

11 Nelson Sudhir Kshiraj, *The Indian Christian...*, 180.

12 http://www.golwalkarguruji.org/download/books/en/Shri_Guruji_and_The_Christian_Missions.pdf, (accessed on 24/01/2011).

13 Gnana Robinson, "Why is Fundamentalism a Problem Today?" in Andreas Nehring, *Fundamentalism and Secularism* (Madras: Gurukul Lutheran Theological College & Research Institute, 1994), 9.

14 Cf. George Ninan, "An Attempt to Define Secularism and Fundamentalism in Indian Context" Andreas Nehring (ed.), *Fundamentalism and Secularism: The Indian Predicament* (Madras: Gurukul Lutheran Theological College & Research Institute, 1994), 47-48.

the Christian faith.[15] It seems that the polarization between liberals and conservatives gave birth to the fundamentalist movement. For instance, some Christians proudly claimed themselves to be fundamentals in the sense that they strongly uphold beliefs in the strict and literary interpretation of the Bible or they strictly maintain the ancient fundamental doctrines of Christianity.[16]

"Religious Fundamentalism" as the new incarnation of religion and more recently as religious extremism has become for great alarm among human communities across the globe. It is a powerful return of religion as a potential social and political force.[17] Globalization has shaken the very foundations of religious traditions. Therefore, it is viewed as a fundamentalist religion of consumerism and a new form of idolatry. It has raised a serious challenge to the very existence of all religions.[18] Given the resurging trend of fundamentalism, the topmost priority of evangelization must be one of peace-making and reconciliation.[19] Religious fundamentalism is an ideology and a movement claiming to pursue the noble objective of defending a particular religion from forces which are believed to weaken or destroy it. It is a phenomenon which claims that certain features of a particular religion are representative of, or equivalent to, the entire religious tradition. A particular religious element is presented as symbolizing the core or nucleus of the tradition, thereby distorting the essence or the main teachings of the religion.[20] For instance, the veneration of a location, traditionally believed to be the birthplace of one of the incarnations of God, though having no historical certainty, is given such exaggerated importance that the essence of that religion is identified with it. Or again, the emphasis on the charismatic manifestation of some supernatural gift of the Holy Spirit in one' s life as constructing *the* qualification mark of genuine Christian-ness.

One of the important features of religious fundamentalism according to Paul F. Knitter in the context of religious plurality is that the claim made by

15 J. I. Parker, *Fundamentalism and the Word of God: Some Evangelical Principles* (Grand Rapids, Michigan: William B. Eerdman Publiching Co., 1958), 24.

16 Rosiamliana Tochhawng, "Religious Fundamentalism and Ethnic Communalism in North East India: A Challenge for Christian Solidarity" in *Mizoram Theological Journal* VIII/8 (Octo.-Dec. 2004), 30.

17 R. Sahayadhas, "A Theological Response to Religious Fundamentalism" *The Theology of Our Times* 13 (September 2010), 26.

18 S. G. Kochuthara, "Fundamentalism: The only way to Redeem Religious Ethics," *Journal of Dharma,* 35 (2010), 338.

19 Antony Lawrence, "Urgency of a New Paradigm of Evangelization in the Postmodern Globalized world" *Vidyajyoti Journal of Theological Reflection (VJTR),* 78/2 (February 2014), 125.

20 Cf. Roger Gaikwad, "The Role of Theological Education in Response to Religious Fundamentalism and Ethnic Communalism in North East India" in *Mizoram Theological Journal* XI&XII/3 (July-Dec. 2005), 44.

adherents of a particular tradition that their religion has exclusive possession of the truth; therefore, all other religious traditions are false, erroneous, human-made or even inspired or authored by evil forces. This characteristic gets all the more poignantly articulated when members of a particular religious tradition engage themselves in proclaiming their faith, calling upon others to give up their respective faiths and to embrace the faith of the preachers. This activity is based on the principle of the extension of one's own religion and the extinction of others. Such a stance appears unjustified and disrespectful to followers of other religious traditions.[21] K. C. Abraham, in his introduction to the book *Religious Fundamentalism: An Asian Perspective,* says that in a religiously pluralistic society, if people belonging to one particular tradition use their religious affiliation, or are so manipulated to use their religious way of life, as an instrument to exercise political power over others, then such religious fundamentalism degenerates into communalism.[22] This communalism generates suspicion, fear, and hatred in the minds of the followers of one religion towards other religions and their adherents. The attitude of superiority with the concept of fullness remains the greatest obstacle for authentic and honest dialogue, given the presence and action of God in other religions and cultures. To what is full one cannot add more; to what is final no changes can be made.[23] As Koyama rightly points out that Christianity exhibits "crusading mind" and not "crucifying mind;" and it suffers from a "teacher complex."[24]

Fundamentalism, though originated in the Christianity of the West, is also a phenomenon in all the religions.[25] "Fundamentalists" are not just religious conservatives; they are conservatives who are willing to take a stand and to fight. In reality, the meaning of the term fundamentalism seems to connote loyalty to the fundamentals of religion and ideology. However, the word 'fundamentalism' also has a negative connotation as 'religious fundamentalism' to those who are terrorizing and troubling

---

21 Cf. Paul F. Knitter, *NO Other Name? A Critical Survey of Christian Attitudes Towards the World Religions* (Crezon City: Claretian Publications, 1985), 75-76.

22 Cf. K. C. Abraham, "Introduction" edited by John S. Augustine, Religious *Fundamentalism: An Asian Perspective,* (Bangalore: SATHRI, 1993), xii.

23 Pluralism does not aim to establish the equality of all religions and validity of their teachings; it rather seeks to promote the mutuality of all the religions in an effort to further the well-being of the religions of the world. This is based on the conviction that dialogue is both possible and necessary. Cf. Paul F. Knitter," The Transformation of Mission in the Pluralistic paradigm," *Concilium* 1 (2007), 94-96; also cf. Antony Lawrence, "Urgency of a New Paradigm of Evangelization"..., 125-127.

24 K. Koyama, "What Makes a Missionary? Toward Crucified Mind not Crusading Mind," Edited by G. H. Anderson & T. F. Stransky in *Mission Trends No. 1,* (Grand Rapids: Eerdmans), 117-132.

25 George Ninan, "An Attempt to Define Secularism and Fundamentalism"...,49.

other in the name of religion as Christian fundamentalism,[26] Islamic fundamentalism,[27] Hindu fundamentalism[28] etc. Selva Rathinam says that Christians rightly affirm the uniqueness and the universal salvific power of Jesus Christ, but in British India, the missionaries went further and accused the Hindus as 'idol worshipers'. Such religious prejudice is not uncommon among the fundamentalist Christians even today.[29] Some aspects of Hindu fundamentalism are a protest against a majority with a minority complex. Hindu fundamentalists teach that the spirit of secularism enshrined in the constitution of India provides an added privilege to the minorities to propagate and spread their religion among the Hindu majority. According to

---

26 The Christian church's vision and understanding of the mission continues to be western religious imperialism and more Christian colonialism as practiced by some western missionaries of the 18th and 19th centuries. They are all still limited to the conversion/proselytization (the term "proselytism" has close affinity with religious "conversion". So much so that to 'convert' would be also to 'proselytize:' the one leads to the other), baptism, and the organizational structure of the church with the slogan that "India for Christ," "Winning India for Christianity" at the cost of other religions in India, instead of "Christ for India." Cf. M. Abel "India, Yesterday and Today" in T. Dayanandan Francis, ed., *The Good News of Jesus Christ in the Indian Setting,* (Chennai: CLS, 2000), xxix.

27 The history of Islam also shows fundamentalistic trends and fanatic actions. The Islamic fundamentalism has its roots in India in 10th/11th century, as the Muslims became the ruling elite and the resurgent Islamic civilization clashed with the Hindu society. History is full of the accounts of bitterness, bloodshed, destruction of Hindu temples, and the treatment of Hindus as second-class citizens. However, after Independence and formation of Pakistan, the Muslims in India found themselves as a scattered, politically powerless, minority-community. Islamic fundamentalism shows its ugly face in the revival and implication of the *Shariat* as the supreme law of the land. In the mid twentieth century, this term was mostly used to refer to Muslim fundamentalists as they emerged as a militant force the world had to take seriously. Cf. George Ninan, "An Attempt to Define Secularism and Fundamentalism"..., 49ff.

28 It is often claimed that Hinduism having no founder, nor a revealed book, nor a doctrine, nor an organized religion, and it cannot promote fundamentalism. It was the religious movement of the 19th century which took upon itself, to define Hinduism and thereby develop the characteristics of a religion. It is only recently the word started being applied to the Hindu community in India, is an idea developed in reaction to the external threat by Christianity and Islam; the Arya Samaj attained the characteristics of a fundamentalist movement, with the *Vedas* as revealed scripture, and claim as the true religion in its well defined essentials of faith and practice. It also attained the characteristics of a missionary movement claiming uniqueness and absolute superiority over other religions. The Arya Samaj and its fundamentalist posture led to the formation of the Hindu Mahasabha, Rashtrya Swayamsevk Sangh (RSS) and recently the Vishwa Hindu Parishad (VHP) and their political wing the Bhartya Janata Party (BJP), all concerned with Hindu identity and *Hindutva*. Cf. George Ninan, "An Attempt to Define Secularism and Fundamentalism"...,54.

29 Selva Rathinam, "Insights from the Interaction between the Two Testaments for Inter-religious Dialogue," *Vidyajyoti Journal of Theological Reflection (VJTR),* 78/1 (January 2014), 65.

Sita Ram Goel, equated the secularism with suicidal of Hinduism, and the death of secularism is the vision of Hindu adherents.[30] The fundamentalists of the *Hindutva*[31] movement in India says that "India for Hindus;" some of the Indian churches with the slogan that "India for Christ," "Winning India for Christianity" at the cost of other religions in India, instead of "Christ for India;" and some of the Christian and Islamic countries already treat people of other faiths as second-rate citizens. Secularism in India does not mean that the state should be hostile to any religion but that it should be neutral between different religions.

3. Secularism and Politics

The latest census (2011) religious data shows there is an increase in the Muslim population.[32] The reaction to this time was not different from the *Sangh Parivar's* response a decade earlier. At that time the RSS chief K. S. Sudershan called upon Hindu couples to produce more than three children to sustain their religious community in India. Now ten years later, the VHP, the religious wing of RSS says that "its stand has been vindicated and it would make a fresh appeal to Hindus to reproduce more." The pioneer newspaper's Delhi edition reported BJP MP from Unnao, Sakshi Maharaj said in a function during *Sant Samagam Mahotsav* in Meerut, Uttar Pradesh that "...the time has come when a Hindu women must bear at least four children in order to protect Hindu religion. Among these four children, the Hindu should send one of them to the Army and give another to *Sant Samaj* for the propagation of Hindu religion."[33] Vasudevanand Saraswati, the Sankaracharya of Badrikashram, while speaking at the *Magh Mela* in Allahabad, says that "it is because of Hindus' unity that Narendra Modi has become Prime Minister. In order to maintain their majority status, every Hindu family should give birth to ten children."[34]

The Government of India had launched a scheme "*Jiyo Parsi*" (live Parsee) to support the Parsee community to grow in numbers, as it alarmed by

30 Sita Ram Goel, *India's Secularism New Name for National Subversion* (New Delhi: Voices of India, 1999), 25ff.

31 The term *Hindutva* is coined by Vinayaka Damodar Savakar, a Hindu nationalist in 1923 who was the prominent in the Hindu awakening of the 20th century. It is understood as an ideology that sought to define Indian culture in terms of Hindu values and it is against the present understanding of Secularism.

32 Though the growth rate of the Muslim population has showed from 29% to 24% between 1991-2001, it is still higher than the national average of 18% for the decade. John Dayal, "Saffronizing the womb" *Indian Currents* XXVII/04 (26 January-01February 2015), 30; also *cf. www.census2011.co.in.*

33 John Dayal, "Saffronizing the womb"..., 30.

34 Quoted by Mary Scaria, "Womb centred politics" *Indian Currents* XXVII/04 (26 January -01February 2015), 34; also cf. John Dayal, "Saffronizing the womb"..., 30.

the predication that the current population growth rate of the Parsees would fall to 23,000 by 2020.[35] The BJP's hidden agenda of making India a Hindu Nation, one wonders if the Modi government would be able to pursue its population control programme as vigorously as it as happening till now.[36] The question arises that will the government is going to lend the same helping hand in the case of other minority groups such as Andaman Tribals, Kashmiri Pandits, Syrian Christians of Kerala, Brus in Tripura[37] etc. All these communities are facing a rapid decline in their population. A study by K. C. Zachariah of the Centre for Development Studies had pointed out that the Syrian Christians of Kerala could decline to 28.51 lakh by 2031. Jose Kottayil, the Secretary, Kerala Catholic Bishop Council (KCBC) says that the church asking its healthy and financially sound members to have four or more children to stem a decline in numbers.[38] Fearing a demographic disaster and losing dominance in Mizoram,[39] two biggest churches in the state the Presbyterian Church of Mizoram and the Baptist church of Mizoram have a long-standing policy that encourages families to nurture more children. The churches and church-sponsored NGOs in Mizoram are influencing people to increase birth rate than the ideal norm of two children per family in order to maintain their demographic hold on the state administration.

As we noted above some of these fringe groups have been raising the bogey of declining their population, and asking their women to produce more children in order to counter 'the planned growth of a particular religious/ political community. Going against the national policy of population control, religions can lead to serious consequences on national integrity as well. The campaigns encouraging procreation with the *religious* and *political* motive can

35 Aasha Khosa, "Parsee on the Brink" *Indian Currents* XXVII/04 (26 January-01 February 2015), 46.

36 Cf. Aasha Khosa, "Parsee on the Brink"..., 47.

37 There are 31,000 Brus evacuees living in six evacuee camps in Kanchanpur sub-division of North Tripura Distrist, demanding the status like Kashmiri Pandits or Tamil refugees to Union Home Minister Rajnath Singh 0n February 14, 2015. They had fled their ancestral homes in Mizoram and have been staying here since October 1997; cf. "Mizo bodies object to Brus' demand for Kashmiri Pandits status," *Newslink* (Aizawl), 18th February, 2015, 1.

38 In a latest Censes shows that the number of Christians have been in stedy decline as 18% of the Kerala's population.

39 Mizoram total population is about 11 lakh (2011), with the birth rate going down every year, while the national population has crossed the 1.21-billion mark with a birth rate of 51 births every minute. The population density in the state is 52 per sq km as compared to 324 per sq km at the national level. The total number of children (0-6 years) in the state is 1, 65,536 out of which 81,571 are girls and 83,965 are boys which accounts for only 15.17 per cent of the total population and shows a decline from 16.2 per cent just a year earlier. Cf.http://en.newsbharati.com/Encyc/2012/7/13Mizo-Church-Fear-demographic-Disaster-Encouraging-childbirths.xhtml, (accessed on 12/02/2015).

only serve to create tensions between the religious communities. As we are living in a postmodern context it is ridiculous to think of the religions in India to tweak the birth control policy to grow more children to preserve a race and a religious community which lead us into a dangerous situation. Manjari, the writer, rightly observes that conversion for the poor and oppressed is not about the religion but about getting better access to resources and rights-and religion is a utilitarian route to such an option. If not these, then the reason for conversion by the vulnerable sections is a threat; in the given political context in the country, this is possible perhaps only by the workers of the *Sangh Parivar*. The weak and vulnerable have no choice but to convert in the face of threats and intimidation used by VHP, *Bajarang Dal* etc. The interesting thing to observe is that the religion or the religious values are again absent in this whole exercise of *ghar wapsi* expect as a cover-up.[40] She further pose the following questions to the RSS and its affiliates:[41] If the whole logic of "reconversion" is to bring back the indigenous people who earlier moved out the Hindu fold to escape social oppression and humiliation, does it not make more sense to work towards improving their economic well-being and dignity; to work towards losing the hierarchies and stratifications that blight their daily lives at the local level, rather than subjecting them to a set of rituals under the garb of *ghar wapsi* and then abandoning them to the same fate of poverty and humiliation? Moreover, if the country has voted for BJP, the electoral front of the *Sangh Parivar*, to power with such a strong majority, what is this insecurity about numbers and power which bother them even now? It seems that the politicization of religion and religionization of politics must be critiqued and the relation of religion and politics in India should be analysed within the framework of secularism. That is what is currently happening with the *Gau Rakshak Dal* (cow protecting activist) in the states like Haryana and Gujarat.[42]

III. Reconstructing Christian Mission in the Context of Indian Secularism

1. Christian Mission and Nationalism

It was crucial for Asian/Indian Christian leaders in the mid-twentieth century were to show that Christianity and nationalism could co-exist. Many missionaries were sceptical or hostile to this project, at least when it became too 'political' and radical. According to K. P. Aleaz, it was neither Aurobindo nor Gandhiji but the Indian Christians like S. K. George, Brahmabandhav Upadhyaya are the ones who initiated the National Movement.[43] It is evident that

40 Manjari Katju, "The Politics of *Ghar Wapsi*..., 24.

41 Manjari Katju, "The Politics of *Ghar Wapsi*..., 24.

42 Cf. Pragya Singh, "Four Stomachs to Fill" *Outlook* (15August, 2016), 32-41.

43 K. P. Aleaz, *Religions in Christian Theology*, (Kolkata: Punthi Pustak, 2001), 288.

Indian Christians nurtured the nationalism which was instrumental in leading the freedom struggle against the British colonial rule in its initial stages.[44] This was because the Indian Christian totally identified with his motherland and the Culture. According to Nelson Sudhir Kshiraj, an Indian writer, "while the Hindus have fought only one war, that for the freedom of India, the Indian Christians have fought two wars, the National freedom struggle as well as the freedom of the church of India to become the Indian National Church."[45] The misconception of the majority of the Hindu mindset in the past was that Christians in India have been viewed as alien to Indian culture and as pro-British elements and propagators of the western culture.[46]

Though there have been positive and negative outcomes, from the postcolonial perspective of Indians, the modern missionaries were often seen as agents of colonialism, and Indian Christians as betrays their own cultures. Another set of problem arose out of the principle of comity[47] adopted by Christian missions, by which they divided the land and identified the people with denominations, which leads to the disunity among the Christians took the form of denominational rivalries. The third set of problems arose out of the lack of adequately contextualizing the gospel and churches. Christianity came like a potted plant dependent on outside nature and support. Many Indian saw it as a foreign religion, and as a religion of untouchable. The lake of contextualization causes the lake of depth in witness and discipleship and little transformation of the Indian worldview in the light of the gospel.[48] Today many Hindus recognize Church in India as *Vidheshi* (Foreign). Some years back, K. S. Sudarshan, the RSS Chief has called on Christians in India to

---

44 Shri Bomesh Chandra Banerjee, the first president of the Indian National Congress was a Christian; and the participants in the Round Table Conference, Shri S. K. Dutta and Shri Gokulnath Chatterjee were also Christians. cf. Nelson Sudhir Kshiraj, *The Indian Christian*, (Jabalpur: NSK Publications, 2002), 19.

45 Today the Church of India is independent and includes the Church of North India, the Church of South India, the National Council of Churches in India and others. Cf. Nelson Sudhir Kshiraj, *The Indian Christian...*, 19.

46 Shri Guruji observes that one wonders why Christian proselytization should lead to an excess of love with western countries. The converts were given not only a psychological affinity towards the western countries but were weaned away from national society. The language, the script, the dress, other modes of life, the fasts and the festivals, the names and nomenclature all undergo a change. The demand of the Goan Catholics to adopt Roman script for Konkani in place of Devnagari is the reflection of this attitude. cf. http://www.golwalkarguruji.org/download/books/en/Shri_Guruji_and_The_Christian_Missions.pdf, (accessed on 24/01/2011).

47 The mutual recognition among Christian Missions of one another's laws, customs, and institutions.

48 Paul G. Hiebert, 'The Christian response to Hinduism' in *Missiology for the 21st century*, edits. Roger E. Hedlund & Paul Joshua Bhakiaraj, (New Delhi: ISPCK/MIIS, 2004), 331.

disassociate themselves from the stronghold of foreign Churches and set up a *Swadeshi* or national Church on the line of Orthodox Syrian Church and Mar Thoma Church of Kerala.[49] The Orthodox Church in India lives at peace with follower of other religions like Hindus, Muslims, Sikhs, Parsees, Jains, and Buddhists etc. They are not aggressive in trying to convert the others but are prepared to live with them in peace and concord, and with respect. For this reason, they are often accused by more aggressive Protestants and Catholics of being imperfect or lacking in Missionary passion.[50]

2. Christian Mission and Religious Conversion

Some religious traditions are said to be 'proselytizing'[51] or evangelizing by character; fundamental to their system of beliefs is the desire and need to bring the unbeliever (sic) into the fold.[52] India is familiar with the concept and fact of conversion from one religion to another.[53] Today's Christian Mission is by and large understood as converting/proselyte people of other faiths into the Christian faith and 'planting' new Churches. Here the danger is that the Local Church is losing sight of the larger universality of Church.[54] M. M. Thomas,[55] advocates for conversion without communalism. And he further says nobody can convert another; it is his/her fundamental right to choose other faith or ideology. And he positively recommended that we have to make a legal provision to bring peace in inter-communal conflict.[56]

In recent years, there have been many attempts to stop conversions through legislation are the bills introduced in various State Legislatures in

---

49 Samuel George, "Churchless-Christ (A Hindu 'Plea'): A Christian Theoplogical Response." *Doon Theological Journal*, Vol. 6, No. 1, (March 2009): 38-64. "The Syrian Church in India is purely indigenous. Its men and money are Indian. It is born and brought up on Indian soil. It is nurtured in the Indian culture and Indian traditions. It always tries to interpret the cause of Christ in a way that Indian can understand...In dress, food, and living, the Syrian Christians are Indian and Indigenous." Cf. Roger E. Hedlund, "Indian Instituted Churches: Indigenous Christianity Indian style"..., 5.

50 Poulos Mar Gregarious, *Introducing the Orthodox Churches*, (New Delhi: ISPCK/ Mar Gregarious Foundation [OTS], 1999), 3.

51 Try to convert somebody to a religious faith or political doctrine.

52 Rowena Robinson and Sathiynathan Clarke, *Religious Conversion in India: Modes, Motivations and Meanings* (New Delhi: Oxford University Press, 2003), 9.

53 Joseph Mattam and Sebastian Kim, *Mission and Conversion: A Reappraisal* (Mumbai: St. Pauls, 1996), 101.

54 Here the Universal Church should understand as the Reign of God. Jesudas M Athyal, *Relevant patters...*, 179.

55 M. M. Thomas was an Indian Christian Theologian, the Director Emeritus of the CISRS, and Moderator of WCC.

56 M. M. Thomas, "Inter-Religious Conversion" in *Religion, State, Communalism: A Post Ayodhya Reflection*, J. John and Jesudas Athyal edits (Madras: A E I T C A, 1995), 95.

order to control conversions.[57] In this context, we must explore the possibility whether a person who is willing to follow Christ from Hinduism or Islam can remain within the framework of the Hindu/Muslim religio-cultural structure at the same time as being fully committed to Jesus Christ, which bring real transformation/Conversion on the lives of the people.

In the context of the History of Christian Mission in India, Conversion and Baptism, invariably involve a radical break with one's religion and cultural past. In the highly pluralistic context of India, the search for relevant patterns of mission and evangelism in most cases is also an encounter between the Christian faith and Other faiths, raising questions of Gospel and Culture at the Theological level. The fundamental relation between *religion and culture* also thus becomes central to our search for new paradigms of Mission and Evangelism. Is it possible to accept the Lordship of Christ and remain culturally as Hindus? Can Christ-centred fellowships within other religions be a substitute for the organized Church?

According to James Kottoor, whether one calls it "conversion" or "*Ghar Wapsi*" in both the end aimed at is a change of mind and heart. Among the world religions-Hinduism, Christianity and Islam - it is generally accepted that Hinduism is the most open or catholic of all religions, tolerating or welcoming people of all faiths and even of no faith. It is not proselytizing in any sense. Christianity and Islam are considered proselytizing religions. It reached its heights during the (Jihad), Crusades and inquisition.[58] That was history, not any more. Now, as a more enlightened religious institution, it has openly acknowledged its past stupidities and continues to ask pardon for them.[59]

57 There is some doubt about the meaning of deals with Article 25 of the constitution of India which confers on all persons the right "freely to profess, practice and propagate religion." Does it include the right to convert another person to one's religion? The debate on Conversion in the Constituent Assembly centered on the following points that freedom to profess; to practice; and propagate one's religion; but restriction on Conversion." P. D. Mathew, "Conversion: Legal Perspective" in *Jnanadeepa*, ed. Kurian Kunnumpuram, 3/1 (January, 2000), 51-64.

58 According to Shri Guruji, Conversion is not only sanctioned and glorified by Christian theologies but is also practiced by their followers with earnestness. The Christians, like others, have got a right to have their own belief systems. But what right do they have to thrust them upon others? Quite a few missionaries not only justified but also recommended this crime of conversion as a basic "human right." And he asserts that a human right cannot be an exclusive right of a Christian but can reasonably be claimed by the Mussalman or for that matter by a Hindu also. It is not and cannot be one-way traffic. It takes the form of a game of numbers. Can this promote national harmony? cf. http://www.golwalkarguruji.org/download/books/en/Shri_Guruji_and_The_Christian_Missions.pdf, (accessed on 24/01/2011).

59 James Kottoor, "The Real Conversion" in *Indian Currents* XXVII/2, (January 12-18, 2015), 39; also K. P. Aleaz says if the colonial missionary understandings were accompanied by the exploitation of indigenous people, genocide, land theft, slavery and oppression which

And he further acknowledges the words of Pope Francis "Proselytizing", as the worst form of cancer or leprosy sullying the church's fair image. He is a shining example in many areas to the whole world, not just to the Catholic world.[60] Christian mission is no more to condemn other religions, rather affirm the Liberative elements in them, overcoming the existing misinterpretations of these by their own adherents of vested interest. The Christian missionary upholds the Liberative elements in other faiths to fights against the evils manifested today through a viable theology of mission, as well as through the proclamation of the Liberative elements even in other religious faith experience.[61]

3. Christian Mission and Caste and Communalism

According to Thomas, the Christian Church in India, as quoted by Jacob Thomas: "got itself isolated from the larger community into mission compounds and denominations, and began to rust and inbreed, turning into an exclusive Christian caste or closed communal group instead of being an open, outgoing, fellowship in the larger society"[62] As a matter of fact, Christians cannot deny the fact that unfortunately the Church too is polarized along caste lines. There is no great value in having excellent educational, medical and welfare projects and facilities if we exclude our own Christian brothers and sisters from deriving the maximum benefits from them. The forms of alienation of indigenous Christian converts are many. Fr. A. F. Nallappan, a Catholic Father, in his response to the reality of caste, he brings out some of the realities in the life of an indigenous Christian converts. The first isolation is by birth; without choice, they are 'placed socially, economically, culturally, and politically, at the bottom of the hierarchical society;' the second is by baptism into a 'community of fellowship' where there is no equality and unity. Hierarchical leadership has hardly any representation from the indigenous community, though numerically they are about 60 per cent of the Christian population. Of course, they are found in ecclesiastical institutions as scavengers, near to the ground and unskilled workers with the same kind of social treatment as in their own society; third, by the government which denies reservations, so that the

---

continues in today's world in more sophisticated ways the first step in Christian mission is to seek forgiveness for the damage done and being done. There is a need further to seek forgiveness for the misinterpretations of the theological concepts of other faiths carried out by Christian missionaries and theologians in India even today. Further, Indian Christian mission is not anymore for pointing out the defects in other faiths to be corrected by Christian faith, as if Christianity is free from all defects. cf. K. P. Aleaz, *Religions in Christian Theology* ..., 297-298.

60 James Kottoor, "The Real Conversion"..., 39.

61 Cf. K. P. Aleaz, *Religions in Christian Theology*..., 293.

62 T. Jacob Thomas, *Ethics of a World Community*..., 183.

indigenous Christian converts are not even equal to other indigenous people in India; the fourth separation and clever exploitation is through the denial of knowledge about funds and projects in their name and the unavailability of institutional service of the Church. Such is the plain reality of being an indigenous people and worse, being an indigenous Christian converts.[63] While the indigenous people trying to overcome through social, cultural, political, economic emancipation; but the Christianity in India is reminding the past history through discrimination.

Thomas advocates a new form the Christian church in India as a Christ-centred fellowship of faith in Hinduism or as a Christ-centred Secular fellowship. It does not mean that he is rejecting the concept of the church, as he is sometimes criticized for doing; but he is rejecting the present form of the church in India as a religious community, which makes Christianity another caste in the Hindu caste hierarchy. Therefore, Thomas argues that:

> "the Fellowship of Christian faith stay within the Hindu religious community, to transform its religious and social patterns in the light of Christ and thus to make Indian society (which is largely Hindu and may remain so in many of its cultural aspects) a common framework for all religions to become truly religious without being communal."[64]

Thomas has distinguished between the questions: Whether the church is necessary? and What forms the church should take? To him, the former is a rather "outdated question of liberal theology," and the latter is a "relevant question of post-liberal and even post-neo-orthodox theology."[65] More importantly, it is also relevant questions that how Jesus Christ and His Gospel can be the unifying factor of entire humanity?

In order to meet the challenges of caste and communalism which Hinduism has forced upon Christianity, Thomas conceives the possibility of the church taking "form as a Christ centred fellowship of faith and ethics in the Hindu religious community."[66] Indian thinkers like Keshub Chunder Sen and K. Subba Rao also envisaged this kind of Christ centred fellowship within the Hindu religious community. Hans Staffner, in his book, *The Significance*

---

63 C. B. Webster John, *The Dalit Christians,* New Delhi: ISPCK, 1996. cf. J. Almeida, 'Christian response to the reality of caste and dalits' in *Missiological approaches in India,* edits. by Joseph Mattam and Krickwin C. Marak, (Mumbai: St. Pauls, 1999), 259.

64 M. M. Thomas, *Some Theological Dialogues* (Bangalore: CISRS, 1977), 134; also quoted by. T. Jacob Thomas, *Ethics of a World Community...,* 185.

65 M. M. Thomas, *Salvation and Humanization...,*38.

66 M. M. Thomas, *Salvation and Humanization...,* 40.

of Jesus Christ in Asia,[67] says that there are three groups of prominent Indians who became the admirers of Jesus Christ differ in the degree of their personal commitment to him. The *first* group as great patriots and social reformers who strove to promote peace and harmony in their country instinctively felt a kinship with the spirit of Christ and pointed to Christ as a teacher and model to be followed. Though they did not regard themselves as Christians, but they recognized the great contribution which the teaching and example of Jesus Christ could make to the social progress of their country. The *second* group regarded themselves as followers of Jesus Christ but did not see their way to join any of the existing churches. And the *third* group became baptized Christians, but culturally remained loyal to the Hindu society. According to Barrett,[68] as quoted by Hedlund, from 1858 to 1975 India had more than 150 Hindu-Christian movements or churches as well as modern Neo-Hindu groups of devotees of Jesus who explicitly acknowledge Jesus, and a number of more strictly Christian movements from which we can be trace out Indigenous Christianity in India. Christianity and Hinduism are usually known as rival religions in India. A peaceful alternative is visible in their interaction in the context of the Christ centred movements like *Jesu Darbar* and *Khrist Bhakta* movements.[69] These Christ centred movements are fascinating as it enables the people from the predominantly Hindu culture to remain faithful believers in Christ without discarding their loyalty to Hindu culture and even Hindu "religion." However, this new assemblage brings with it fresh challenges to both Christianity and Hinduism.

Conclusion

It seems that 'secular' is the space where 'sacred' is celebrated in the harmony of religions. It also seems that the modern form of grand narratives like "secularism," "Fundamentalism" "Individualism" "democracy" etc., needs to be reconstructed in order to develop alternatives in the Christian mission. Mission in postmodernism will challenge the validity of all the meta/grant narratives of the modernity with their dominant value systems of the world and the churches; and will encourage the small narratives with their traditions and

67 Hans Staffner, *The Significance of Jesus Christ in Asia*, (Anand: Gujarat Sahitya Prakash, 1984), xvii+264.

68 David B. Barrett, George T. Kurian & Todd M. Johnson eds. *World Christian Encyclopedia*, (Nairobi: Oxford,1982)15; doted by Roger E. Hedlund, "Indian Instituted Churches: Indigenous Christianity Indian style" O. L. Snaitang, *Churches of Indigenous Origin in North East India,* (Delhi: ISPCK, 2000), 5.

69 Cf. Ciril J. Kuttiyanikkal, Khrist Bhakta Movement: A Model For An Indian Church? Inculturation in the Area of Community Building, (Germany: LIT VERLANG, 2014); cf. *http://www.freebook-finder.net/finder/ciril-j-kuttiyanikkal-khrist-bhakta-movement-a-model-for-an-indian-church,* (20/07/2015).

the rise of new cultural, religious and secular movements, liberation movements of indigenous people for their rights. Reconstructing postmodern Christian mission in the context of secularism is to enable people to imagine, dream or share a vision of new alternative relationship which free from all the meta-narratives in order to act and learn together as part of the one body of Christ (Gala. 3:28). The need of the hour is that Christianity should be *Indianized* not India *Christianized.* Reconstructing of Christian mission also provides hope for alternatives where Christianity and Secularism create common objectives and Mission of the churches in Asia general and India particular. It will also provide alternatives for the mission of the churches to engage in dialogue and collaboration with the men and women of all cultures, ideologies and religious traditions, to promote peace and harmony by witnessing to the presence and growth of the kingdom of God in the world at large and Asia/India today. If one put it in the words of M. M. Thomas, it seems that the need of the hour is *neither* the question of liberals Whether the Christian Mission is necessary? *nor* the relevant question of postcolonial and postmodern contextual theology that in What way Christian Mission should do? But, more important question is that How Jesus Christ and His Gospel can be a unifying factor of entire humanity?

12

TOWARD THE MISSIOLOGICAL INTEGRITY OF CREATION AND REDEMPTION

Suk Tae Yun[1]

I. Introduction

Missiology has divided into the ecumenical missiology and the evangelical missiology. The underlying concepts of both missiologies would be "creation" and "redemption," respectively. The ecumenical missiology is based on the theology of creation, and the evangelical missiology on the theology of redemption. Due to the difference of emphasis, however, it has been challenging to obtain missiological integrity of creation and redemption. To gain it, we are required to understand creation and redemption, more comprehensively and mutually, which are integral relationship. For this, we study the two creation stories in Genesis 1-2:4a (hereinafter referred to as "Gen. 1") and 2:4b-3:24 ("Gen. 2-3"), which are the seeds of the theologies of creation and redemption.[2]

To begin with, as comparing Gen. 1 with *Enuma Elish*, which is the creation story of ancient Babylonia, we investigate how the author (s) of Gen. 1 unfolds his theology of creation and what its soteriological meanings are. Then we deal with Gen. 2-3, which has to do with the original sin of human beings,

1 *Rev. Dr. Suk Tae Yun Ph.D. is holding his Doctor of Philosophy from the Asbury Theological Seminary, Kentucky. Currently he is a Visiting Scholar at Madras Theological Seminary & College, Chennai.*

2 Bernard Och, "Creation and Redemption: Towards a Theology of Creation," *Judaism: A Quarterly Journal of Jewish Life and Thought*, 1995 Spring, vol. 44, no. 2, 226.

especially in terms of the distortions against God and the creational order of humanity and nature embodied in Gen. 1. Then, mentioned is the creational meaning of Gen. 3:15, which is regarded as "Protevangelium." In conclusion, we claim that the stories of creation and redemption are fundamentally not separable and must be mutually understood, not only because Gen. 1 already implies the redemptive aspects and Gen. 2-3 the creational ones but because redemption is ultimately directed to the restoration of creation. In so doing, we can demonstrate the holistic missiological ground for doing missions, without being on only one side of either creation-focused missiology or redemption-focused missiology.

II. Two Creation Stories: The God of Creation and Redemption

1. Comparing with *Enuma Elish* of Babylonia Gen. 1

Both stories of creation in Genesis can be seen as being edited and finalized in different periods and with different backgrounds, based on Moses' traditions handed down from Moses. Most biblical scholars say that Gen. 2-3 is a Yahweh document (J source) edited during the monarchy, especially after Solomon's death (930 B.C.E.), and Gen. 1 is a priestly document (P source) edited by the priests after the Babylonian exile in 587 B.C.E.[3] If so, Gen. 2-3 precedes Gen. 1 over hundreds of years. However, because Gen. 1 is about the beginning of the cosmos by content, it finally took the very first chapter of Genesis.

Regarding the historical background of Gen. 1, Kim Jeongjoon says that it has to do with the Jews' harsh experiences as captives to Babylonia, and its author reveals for those who knew the Babylonian creation story the fact that God's creation is different from it.[4] By speaking about the only Creator God who is entirely different from the Babylonian gods and goddesses, the author seems to try to console Jews who are frustrated by captive lives and experiencing chaos and to give them a steady point of view of God.

It has been understood that the story of Gen. 1 is related to the Babylonian creation story *Enuma Elish*. From the middle of the nineteenth century, thousands of tablets that recorded the law, administration documents, literature of the ancient Near East began to be excavated. Among them, seven tablets record the creation story of Babylonia, and it was called *Enuma Elish* ("When on high") later. Its content seems to have passed down from the Sumerian Empire in 3000 BCE through the Akkadian Empire to the Babylonian Empire with slight modifications. Therefore, it can be said

3 The J document refers to a document known through the Yahwists who call God YHWH. "J" of the J document is the first letter of the German word Jahwist and "P" in the P document is the first letter of Priestly.

4 Kim Jeongjoon, *Study on the Pentateuch and the Prophets* (Korean) (Seoul: Korea Theological Study Institute, 1988), 41.

that *Enuma Elish* reflects the longstanding thought of the beginning of the cosmos of the ancient Near East.

After *Enuma Elish* was publicly known, scholars discovered many similarities to Gen. 1 and, based on them, they claimed that Gen. 1 came from Enuma Elish. For example, as regarding especially Gen. 1:2 ("Now the earth was formless and empty, darkness was over the surface of the deep, and the Spirit of God was hovering over the waters.") as God's combat (*chaoskampt*) with chaos that is expressed by the water (*tehom*) on the surface, Hermann Gunkel insisted that Gen. 1 originated from the story of Marduk's combat with Tiamat in *Enuma Elish.*[5] Samuel R. Driver alleged that Gen. 1 is the Hebrew version of *Enuma Elish.*[6] Other scholars, however, dispute Gunkel's and Driver's argumentation by claiming that the two stories just share the typical way of thinking of the ancient Near East about the beginning of the cosmos. Some of them analyze apparent differences between both and conclude that Gen. 1 has an independent origin regardless of *Enuma Elish.*[7] *We agree with this conclusion. Besides, when the Jews were living as captives to Babylonia, most Jews followed the Babylonian religion, except for Shadrach, Meshach, and Abednego (Dan. 3), for example.*[8] *If so, the author seems to have contextualized his creation story to react and confront such a crisis situation.*

By comparing between Gen. 1 and Enuma Elish, we need to see how the author of Gen. 1 confronted against the creation story of Babylonia and demonstrated Israel's own and unique theology. In particular, we need to focus on the differences between the two. As the first difference, we can point out that the creation in *Enuma Elish* is related to the struggle with primordial divine chaos groups or the war among gods and goddesses.[9]

> In the beginning, there was only undifferentiated water swirling in chaos. Out of this swirl, the waters divided into sweet, fresh water, known as the god Apsu, and salty bitter water, the goddess Tiamat. Once differentiated, the union of these two entities gave birth to the

---

5 Hermann Gunkel, *Creation and Chaos in the Primeval Era and the Eschaton: A Religio-Historical Study of Genesis 1 and Revelation 12*, trans. by K. William Whitney Jr. (Grand Rapids: William B. Eerdmans, 2006).

6 Samuel Rolls Driver, *The Book of Genesis with Introduction and Notes*, 6th ed. (London: Methuen & Co., 1907), 31.

7 Richard J. Clifford, *Creation Accounts in the Ancient Near East and in the Bible* (Washington: Catholic Biblical Association of America, 1994). Babatunde A. Ogunlana, "Inspiration and the Relationship between Genesis 1:1-2:4 a and *Enuma Elish*," *Baptist Theological Seminary, Kaduna Insight* (BTSK Insight), 2016, 99.

8 Richard Clifford, *Fair Spoken and Persuading: An Interpretation of Second Isaiah* (New York: Paulist Press, 1984), 13.

9 Othmar Keel and Silvia Schroer, *Creation: Biblical Theologies in the Context of the Ancient Near East*, trans. by Peter T. Daniels (University Park, PA: Eisenbrauns, 2015), 97.

> younger gods. These young gods, however, were extremely loud, troubling the sleep of Apsu at night and distracting him from his work by day. Upon the advice of his Vizier, Mummu, Apsu decides to kill the younger gods. Tiamat, hearing of their plan, warns her eldest son, Enki (sometimes Ea) and he puts Apsu to sleep and kills him. Tiamat, once the supporter of the younger gods, now is enraged that they have killed her mate. She consults with the god, Quingu, who advises her to make war on the younger gods. Tiamat rewards Quingu with the Tablets of Destiny, which legitimize the rule of a god and control the fates, and he wears them proudly as a breastplate. With Quingu as her champion, Tiamat summons the forces of chaos and creates eleven horrible monsters to destroy her children. Ea, Enki, and the younger gods fight against Tiamat futilely until, from among them, emerges the champion Marduk who swears he will defeat Tiamat. Marduk defeats Quingu and kills Tiamat by shooting her with an arrow that splits her in two... Out of Tiamat's corpse, Marduk creates the heavens and the earth... (https://www.ancient.eu/article/225/enuma-elish---the-babylonian-epic-of-creation---fu/).

By contrast, there seems no war or violence among gods in Gen. 1. The creation of God is not such a story that the sun, moon, stars, and humans are created from the enemy god's corpse gained from war among gods. There could not be a fierce and bloody struggle at the outset, because the only Creator God was acknowledged. Gen. 1:1 ("In the beginning, God created the heavens and the earth.") seems to make an end to the era of gods and goddesses and inform the beginning of the era of God who is preexistent, omnipotent, and creates from nothing. Then in a peaceful and controlled atmosphere, the sun, moon, and stars are created by God's word ("*logos*").

William Lasor *et al.* argue that the author confronts the view of gods of the ancient Near East by saying that the sun, moon, stars and so on for Babylonians to believe as gods, who dominate human destiny were created as simple luminous bodies (Gen. 1:16-18) by God's command. The primeval mother goddess Tiamat (sea) and earth are also simple natural creatures created by God (Gen. 1:10).[10] Joo Wonjoon claims that Gen. 1, as "the charter of demythologizing," is where the demythologizing for sky god, wind god, mount god, water god, moon god, sun god, mercury god, and so on of the ancient Near East is compiled. For instance, God plunges the authorities of these great gods by making them as natural creatures only in four days. Joo

10 William S. Lasor, David A. Hubbard, and Frederic Wm. Bush, *Old Testament Survey: The Message, Form, and Background of the Old Testament* (Grand Rapids: William B. Eerdmans, 1982), 126.

argues that in this sense, Gen. 1 is the conclusion of Israel's theological project to confront against other religions and myths and to keep its own belief in creation.[11] Consequently, Gen. 1 stands against the Babylonian religion by reaffirming that because the cosmos was created by God, not by Marduk of Babylonia, all creatures belong to God, and they are ruled by God.

Beyond this historical background, Gen. 1 provides us with essential points of view for the theology of creation. As mentioned earlier, it reminds us of the only Creator God. The creation of God has nothing to do with conflict, war, and violence. Instead, it is experienced as the act of love. In particular, Martin Luther says that creation comes from God's love. In *1518 Heidelberg Disputation*, he argues, "the love of God does not find, but creates, that which is pleasing to it" (Theses 28). Jürgen Moltmann mentions, "God withdraws himself from himself to himself to make creation possible. His creative activity outwards is preceded by this humble divine self-restriction... God's creative love is grounded in his humble, self-humiliating love. This self-restricting love is the beginning of that self-emptying of God." "Creation is not a demonstration of his boundless power; it is the communication of his love, which knows neither premises nor preconditions: *creatio ex amore Dei*."[12]

God had no duty to create the world, because the Father God, the Son God, and the Spirit God exit in the perfect love, the Triune God never needs other creatures.[13] The Bible does not say that God created the world because of His inner need or His loneliness. Irenaeus of the 2nd century pointed out, "in the beginning, God formed Adam, not as if he was in need of man, but that he might have someone upon whom to confer His benefits."[14] Panentheists like a process theologian John B. Cobb and an eco-feminist theologian Sally FcFague insist that God cannot exist without human beings or that the world is essential to God. However, if the world exists because God chose to create it with His freewill, not because God needed it, Panentheists' argumentation is incompatible. The creation of the world, as Karl Barth spoke, like a miracle. According to him, the miracle is not that God exists, but that the world exists.[15] In summary, faith in God as the creator is perceived and experienced as "the

---

11 Joo Wonjoon, *The Old Testament and Gods: The Myth of the Ancient Near East and the Spirituality of the Ancient Israel* (Korean) (Euijeongbu: Hannim Bible Study Institute, 2018), 97, 94.

12 Jürgen Moltmann, *God in Creation: An Ecological Doctrine of Creation*, trans. by Margaret Kohl (London: SCM Press Ltd, 1985), 88, 76.

13 Charles P. Arand, "The Unbounded Creator and the Bounded Creatures," *Lutheran Quarterly*, vol. 31, 2017, 273.

14 Arand, Ibid.

15 Elizabeth Achtemeier, *Nature, God and Pulpit* (Grand Rapids: Eerdmans, 1992), 40.

all-embracing framework, as the fundamental, all-underlying premise for any talk about God, the world, Israel, and the individual."[16]

The second difference between *Enuma Elish* and Gen. 1 appears in the understanding of human beings. Humans in *Enuma Elish* were created as slaves to serve gods. They are only insignificant creatures.

> When Marduk heard the gods' speech. He conceived a desire to accomplish clever things. He opened his mouth addressing Ea. He counsels that which he had pondered in his heart, "I will bring together blood to form bone, I will bring into being Lullû, whose name shall be 'man'. I will create Lullû—man… "Quingu is the one who instigated warfare, who made Tia-mat rebel and set battle in motion." They bound him, holding him before Ea. They inflicted the penalty on him and severed his blood-vessels. From his blood he (Ea) created mankind, On whom he imposed the service of the gods, and set the gods free. After the wise Ea had created mankind. And had imposed the service of the gods upon them— (Tablet VI).

By contrast, humans in Gen. 1 were created in God's image and likeness (Gen. 1:26-7). This shows us Israel's most distinctive viewpoint among other worldviews. Gen. 1 offers an astounding meaning of the status of human existence. Because humans were created in God's image, they have the highest value and dignity by nature. Only after the creation of humans in His image, God said that the world is "very good." The creation of the world is completed only after the creation of them. Unlike *Enuma Elish*, humans in Gen. 1 are never slaves. Rather, they have enough right to be fruitful, increase in number, and rule other creatures. God grants them the right as vicegerents to rule other creatures on behalf of God.[17]

> God blessed them and said to them, "Be fruitful and increase in number; fill the earth and subdue it. Rule over the fish in the sea and the birds in the sky and over every living creature that moves on the ground (Gen. 1:28).

Not slaves for gods, they are God's agents and partners to manage and run the world that belongs to God. Like this, Gen. 1 demonstrates that the things that the Babylonians serve as gods are natural creatures created by God's word and wisdom and elevates the position of human beings to the level of a king to rule nature. In a word, it delivers man from the Babylonian gods.

---

16 Rolf Rendtorff, *Canon and Theology: Overtures to an Old Testament Theology*, trans. by Margaret Kohl (Minneapolis: Fortress, 1993), 107-8.

17 Walter Bruggemann, "From Dust to Kingship," *Zeitschrift für die Alttestamentliche Wissenschaft*, vol. 84, 1972, 1-18.

Gen. 1 continues to show the different thoughts of God and humanity from Enuma Elish. While human in *Enuma Elish* has a status to have to work for gods, God in Gen. 1 reversely works for and serve humans. God is like the anthropocentric God. He made all things for humans. God creates the cosmos for human and put him in the position of the center of creation. Above all, the world is the habitable place (*oikoumene*) in which man can reside. The heaven and the earth in *Enuma Elish* are places that gods reside. It is said that the cosmos is made as residences that gods enjoy and live: "He fashioned heavenly stations for the great gods, and set up constellations, the patterns of the stars... He established the heavenly station of Ne-beru to fix the stars' intervals." (Tablet V). In contrast, the world in Gen. 1 is a great residence for human (Isa. 45:18). God did not make any evil things in this residence. All creatures in this "house" reflect the goodness of God because they are God's works (Gen. 1:4, 10,12, 18, 21, 25, 31). So, the world is the place of *shalom* that human lives with God. Gregory of Nyssa described God as a host who goes about and makes all the preparations necessary to provide an incredible place for his human creatures to live. He portrays God as a host who prepares "a royal lodging for the future king (and this was the land, and islands, and sea, and the heaven arching like a roof over them), and when all kinds of wealth had been stored in this palace."[18] Similarly, Martin Luther depicts God, who sets up a house with the sky as the ceiling, the oceans as the walls, and then fills it with everything we need for life with God and with each other here on earth.[19]

God did not stop His creation by making a beautiful house for man. Then He feeds man. "I give you every seed-bearing plant on the face of the whole earth and every tree that has fruit with seed in it. They will be yours for food" (Gen. 1:29). While human in *Enuma Elish* was created as one who has to labor on behalf of gods and feed them, in Gen. 1, reversely, God provides man with food. God feeds man, not that man feeds gods. Genesis 1 puts the status of man back to the fold. Regarding God's attitude for humans, John Stott says that it always is "positive, constructive, enriching" and that "His principal and characteristic work is to bless people with salvation."[20]

The third and last difference between *Enuma Elish* and Gen. 1 is about rest (Sabbath). Even after creation finished, God's work continues. His work reaches the climax in rest on the seventh day. Gods' rest in *Enuma Elish* is gained by terminating chaos with murdering enemy gods and by creating

18 Arand, Ibid, 275.

19 Arand, Ibid.

20 John R. W. Stott, "The Living God is a Missionary God," *Perspectives on the World Christian Movement: A Reader*, ed. by Ralph D. Winter (Pasadena, William Carey Library: 2009), 9.

humans who can labor instead of low-gods. In contrast, God in Genesis works for humans and then takes rest for them. God is everlasting. "He will not grow tired or weary." He does not need food (Isa. 40:28). Therefore, He does not need to take rest for Himself. He takes rest for humans, not for Himself. The purpose that God takes rest is again, man. David Adams calls God's rest, which can be characterized by the ultimate state of "goodness" and "perfection," "goal of His creative activity." According to him, God's rest reveals His intention that such a state of rest "should characterize all that he had made, and should be the on-going experience of his creation." It also anticipates "the end-time restoration of creation to the state of rest that characterized it as the completion of God's creative activity."[21] More specifically, Walter Brueggemann says that God's rest is the promise of rest for humankind, and it proclaims God's ownership of all creatures as the element to guarantee all people's and all creatures' happiness. All people, including not only the owners but also the slaves and even animals, receive a period to work and take rest as presents."[22]

We have compared Gen. 1 with *Enuma Elish* thus far. All stories of creation do not end with a simple story. They may form a worldview and faith of those who listen to them and greatly impact on their way of thought and behavior,[23] because humankind incessantly imitates and represents the actions of gods in stories of creation through rituals or festivals. For example, *Enuma Elish*, as discussed earlier, continues to remind that the universe was created in conflict, war, and violent situations and that humans were created as slaves to the gods. Ordinary people consider these stories their fate. For them, the value of human dignity is not inherent from the beginning. They are gripped with fear and uncertainty. They cannot help live without hope. They are like a universal orphan who cannot appeal to anyone. The masters of human destiny are gods. Gods determine their past, present, and future. People regard gods as fundamentally evil and unpredictable. For them, justice to the gods is fluid and always changing. When disaster strikes them, it is because certain god (s) are angry or because a devil has been summoned to harass them. It is thought that human is merely victims of the power of the gods. The only way for humans to live a safe life is not to be caught by the gods' 'radar.' To do this, as relying

---

21 David L. Adams, "Some Reflections on the Historicity of the Biblical Creation Account," (a paper presented at the Dies Academicus of the Lutherischen Theologische Hochschule, Oberursel, Germany, Nov. 7, 2013). 20. David Adams and Charles P. Arand, "A Few Reflections on Creation in Genesis 1," https://concordiatheology.org/2018/03/a-few-reflections-on-creation-in-genesis-1/, accessed on February 18, 2020.

22 Walter Brueggemann, *Reverberations of Faith: A Theological Handbook of Old Testament Themes* (Louisville: Westminster John Knox Press, 2002), 180.

23 Arand, Ibid, 132.

on fortune-tellers or spiritual experts,[24] they must find ways to avoid the wrath of the gods or relieve the anger of the gods through sacrificial rituals, which inevitably offer sacrifices (foods) to gods.

The creation story in Gen. 1, however, offers a unique, alternative, and revolutionary worldview. As mentioned so far, Gen. 1 is a story of salvation from gods who oppress humans. It includes a soteriological meaning in that it rejects the story that humans are only slaves to gods and claims that human beings were originally created in the image of God, and so have the highest value and dignity among all creatures.

2. The Second Story of Creation (Genesis 2:4b-3:24): Redemption

The second story of creation in Gen. 2:4b-3:24, as mentioned at the outset, is considered to be a J-source. The redaction process seems to have undergone through Moses, the rise and fall of the Northern Kingdom of Israel, and even the Babylonian captivity.[25] Some scholars say that through this story, Moses explains that the pain of slavery life in Egypt stems from what happened in the Garden of Eden.[26] Scholars, who see the main background of this story as the destruction of the Northern Kingdom of Israel, argue that the story is associated with the Canaanite religion, especially the worship of *El*, the supreme god of Canaan and god of creation or *Baal*, the Canaanite god of abundance. According to them, the event that happened in the Garden of Eden symbolizes the worship of *EL* or *Baal*. For example, according to Nicolas Wyatt, who claims the association with *El* worship, Adam was created as the archetypal gardener, the actual kingship (Gen. 2:15). Adam in the Garden of Eden represents the king of the Northern Kingdom of Israel, where a sanctuary (Shechem) exists. Like the gardener who has to care for the garden, the king must, above all, take care of the sanctuary by keeping God's Torah, thoroughly. But to become a god, the king serves *El*, which must never commit (eating from the tree, Gen. 3:6). Thereby, the king broke the law and committed injustice before God. By punishment, he was banished from the sanctuary and forbidden to return. Consequently, Gen. 2-3 suggests that the destruction of North Israel by Assyria in 722 B.C.E. resulted from idolatry (breaking the first commandment of the Ten Commandments). Wyatt also alleges that this story was easily applied over time to the cause of the fall of the Southern Kingdom of Judah by Babylon and, in particular, Gen. 2:10-14 may have been added at

24 Pierre Gilbert, "The Missional Relevance of Genesis 1–3," *Direction: A Mennonite Brethren Forum*, vol. 43, No. 1, Spring 2014, 52.

25 Nicolas Wyatt, "Interpreting the Creation and Fall story in Genesis 2-3," *Zeitschrift für die Alttestamentliche Wissenschaft*, vol. 93, 1981, 11.

26 David Zac Niringiye, "In the Garden of Eden II: Creation-Community Distorted, Torn Apart," *Journal of Latin American Theology*, vol. 5, No. 1, 2010, 35.

this time to Gen. 2.[27] In any case, the author(s) of Gen. 2-3 seems to say that all the causes of slavery in Egypt and the destruction of northern Israel and South Judah originated primarily from idolatry.

Beyond these historical backgrounds, Christian theology sees that all the catastrophic consequences of humankind are attributed to the event of the good and evil tree in the Garden of Eden (Gen. 3). God in the Garden to appear to symbolize a rich, abundant, and beautiful world to dwell with humans (Gen. 2:17) prohibits humans from only eating the fruit of the tree as allowing all other things. This was to set humanity's distinct creatureliness, even though human has the image of God. This limitation was given with a strict warning that "when you eat from it, you will certainly die" (Gen. 2:17). But, humans rejected their limitations as a creature and, in the end, violated God's command to become like their Creator God (Gen. 3:5). It trespassed the boundaries of human beings.

There can be many ways to talk about Adam and Eve's disobedience to God's command and its consequences, but, above all, we point out that they have destroyed all of the harmonious order of creation. First, humans have caused themselves to distort the Creator God. When God found them immediately after the event, they were hiding (Gen. 3: 8). This means that the relationship between God and humans already began to break. Adam and Eve no longer recognized that God is the Creator, Blessor, Benefactor, Sustainer, and Giver. For them, God is now just a fearful, unsafe, and harmful existence. Therefore, by hiding themselves, they separated themselves from such God and let Him become a *deus otiosus* who has to be far from them. By this, they scandalously distort the identity of God.

This distortion of God's identity resulted in, at least, two successive consequences in the history of humanity, one of which transforms God into something else or creates other gods instead of God. The tree of good and evil was no less than idols because Adam and Eve had already believed in it as a means of realizing their desire to become a god (Rom. 1:25). So, in this story, Adam and Eve appear to be the first prototypical idolaters. It is easy to see that post-Adam people created numerous gods in human or animal images. For example, when Moses went up to Mount Sinai to receive the Ten Commandments, the remaining people made the golden calf and called it Yahweh (Ex. 32: 4). Jeroboam, who established the northern kingdom of Israel, built a temple in Shechem instead of Jerusalem and made two golden calves there (1 Kings 12). Archeology shows that golden calf worship prevailed in northern Israel, judging from numerous excavated bovine idols. The excavated fragments are marked "glyw," which means "Yhwh-Calf," "Yahweh is a calf.,"

27 Wyatt, Ibid.

Or "Calf of Yhwh."[28] God was ascended and idolized in the form of a cow. God, the Creator, became a god made by humans.

Most of the gods, in all ages, have the images of man, animal, or therianthropic creatures, whether it is a manifestation or a symbol of divine beings. Humans not only distort God's identity but also made themselves and other creatures (pantheism) as gods and idols. The apostle Paul points out that man has "exchanged the glory of the immortal God for images made to look like a mortal human being and birds and animals and reptiles." (Rom. 1:23). In *Institutes of the Christian Religion*, John Calvin says that human nature "is "a perpetual factory of idols." "Man's mind, full as it is of pride and boldness, dares to imagine a god according to its own capacity; as it sluggishly plods, indeed is overwhelmed with the crassest ignorance, it conceives an unreality and an empty appearance as God… To these evils a new wickedness joins itself, that man tries to express in his work the sort of God he has inwardly conceived. Therefore, the mind begets an idol; the hand gives it birth."[29] Since the first, second, and third commandment of the Ten Commandments are all related to the prohibition of idolatry, humanity's desire for idol worship seems to be derived from the desolate and fallen human nature after the fall in the Garden of Eden.

Another consequence is the commencement of an action to try to alleviate the wrath of God for human sin. Essential to the sacrifice is the act of offering food and animals to God. However, God neither spoke about nor commanded any sacrifices (Jer. 7: 22-23). God did not want sacrifice (Hos. 6: 6). Offerings are of no benefit to God (Isa. 1: 11-13). Through this act, the identity of God is distorted again from the feeder of humans and animals (Gen. 1:22, 28) to the eater or the God who needs nourishment. God is also transformed from God as the source and Giver of rest to the One to have to be alleviated by human sacrifices. Behind this act of sacrifice lies the desire for man to take the place of the Benefactor, not the beneficiary. Darrell Ferguson says that "their sin is to think of God as a beneficiary," not Benefactor.[30] Quoting Acts 17:24-25 ("The God who made the world and everything in it is the Lord of heaven and earth and does not live in temples built by human hands. And he is not served by human hands, as if he needed anything. Rather, he gives everyone life and breath and everything else".), John Piper warns to "beware of serving God as a benefactor."[31]

---

28 Graham I. Davies, *Ancient Hebrew Inscriptions* 3.3.041. K. Koenen, "Der Name GLYW auf Samaria-Ostrakon nr," in Vetus Testamentum vol. 44, 1994, 396-400.

29 John Calvin, *Institutes of the Christian Religion*, 1.11.8.

30 Darrell Ferguson, *What's So Great About God* (Grand Rapids: Zondervan Press, 2011), 206.

31 John Piper, *Desiring God: Meditations of a Christian Hedonist* (Colorado Springs: Multnomah Books, 2011), 168.

Often, certain people were sacrificed as food for gods. The story of Abraham's attempt to sacrifice his son Isaac reflects the ancient Near Eastern religious practice to sacrifice humans. God's substitution of the prepared sheep forbade human sacrifice. However, until recently, quite a few people have been sacrificed to be regarded as the best foods to nourish the gods, and human sacrifice is now somewhere performed in the name of god (s).[32] This kind of act means that humans created gods and idols with their own hands, but are now their slaves under their control. This destroys the natural order given by the Creator God by lowering human dignity and the position of being under other natural creatures. Unsaved humans are still trying to become like God through idolatry, but the result is only living as slaves to idols, whether they are human, animal, or things like money (mammonism).

In conclusion, the original sin of human has resulted in the distortion of God, human beings, and nature (creation). As God's warning (Gen. 2:17), humans live the curse of death (Rom. 5:12, 6:23) in the distorted order of creation.

2.1. The God to Create Redemption Genesis 3:15

God, however, continues to work for man even after creation. Most notable is the declaration that He will redeem humankind from sin and curse. "I will put enmity between you and the woman, and between your offspring and hers; he will crush your head, and you will strike his heel" (Gen. 3:15). This declaration is called the protevangelium in the sense of the first gospel proclamation of the Bible.

Adam and Eve's sin was not only disobedience to God but also obedience to the serpent (Satan). Regarding the identity of the snake in Genesis 3, some scholars claim that one cannot identify the snake with Satan. They assume that at the time this story was written, the concept of Satan was yet to come. Therefore, the snake could not represent Satan or Satan in the form of a snake but is merely a symbol of chaos and disorder.[33] They also argue that there is no direct basis for identifying the snake and Satan, even in the New Testament.[34] But judging from the fact that Satan entered Judas Iscariot (John 13:27), or nearly two thousand demons came out of a man and entered a herd of swine again (Mark 5:1-13), we can assume that Satan in Eden took a snake body specifically to achieve his purpose. In the Bible, Satan is expressed as "the

32 "Feeding the Gods: Hundreds of Skulls Reveal Massive Scale of Human Sacrifice in Aztec Capital" https://scim.ag/2K2uixU, accessed on 2020-01-10.

33 Karen Randolph Joines, "The Serpent in Gen 3," *Zeitschrift für die alttestamentliche Wissenschaft*, 87 No. 1, 1975, 8.

34 Shawna Dolansky, "How the Serpent Became Satan," https://www.biblicalarchaeology.org/daily/biblical-topics/bible-interpretation/how-the-serpent-became-satan/ accessed on 2020-02-01.

prince of this world" (John 12:31, 14:30, 16:11), "the tempter" (Matt. 4:3), "a murderer from the beginning," "Father of lies" (John 8:44), "the god of this age" (2 Cor. 4:4), "the ruler of the kingdom of the air" (Eph. 2:2), "a roaring lion looking for someone to devour" (1 Pet. 5:8, Job 2:2), "the spiritual forces of evil in the heavenly realms (Eph. 6:11-12). Satan and his offspring do the same to humans as Satan did to Adam and Eve as traveling throughout the world (Rev. 20:7-10). Those who do not overcome this temptation deny God and become slaves to Satan.

This unfortunate thing happened in the event of the tree of good and evil, and in the circumstances that the same would continue to occur in the history of humanity, God creates redemption from nothing like a creation from nothing. Through the protevangelium, hinting Christ as the new Adam and Redeemer, God proclaims that Christ would defeat Satan ("he will crush your head" Cf. Rev. 20:10). Through the redemption of Christ, humans turn from their sin and come to acknowledge that God is the only Creator, Blesser, Benefactor, Sustainer, and Giver. The image of God will also be restored, and humans will dwell with God (Rev. 21:3). Their status as a steward is also restored. Thus, they may participate in God's creative mission to restore the creational order, goodness (beauty), righteousness, and an abundance of the created world until the Second Coming of Christ, "without worshiping the beast and his idol" (Rev. 20: 4, 21:8).

In conclusion, the two creation stories that we have discussed so far are about the beginning of God's creative work and the beginning of God's redemptive work. As James Chukwuma Okoye says, the act of creation was an act of salvation, and the redemption itself was a new act of creation.[35] This process of redemption is directed toward the completion of creation. Therefore, if we neglect this relationship and emphasize only the creation theology, then the covenant proclaimed in Genesis 3:15 will be overlooked, and thus it will be a lack of Christology. On the other hand, if we emphasize only the redemption theology, we can only emphasize individual spiritual salvation. If redemption is directed toward the restoration and completion of creation, salvation must extend beyond an individual experience to the creational restoration of society, community, nature, and the world. Thereby, we may secure God-desired salvation, that is, the integrity of creation and salvation, in mission fields.

35 James Chukwuma Okoye, *Israel and the Nations: A Mission Theology of the Old Testament* (Maryknoll: Orbis Books, 2006), 24.

13

KOSUKE KOYAMA'S 'STRANGER-CENTRED' MISSIOLOGY A PARADIGM FOR MISSION IN INDIA

Samuel George[1]

Dr. Onesimu is Professor of Christian Theology & Missions, and Principal of Madras Theological College (Senate of Serampore College (University)), Chennai, India. It was in 2013, when I was the Principal of Master's College of Theology (Senate of Serampore College (University)), Visakhapatnam that I first met Dr. Onesimu. Since then on many occasions we have had the opportunity to be together in Senate and other meetings. Over the years, I have come to know more about him and admire his passion for theological education and commitment to Christian missions. I congratulate him for attainting such a distinction both in his personal and ministerial life. I also appreciate the editors of this Festschrift by honouring an ardent colleague in the field of theological education. This short reflection is my humble tribute to the life and ministry of Dr. Onesimu.

Introduction

Asian Christian Theology and Missiology is incomplete without the colossal contribution of the Japanese theologian, Kosuke Koyama. Born (December 10, 1929) in Tokyo to Japanese parents, he lived 16 years under Meiji rule and

1 *Dr. Samuel George (Jammu and Kashmir) is Professor of Christian Theology at Allahabad Bible Seminary (Serampore University), Uttar Pradesh. Earlier he served as a missionary theological educator in Jammu, Punjab, Chandigarh, Uttarakhand, Andhra Pradesh, and Kerala. He can be contacted in the Email ID: samuelgeorge@outlook.com*

the rest under the New Constitution of Japan. He seems to have inherited a deep sensitivity from his keen observation of his national life. The 'Divinity' of the Emperor, which he calls 'idolatry; Japan's military policy and the pain of Hiroshima had affected his theological reflection deeply.[2] Doh-Shin-Kwai Church, Nakano, Tokyo nurtured him in Christian fellowship and gave him both a missionary and theological vision. His primary theological education was from Tokyo Union Theological Seminary. Upon graduation, he was made a minister of the United Church of Christ of Japan. In him we find the influence of Luther, Calvin and Karl Barth. His mentor was Prof. K. Kitamori whose book *Theology of the Pain of God* had a very deepening impact on Koyama in developing a theology-missiology of the cross.

After his successful completion of theological studies in the United States of America he was a Kyodan missionary (1960-1968) to the Church of Christ in Thailand. He also taught at Thailand Theological Seminary at Chiengmai. From 1968-74 he was the Director of the Association of Theological Schools in South East Asia, later Dean of the South-East Asia Graduate School of Theology and Editor of the *South-East Asia Journal of Theology*. He also worked as Senior Lecturer of phenomenology of religion at University of Otago in Dunedin, New Zealand. From 1980-1996 he was John D. Rockefeller Professor of Ecumenics and World Christianity at United Theological Seminary New York. He is a prolific and engrossing writer. Some of his major works are: *Water Buffalo Theology* (1974), *Theology in Contact* (1975), *No Handle on the Cross* (1977), *Three Miles an Hour God* (1980), *Mt. Fuji and Mt. Sinai* (1985). He breathed his last on March 25, 2009.

This essay is an attempt to engage with the mission theology of Koyama from an Indian context.

Koyama's Theology of Mission

More than most, Koyama was keenly aware of the missionary context in which, Christianity of this era finds itself. He explores means by which, Christianity can meaningfully address the modern context. He clearly recognizes that theology must be deeply intercultural. Accordingly, he brings those Asian experiences and insights, which he can convey, into dialogue with the Christianity promulgated by the West.

The language he employs is one of his major contributions to Christian theology in the current era. He communicates in a way that enchants the young,

2 Batumalai Sadayandy, *A Prophetic Christology for Neighbourology* (Kuala Lumpur: Seminari Theoloji Malaysia, 1986), 102.

intrigue the mature, and upset the theologians. His theology can be termed as user-friendly.[3]

History

History in a general sense can be termed as the continuum of events occurring in succession leading from the past to the present and even into the future, which affects the whole of human existence. History is always shared. History gives identity. History finds an important place in Koyama's theology of mission. According to Koyama "mission is to relate God's history of shared self-identity with people's history of shared self-identity."[4] For him biblical history becomes a primary tool for Christian proclamation. God is passionately attached to human history. The wrath of God is provoked by the historical violation of God's love and holiness. God can be moved to wrath because he is God in history.[5] God is engaged in history through creation and through God's particular covenant with Israel in it, God is committed to redeeming human history and restoring God's people within it.[6] God ultimately involved in the human history in the incarnation of Jesus Christ. Koyama opines "in Christ, man [*sic*] began to see the glory of God, not as the man [*sic*] who aspires to reach beyond history, but as a man [*sic*] who lives in history."[7]

Christianity seeks to express God's involvement in history through Jesus Christ. As such, it is an intensely historical religion, i.e., having a specific historical event at the origin and centre of its message. And this must be related in a slow and costly manner. This requires a deep involvement in and acceptance of the different stories of human life, for which repentance and a willingness to learn are essential.

God's own participation in human history culminated in a willingness to be "nailed down 'full stop'" (*Three miles an hour God*, 7.) for the sake of humanity.[8] When the biblical idea of history and biblical account of the God who shapes and participates in that history are set out in terms which are meaningful to people with other concepts of God and history, Koyama believes that Christianity will become more comprehensible and acceptable to other people.

3 Merrill Morse, *Kosuke Koyama: A Model for Intercultural Theology* (Frankfurt: Peter Lang, 1991), 273-274.

4 Kosuke Koyama, *Water Buffalo Theology* (Maryknoll, NY: Orbis Books, 1974), 12.

5 Ibid., 103-104.

6 Ibid., 148.

7 Ibid., 152.

8 Morse, *Kosuke Koyama: A Model for Intercultural Theology,* 141.

Missiology of *Theologia Crucis*

Theologia Crucis is a borrowed term from Luther for whom it is the true knowledge of God which comes from the knowledge of the suffering of Jesus Christ.[9] For Koyama a missiology of *theologia crucis* is an understanding of the Christian mission from the event of the cross.[10]

Koyama rejects emphatically the crusading mentality of the Christian mission, from the medieval crusaders to the colonial and triumphalistic Western mission of the last centuries. He proposes to replace the "crusading mind" with "crucified mind".

The heart of all Koyama's theology is his vision of the "crucified mind". It is the prism through which his perspective on all other issues is filtered. The crucified mind takes as the source and model Christ's crucifixion. Koyama seeks to express the extremity of God's love, as well as the response it calls forth from humanity, in terms of Christ's rejection. Jesus was abandoned on the cross, and this self-denial by God through Jesus is the key to reconciliation between God and humanity with each other. The word of the cross is the word that summarizes the mission of Jesus Christ.[11] It is only this ultimate self-denial-the abandonment by God at the cross that could heal and recreate a broken humanity.

In order for this ultimate love to become tangible to humanity, God, again working through human beings themselves, empowers those who perceive and experience this reconciliation to communicate it through their own lives to others. When human beings, empowered in love by God's self-sacrifice, open their lives to risk cf rejection, powerless and suffering, they are participating in Christ's crucified life.

But there is a recurring difficulty in the human response to God's self sacrifice in Jesus, that human beings constantly seek to rely on their own resources ('crusading mind'-a 'lunch box with a handle mentality'-human resourcefulness) rather than to take the risk of sharing in the life of the Crucified one ('handle-less cross'). The crucified mind does not seek to rely on human resourcefulness. It seeks rather to reflect the nature of the crucifixion, which was the ultimate demonstration of non-handle-mindedness i.e., of giving up efficient, self-centred control over life.[12] Koyama in the process do not intend to reject the crusading mind. He says this lunch-box-carrying crusading mind

9 Kosuke Koyama, "Extend Hospitality to Strangers-A Missiology of Theologia Crucis," *International Review of Mission* LXXXII, no. 327 (July/October 1993): 285.

10 Lars Lindberg, "Koyama, the Cross, and Sweden in Dialogue," in *The Agitated Mind of God: The Theology of Kosuke Koyama*, eds. Dale. T. Irvin & Akintunde. E. Akinade (Maryknoll, NY: Orbis Books, 1996), 89.

11 Koyama, *Water Buffalo Theology*, 180.

12 Morse, *Kosuke Koyama: A Model for Intercultural Theology*, 148.

must be carefully and kindly dealt with in the community of faith. It has a God given role to play in the mission. It must be guided and illuminated by the 'crucified mind'.[13] The crusading mind must be placed in the light of the crucified mind in order to be 'crucified and risen'. Resourcefulness must be theologically judged and contextualized in order to become genuinely resourceful. Resourcefulness must then be crucified.[14]

Within this overall perspective Koyama emphasizes how it is especially crucial that Christians, who base their faith on the self-denying love of God, proclaim that love through lives consistent with it. "The only way to speak about the crucified and risen name is by participating in Christ's crucifixion and resurrection".[15]

Koyama believes that the attitude of becoming 'the refuse of the world', the off-scourging of all things (1 Cor.4:13)[16] can affect history and accomplish Christian mission. To the degree that the church has been spat upon, she has become alive in mission and healing in history. For Koyama mission with a crucified mind means an informed love for others, full participation in their particular situation, and a willingness to suffer for them.[17]

In truth Christians, have preached Jesus Christ crucified, says Koyama. But in practice Christianity has presented him as bulldozing and crucifying one, which according to him is the "most serious missiological problem today in Asia".[18] For Koyama, the crucified Christ calls Christianity to repent of its crucifying tendencies, thereby becoming "deeply historical". The missiological response of repentance is movement into history, which brings with it the promise of future. "The context of repentance is 'Go therefore…'"[19] Go where? For Koyama, the answer is clear:

> So, Jesus Christ demonstrates his centrality by going to the periphery. Where is the periphery? The periphery is the place without honour, prestige and power…. This understanding of periphery is important. The theology of the cross is fundamentally different from a theology of honour, prestige and power…. The periphery is the place of discipleship. If we follow Jesus we will come to the periphery with him.

---

13 Kosuke Koyama, *No Handle on the Cross* (London: SCM Press Ltd., 1977), 3-4.

14 Ibid., 5.

15 Ibid., 83.

16 Ibid., 93.

17 Morse, *Kosuke Koyama: A Model for Intercultural Theology,* 153.

18 Koyama, *No Handle on the Cross,* 109.

19 Lindberg, "Koyama, the Cross, and Sweden in Dialogue," 95.

> The periphery is the place of the cross... Jesus Christ is the centre; therefore, wherever he is becomes the centre. If he goes to the periphery, the periphery, because of his presence, becomes the centre.[20]

Neighbourology – the significance for Christian witness

'Neighbourology' is the term, which carries what might be called Koyama's "doctrine of human beings".[21] His concern is more existential. The importance of Koyama's concern for people shows sensitivity to human feelings, experiences and relationships-these are the formative ingredients for his whole understanding of the life and mission. In Koyama's experience, we meet God in the communicative actions of our neighbours. He calls us away from theological and theoretical abstractions. He wants us to talk about "the people I know".[22]

He states, "Through my experience I discovered something very basic. I was confronted by my neighbour who is not a *maya* (illusion), but very real."[23] Our sense of the presence of God will be distorted if we fail to see God's reality in terms of our neighbour's reality. And our sense of our neighbour's reality will be disfigured unless it is seen in terms of God's reality.[24] This statement states the significance Koyama attaches to awareness of and love for one's neighbours as being intrinsic to the Christian faith. In Christ Jesus God, who created humanity was personally present as a human, is supreme testimony to the importance God attaches to human being. Koyama holds, God continues to use humanity as an instrument and communicator of God's presence and purpose.[25]

This has special significance for those involved in the task of transmitting the Christian faith. To relate the Word of God to the lives of the people addressed in Christian mission, Koyama proposes that a missionary must undertake two kinds of exegesis: "exegesis of the Word of God and the exegesis of the life and culture of the people among whom he/she lives and works".[26]

Such a situation places the missionary in what Koyama calls a "sandwiched" position 'between Christ's life and theology then take on meaning through interaction with one's neighbours. By submitting and committing

20 Kosuke Koyama, *Mount Fuji and Mount Sinai: A Pilgrimage in Theology* (Maryknoll, NY: Orbis Books, 1984), 251-252.

21 Morse, *Kosuke Koyama: A Model for Intercultural Theology*, 157.

22 Kosuke Koyama, *Three Miles an Hour God* (London: SCM Press Ltd., 1979), 70.

23 Koyama, *Water Buffalo Theology*, 90.

24 Ibid., 91.

25 Morse, *Kosuke Koyama: A Model for Intercultural Theology*, 167.

26 Koyama, *Water Buffalo Theology*, 91.

oneself to the Word of God, he/she tries to communicate the message of the real Christ to his/her real neighbours.[27]

Koyama points that "our neighbours are not concerned with our Christology, but they show, from time to time, their interest in our Neighbourology".[28] This means that our neighbours in Asia are ready to hear our message of Christ if we put it in 'neighbourological' language, though they would reject Christ if we were to present him Christological language.[29]

Koyama says, "'Neighbourology' is in fact, the best vessel to convey Christ. We want to insist on this our missionary experience in South East Asia".[30] Neighbourology carries a responsibility. In order to be able to present Christ in 'neighbourological' terms to our neighbour we must learn, first of all, to see God, whether God be a human being, as someone whom we 'come up against'.[31]

'Stranger-centred' missiology in the inter-religious context

Paul says in Romans 12:13 "extend hospitality to strangers". The word used for hospitality is '*philonexia*' 'to love strangers'. Strangers (*xenos*) mean someone who is 'foreign', 'alien', 'appearing strange', and 'creating distaste'.[32] The way of extending hospitality to the strangers may even become the way towards martyrdom (Phi. 2:8). Christ was crucified because he extended hospitality to strangers so completely.

Our "extending hospitality to strangers" happens "by the mercies of God," and when this happens our life becomes a "living sacrifice," which is "holy and acceptable to God," and it is an essential part of our "spiritual worship." There is a living connection between "extending hospitality to strangers" and "loving your God and loving your neighbour" (Mk. 12:28-34) of which Christ says "there is no other commandment greater than these" (Mk. 12:31). And his directive to love enemies (Mt. 5: 44) is the ultimate of extending hospitality to strangers.[33]

The "form of Christ" (Gal. 4:19) is the form of "extending hospitality to strangers". This form is the essence of the Christian gospel. It is the vision of ecumenism. It is that which inspires Christian mission. Mission is "extending hospitality to strangers".[34] The aim of mission is the creation of community

27 Ibid.

28 Ibid., 91-92.

29 Ibid., 93.

30 Ibid.

31 Ibid., 93-94.

32 Koyama, "Extend Hospitality to Strangers-A Missiology of Theologia Crucis," 283-284.

33 Ibid., 284.

34 Ibid., 285.

centred by the peripherized Christ[35] for all people.[36] Christ creates *koinonia* (communion, contribution, fellowship, partnership, sharing, and participation). Christ's way of extending hospitality to strangers must be the way for the whole world.

Koyama asks how should Christians hear the apostolic exhortation "extend hospitality to the strangers" while leaving in the "Rush Hour of the God's"? Does it mean to be open to all kinds of religious teachings and experiences of salvation? If the aim of mission is the creation of *koinonia* of the whole of humanity centred by the peripherized Christ, what should be our attitude towards people of other faiths?

In the context of "extending hospitality to the people of different religious persuasions," we must primarily look at our human reality, both personal and collective, and not at the doctrinal or institutional aspects of the religions.[37]

Thus, for Christians, the need for repentance appears in the context of inter-religious dialogue. We must renounce our centuries old "teacher's complex". The proclamation of the gospel and teacher's complex do not go together. Christians' understanding of the people of other faiths, then, begins with Christians' own repentance. Only when we repent, can we truly "extend hospitality to strangers."[38]

Koyama still holds that it is imperative for Christians to publicly state what they believe. This is an essential part of "extending hospitality to strangers."[39] Of this we feel that Lesslie Newbigin's clarion call of 'Gospel as Public Truth'[40] has an important validity in the present context of cultural and religious relativism. Later in this paper we will look into this matter more clearly. Missiology of *theologia crucis* must make it clear how the teachings of different religions differ from the Christian proclamation. The *theologia crucis* inspires the Christian act of clarification, which safeguards Christianity from becoming indiscriminately confused with different doctrines.

It is according to the apostolic faith, the Spirit of Christ that energizes our evangelistic proclamation. People of other faiths as enemies of God are not at all central to the Spirit of Christ. The Spirit of Christ does not support the spirit of greed to conquer others and self-righteousness to demonstrate our own superior piety. The gospel message is that in Jesus Christ, God extended

35 The New Testament image of Jesus Christ being a stranger "I was a stranger and you welcomed me" (Matt. 23:35) suggests a revolutionary displacement of "the centre." Christ the centre-person becomes the Christ the periphery-person.

36 Ibid., 287.

37 Ibid., 290.

38 Ibid., 291.

39 Ibid., 292.

40 Lesslie Newbigin, *Truth to Tell: The Gospel as Public Truth* (London: SPCK, 1991).

hospitality to strangers to an unimaginable extent and to an unsearchable depth (Rom.11:33).[41] This is the spirit of the stranger-centred missiology.

Conclusion

Kosuke Koyama's stranger-centred missiology is a workable paradigm for doing mission in the Indian context. India being a land of religious and cultural plurality always poses a challenge to engage in the Christian mission. In such a context, we would like to comment and raise some questions on the model of missiology proposed by Koyama.

- Koyama's theology/missiology is reflective in nature. Throughout his writings there is the constant interaction with imperialism, both past and present, idolatry of power and wealth in national and international affairs, problems faced by racial, and economic, religious and other minorities, ecology in light of the cross of Christ.
- Crucified mind also requires more dramatic action, for e.g., choosing a life of voluntary poverty, disassociating from all positions of power of authority, or something similar. Koyama does not suggest this as a necessary consequence of the crucified mind.
- Crucified mind refers to one's fundamental orientation, to one's trust in God- how that serves as model or invitation for Christians to follow, whatever their position in life.
- Crucified Christ going to the periphery of history is a compelling missiological theme. But it has not been universally heeded or even accepted among Christians of the contemporary world. If it is true that the theology of cross has returned during the 20th century, it is also true that the theology of glory is increasing in our time.
- Koyama's overemphasis on the crucified mind sends wrong signals, as if the 'Western guilt complex' in missions overburdens him.[42]
- It may be true that our neighbours are more interested in our 'neighbourology' than our Christology. But what cannot be denied is that, ultimately, it is our Christology that shapes our Neighbourology.
- Koyama's stranger-centred missiology is 'ambiguous.' It is so because on the one hand he calls for accepting all religions, and on the other he calls for keeping the Christian identity intact. How can these two co-exist?

Koyama's theology/missiology displays a strong sensitivity to socio-political context of Asia. His contribution to an authentic Asian theology is

41 Ibid., 293.

42 Hwa Yung, *Mango or Banana? The Quest for an Authentic Asian Christian Theology* (N. Delhi: Regnum Books, 1997), 165.

enormous. His emphasis on the contextualized Christianity has paved the way for presenting the gospel in a relevant manner in the Asian context. But his stranger-centred missiology also demands a Missiological response.

In recent times, the issue of strangers, 'illegal'-immigrants, and 'others' have become a thorny issue in the Indian political discourse. With the upsurge of 'Right' wing ideological shift in the country this issue has taken a xenophobic turn. For the last few months, I have been reflecting on the theme: an 'inward look' to Christian ministry. **Hospitality as Mission** motif is something that is often ignored and neglected in the mission discussions. The recent influx of African and Asian migrants/refugees into Europe and other western nations and their (western) reactions (more often xenophobic) has brought the aspect of hospitality to the forefront of ministerial and mission discussions. This has particular implications in the context of India especially due to the discussions (often extremely emotionally charged) on 'illegal' migrants like Rohingya Muslims entering India.

Hospitality means: "the friendly and generous reception and entertainment of guests, visitors, or strangers." I want to focus especially on the aspect of **strangers**. Henri Nouwen defines hospitality as the offer of a space where **"change can take place",** a space where **"the stranger can enter and become a friend instead of an enemy."**[43]

Letter to the Hebrews was written to a community that was undergoing intense persecution for the sake of the gospel of Christ Jesus. They could not be sure whether they'd manage to stay as steadfast as before. The author, though unknown, encourages the ever-weakening Hebrew Christians by pointing them to Jesus as the fulfilment of the Old Testament covenant, and as the fulfilment of their lives.

In the face of their weakening defense the writer of the Letter to the Hebrews encourages the demoralized community to keep going. "But we are not among those who shrink back..." (10: 38), instead the writer urges that their strategy must be, assertive, outgoing, and offensive.

In Hebrews 13, we find specifics about how to be assertive, outgoing and offensive. One of the ways it is done is: "to show hospitality." "Do not neglect to show hospitality to strangers, for by doing that some have entertained angels without knowing it." In that context hospitality is a word filled with images of **radical faith**, **action** and **witness**.

Hospitality spoken here in this chapter should not be understood in its current meaning. Today, hospitality is a business. Rather, the hospitality business is one of the biggest industries. It has taken the meaning of 'providing service at a (any!) cost' and sometimes at an exorbitant cost. Also, it should

43 Henri J. M. Nouwen, *Reaching Out: The Three Movements of the Spiritual Life* (New York: Image Books, 1986), 51.

not be understood as an informal get together for tea and cookies, dinner parties, bland conversations and a general atmosphere of coziness. Christian hospitality is radical and at times offensive and subversive. The hospitality as mentioned in the text to the Hebrews has probably lost much of its power and seriousness in our present context.

The Early Christians were encouraged to practice 'hospitality of risk.' Such practice could hold potential danger for those who were the hosts and would expose the 'reality' of the hosts. Hospitality in the Bible is a religious task, something that God wanted them to do, and something that would please God extraordinarily. As a Christian virtue, they are to practice this radical faith in and through their lives. And the current situation (of the Hebrew Christians) of intense persecution demands that they do it more than before.

The writer of Hebrews reminds them of the long tradition they had of radical hospitality. Gen. 18:15 highlights the radical invitation of three strangers by Abraham. From the passage, we learn that Abraham may not have understood who the strangers were, but in the profoundest sense they represent the presence of God, and the consequence is a blessing for barren Sarah: the child Isaac.

The biblical teaching is clear: giving hospitality and loving- kindness to strangers, who are always to be seen as children of God, even the presence of God—with the consequence of blessing—establishes itself as a pattern early on in the Jewish tradition, and hence in Christianity. Moreover, the biblical message is profound: whenever strangers present themselves to us we are to see them as holy ground and do the distinctive and humane thing, which is to share a meal with them. The sharing of meals, which is at the heart of all our faiths, is seen as the way in which God speaks to people through and beyond any barriers that they set up.

Hospitality in the Bible always has the same basic elements: welcome, a gesture of honour, time spent together, washing feet, especially prepared food, water, rest in the shade, shelter, a place to stay for the night, and a blessing.

The passage in Hebrews 13:2 uses the Greek *philoxenia*, which in English means, "entertain strangers". The first element of the word, *philo,* refers to love or friendship, and thus, the passage means more than simple hospitality. *Philoxenia* is not a mere sentimental response to the "other," but truly "love for strangers." This biblical text is therefore, literally exhorting its readers to "love for strangers," as opposed to its antonym *xenophobia,* which translates as "fear or hatred of strangers." This teaching has enormous implications for healing our world from the proliferating disease of xenophobia (racism, prejudice, nationalism, chauvinism).

Radical hospitality is inviting inside and making ourselves available to the strangers to the extent of exposing ourselves of great risks. But in that radical action, the Bible states, "some of have entertained angels unknowingly." Are we willing to open ourselves, our homes, our churches, our institutions, our countries for strangers? In doing so, the Mission of God begins inside our homes, churches, and institutions. Koyama through his writings suggested such a mission paradigm.

PART IV

RELIGIOUS

14

EQUALITY IN HINDUISM

S. Robertson[1]

Introduction

I always distill appreciable Hindu constructs as a part of my commitment to interreligious relations. It continued in my article (subsequently part of a book) on 'Hindu Spirituality' wherein I profusely appreciated certain Hindu values. My doctoral research was to draw insights for a theology of religions from the bhakti tradition of Vaishnava Alvars. However, the communal violence that consumes so many lives, constant anti-minority polemic and the murderous lynching that honored animals more than human beings and brutally killed many poor, weak, aged, vulnerable people who eked a living on animals, changed my perceptions. Added to these are my reading on Dr. Ambedkar, Manu Smriti and Bhavagavad Githa and my own analysis of 'Christian identity and witness in India in the context of Hindutva politics.'

However, with due respect to my topic, I shall attempt, in the first place, a graphic overview of some of the Hindu concepts, of course not complete, on which equality, although difficult, is claimed in Hinduism. I shall also, in the second place, highlight the inequality or hierarch prevalent in Hinduism. This, of course, is an outsider's understanding of Hinduism and hence subject to the necessary limitations.

---

1 *Rev. Dr. S. Robertson is the Principal of the Bethel Bible College, Guntur, Andhra Pradesh. He is the Professor in the Department of Religions.*

1. Equality

The possibility of equality in Hinduism can be interpreted, not without ambiguity, from the following formulations. They are: reality, creation, human life, self, salvation, different ways, Sanskritic Hinduism, bhakti and popular Hinduism.

1.1. Reality

Hinduism, in contrast to the general perception, affirms that 'the Reality is one.' Even the manifold forms of rituals and worships (spirituality) are explained as, varied means of adoration to that One Reality. This is reasonably justified in the context of geographical, cultural, linguistic, climatic, and even economic variations.

There is also unanimity that God has attributes. It is expressive even in Sankara's view that only at the higher level of spiritual realization, God can be realized as formless. Another commonality is the acceptance that God is both transcendental and immanent. In the words of Radhakrishna "God is neither completely transcendent not completely immanent."[2] It is further explained as "an intelligent Hindu thinks of god as residing within himself, controlling all his actions as the 'inner controller' and at the same time god is outside him, manifest in innumerable ways, known and unknown."[3]

These considerations are at a higher level and give the impression that Hindus are one and they are equal in accepting one God, the attributes of God and God's transcendental and immanent natures.

1.2. Creation

Starting from *Purusa sukta*, there are different creation narratives in Hinduism, each claiming that creation is from God - created, emanated, evolved, an illusion. Even Manu says "He, desiring to produce beings of many kinds from his own body, first with a thought created the waters, and placed his seed in them."[4]

Hinduism holds that the world is a 'spiritual entity.'[5] The theory that five elements[6] constitute creation is also in the same line. Often earth is called the mother. Therefore, it can be assumed that everyone is equal in being part of

---

2 S. Radhakrishna, *An Idealist View of Life*, Fourth impression, 2nd edition (London: George Allen & Unwin Ltd., 1951), 106.

3 Jitendra Nath Banerjee, "The Hindu Concept of God", *The Religion of Hindus*, ed. by Kenneth Morgan, Reprint (Delhi: Motilal Banarsidas, 1986), 48.

4 *Manu Smriti* 1:9. N. C. Panda, ed., *Manu Smriti* (Delhi: Bharatiya Kala Prakashan, 2014).

5 A. K. Banerjee, *Discourses on Hindu Spiritual Culture* (New Delhi: S. Chand & Co.1967), 133.

6 *Manu Smriti* 1:27.

this creation. The Indian Hindu scholars are unanimous in their commitment to represent Hinduism as world-affirming in contrast to the Christian notion that Hinduism is world negating.

1.3. Human Life

Hinduism 'postulates no absolute distinction between divine and human beings.'[7] Human beings are divine and God lives in them. The concept of *rta* in the Vedas, in addition, explains that humanity is not only divine but also is in harmony with nature.[8]

1.4. Self (Soul)/Karma Samsara/Karma Janmantra

The idea about the soul that it is 'immortal and eternal' is another expression of equality in Hinduism.[9] It is further strengthened by the doctrine of Karma Samsara that all souls will be subjected to *janmantra* until final *Moksha*. The theory of *karma* answers the questions of differences and reiterates that each one inevitably undergoes its effect.

1.5. Salvation/Goal

The chief goal of Hinduism is attaining salvation/liberation/moksha of the soul from the world (*samsara chakara*). In the process, peace (*santhi*) is guaranteed. It is for everyone and it is attainable in this world itself (*Jivan Mukti* and *Jivan Mukta*). It is said, "the Jivan-Mukti or liberation-in-life 'ideal' has been customarily enshrined as the highest vision of life in the Indian Tradition."[10] It is also expected that a liberated person leads others to salvation. Moksha is also is one of the four goals of life (*purusarthas*), which is equally expected of all.

1.6. Different Ways

Hinduism cares everyone equally can be illustrated from the principles of *adhikāra*[11] and *ishta-devata.*[12] The first one is called the doctrine of spiritual

7 C. J. Fuller, *The Camphor Flame: Popular Hinduism and Society in India*, Revised and expanded edition (Princeton and Oxford: Princeton University Press, 2004), 3.

8 Rajendra P. Pandeya, "The Vision of the Vedic Seer", *Hindu Spirituality; Vedas through Vedanta*, First Indian Edition (Delhi: Motilal Banarsidass, 1995), 21.

9 S. Balakrishnan, *Introduction to Hinduism (*Great Britain, Cambridge: Cambridge University Press, 1996), 25.

10 J. G. Arapura, *Hermeneutical Essays on Vedantic Topics (*Delhi: Motilal Banarsidass, 1986), 124.

11 D. S. Sarma, "The Nature and History of Hinduism", in *Religion of the Hindus*, edited by Kenneth Morgan (Delhi: Motilal Banarsidass, 1996), 5.

12 Giorgio Bonazzoli, "Puranic Spirituality", in *Hindu Spirituality, Post Classical and Modern* edited by K. R. Sundararajan and Bithika Mukerji (London: SCM Press, 1997), 166.

competence and the second is the doctrine of chosen deity. Hinduism proposes that a seeker of religious truth should choose a means of realization according to his/her ability. If anyone follows a path that is beyond his/her capacity, he/she will meet spiritual death. Similarly, a devotee can choose any deity of his/her own choice.

1.7. Sanskritic Hinduism

M. N. Srinivas, in his book, *Religion, and Society among the Coorgs of South India* suggests that 'Sanskritic Hinduism' presents certain common characteristics of higher Hinduism which seem to be equal to all. They are, 'worship of great deities like Vishnu and Shiva, the pan-Hindu sacredness of rivers, the importance of major pilgrimage centers, the currency of the two classical epics (the *Ramayana* and the *Mahabharata*), the sanctity of the cow, belief in the concepts of *karma* and *dharma,* and the preeminent role of Brahmans.'[13]

1.8. Bhakti/Devotionalism

Bhagavad Gita, emphasis on the 'grace'[14] of God and 'devotion of God.'[15] These have become foundations of *bhakti marga* which centers on the doctrine of grace.

Devotionalism seems to be revolutionary, and it insists that 'true Brahmanhood is achieved by devotion to god, not given by birth.'[16] In a way, everyone can equally be recipient of God's grace.

To avoid possible limitations (caste hierarchy and strict religious observances) in practicing bhakti because of its requirements, *Alvars* in the south propounded *prapatti*, which people of all class and grade could practice. They constantly maintained that the ultimate reality is one and that is Tirumāl, who used Tamil and Tamil poetical skills to convey the content of Sanskrit religious texts. The presence of a woman and people from different caste groups in the band of Alvars are radical reformations. They have also revealed the inherent riches and divinity of nature in their poems.

1.9. Popular Hinduism

Popular Hinduism, like in every religion, is a social and cultural construction.[17] There are innumerable religious developments like Ayavazi, Aathi parasakthi,

13 C. J. Fuller, 28.

14 S. N. Dasgupta, "Classical Forms of Devotional Mysticism", *Hindu Mysticism,* Republished (New York: Frederick Ungar Publishing Co,1959), 119.

15 A. L. Basham, *The Origins and Development of Classical Hinduism,* ed. and annotated by Kenneth G. Zysk (Delhi: Oxford University Press, 1992), 91.

16 C. J. Fuller, 157.

17 C. J. Fuller, 7.

Narayana Guru, Linkayats, Dalit religion, etc., to enforce equality in Hinduism. I am not in a position to assess their success.

Having presented, as much as possible, the seeming sources for equality claims in Hinduism, let us proceed to the second part of the paper.

2. Inequality

You would have already realized my struggle with the first part of the paper and I am sure that it can be overcome in the second part. My quest for equality in Hinduism helped me to consider the opposite of it as well. Let us start with religion.

2.1. Religion-Hinduism/Dharma

The word Dharma is used in most cases as religious ordinances or rites. Hindu dharma/religion is 'really Law or at best-legalized class-ethics.' It is 'misrepresented to the people as religion.'[18] "By "Dharma" the Hindus mean 'right, duty, law' and also 'religious custom and usage.'[19] It is true that "customs have been recognized from the very beginning as a source of the Hindu Dharma."[20]

Ambedkar writes that in Hinduism 'religion, in the sense of spiritual principles, truly universal, applicable to all races, to all countries, to all times, is not to be found' and 'I have, therefore, no hesitation in saying that such a religion must be destroyed.' He goes on to say that "You will succeed in saving Hinduism if you will kill Brahmans."[21] His anger germinated from the view that all the inequalities in Hinduism and society are the product of one group and there is no equality in Hinduism.

2.2. Sanskritic Hinduism

The Sanskritic Hinduism, opposed to its claim of equality, is 'the religion of the high castes' derives universality from its roots in the Sanskrit scriptural tradition mainly perpetuated throughout the country by the Brahman literati.'[22] The reality of this is true in the division of Hinduism as 'higher Sanskritic and lower non-Sanskritic strata' or great and little traditions. The hierarchy and inequality are right through Hinduism.

For example, 'the temples of great deities like Vishnu and Shiva, tend to attract more high-caste worshippers, and they are mainly served by Brahman

---

18 B. R. Ambedkar, *Annihilation of Caste*, 2nd ed. (New Delhi: Samyak Prakashan, 2018), 75.

19 Rajbali Pandey, *Hindu Samskaras: Socio-Religious Study of the Hindu Sacraments,* 11th Reprint (Delhi: Motilal Banarsidass Publishers Private Limited, 2018), 7.

20 Rajbali Pandey, 11.

21 B. R. Ambedkar, *Annihilation of Caste*, 75-78.

22 C. J. Fuller, 25.

priests, who make only vegetarian offerings and use Sanskrit as the ritual language'. On the other hand, 'the temples of many other deities tend to be patronized by the low castes, and they generally have non-Brahman priests, who make both vegetarian and non-vegetarian offerings and use vernacular languages in ritual'. The bitter fact is that 'the separation is reinforced by the higher-status groups.'[23]

2.3. Bhakti

The so-called bhakti tradition, contrary to expectations, has resorted 'to institutionalized inequality.'[24] Often the devotees greet the gurus 'by prostrating at his feet'. In other words, 'hierarchical inequality is embedded within the structure of all devotionalist orders, which can never be fully egalitarian."[25] The entry of *Ācāryas* once again brought Sanskrit and Brahmanic control into prominence.

2.4. Samskaras

Samskaras are Hindu sacraments (of purification). Many social and cultural elements have entered into the religious ceremonies to mould the Samskaras.[26] Most of them are domestic rites and ceremonies based more on precedence and popular traditional usages than on any definite written code.[27] In other words "really speaking, customs were the only source of the Samskaras before they were codified in the Girhya manuals."[28] Yet they were binding on the Hindu householder. Samskaras mark the transition from the Vedic to Smarta (smriti) and Pauranika Hinduism where 'greater restrictions are placed on social sides of the Samskaras.'[29] There is a greater amount of inequality in terms of age, duration, rites, and ceremonies according to caste. For example, "the corpse in its hands, should have a piece of gold if it is of a Brahman, a bow if of a Kshttriya, a jewel if of a Vaisya."[30]

Even different forms of marriages are suggested for different castes. All the once-born and women are not entitled to Samskaras.

23 C. J. Fuller, 28.

24 C. J. Fuller, 158.

25 C. J. Fuller, 164.

26 Rajbali Pandey, *Hindu Samskaras: Socio-Religious Study of the Hindu Sacraments*, vii.

27 Rajbali Pandey, *Hindu Samskaras: Socio-Religious Study of the Hindu Sacraments*, 1.

28 Rajbali Pandey, *Hindu Samskaras: Socio-Religious Study of the Hindu Sacraments*, 11.

29 Rajbali Pandey, *Hindu Samskaras: Socio-Religious Study of the Hindu Sacraments*, 8.

30 Rajbali Pandey, *Hindu Samskaras: Socio-Religious Study of the Hindu Sacraments*, 251.

2.5. Caste Constrains and Influences

Inequality is pervasive in Hindu literature. Ambedkar writes that "the literature of the Hindus is full of caste genealogies in which an attempt is made to give a noble origin to one caste and an ignoble origin to other castes."[31]

It is traditionally claimed, as opposed to the current trend, that Hinduism is not a missionary in nature. The reason given is that 'caste is inconsistent with conversion.'

Since Hindu Society is 'a collection of castes and each caste being a close corporation there is no place for a convert.' Therefore, so long as caste remains '*shudhi* will be both folly and a futility.'[32] This we see in many contentious discussions related to religious mobility.

Another main reason for this divide and inequality is that Hinduism 'postulates no absolute distinction between divine and human beings.' Often 'human beings are seen as actually divine in one way or another', and the same 'gesture is made to deities as well as people', 'so that human superiority is justified by god-like attributes.' Or 'the gesture tends to disguise behind a religious veil the objective bases of social inequality that lie', 'in unequal control over politico-economic resources.'[33]

2.6. Hindu Society

Ambedkar says that the 'Hindu Society is a myth.' The name Hindu is itself a foreign name given by the Mohammedans to the natives for the purpose of distinguishing themselves. It does not occur in any Sanskrit work 'prior to the Mohammedan invasion.'[34] Hindus did not feel the necessity of a common name because 'Hindu society as such does not exist.' 'It is only a collection of castes'. Similarly, 'one of the most fundamental principles in Indian society is hierarchical inequality.'[35] Therefore, it is in place to look for the reasons behind these inequalities and hierarchies.

2.7. The Varna and Caste Hierarchies

The 'hierarchical inequality' in Indian society is most distinctively expressed 'by the concepts of *varna* and caste'. It begins with the *Purusha sukta*.[36] For Ambedkar Caste is a 'human institution'[37] and it is different from varna. Varna

31 B. R. Ambedkar, *Annihilation of Caste*, 43.

32 B. R. Ambedkar, *Annihilation of Caste*, 46-47.

33 C. J. Fuller, 3-7.

34 B. R. Ambedkar, *Annihilation of Caste*, 41.

35 C. J. Fuller, 12.

36 C. J. Fuller, 12.

37 B. R. Ambedkar, *Castes in India: Their Mechanism, Genesis and Development* (New Delhi: Samyak Prakashan [1917], n. d), 9.

is necessary because it 'is an ideal model for the caste system despite the latter's more complex structure.'

The word 'caste' is a translation of *jati* in all the main Indian languages. It 'literally means "kind" or "species," so that the social unit that we describe as a 'caste' is but one of these kinds.' It is not an abstract, but 'a visible dimension of everyday life.'[38]

Vivekanand Jha defines caste 'as a system of social stratification characterized by hierarchy, heredity, the pursuit of one or a few particular occupations, inequality, endogamy, restrictions as to taking food and drink from the outsiders, and the notion of purity and pollution associated with hierarchy.'[39] While dealing with the caste inequality it is a huge surprise to read that 'due to the distribution of the people into castes that India did not lapse into a state of barbarism.'[40]

2.8. Chaturvarnya and Guna

Chaturvarnya is the division of society onto four classes instead of the four thousand castes that we have in India'. It is claimed that varna 'is based not on birth but on *guna* (worth).'[41] This has support in Manu,[42] Githa,[43] philosophy and all the Hindu religious literature. The theory of *guna* is nothing but presenting inequality in creation.

Ambedkar writes 'my whole being rebels against it'[44] because the *varna* is closer to class where caste is birth. The *varna* and *guna* forms of explanation reinforces inequality.

2.9. Brahmin-Twice Born

As caste is based on birth the inequality is infused into the creation itself that "man is stated to be purer above the navel (than below); hence the Self-existence (*Svayambhu*) has declared the purest (part) of him (to be) his mouth."[45] This is a vivid systematic effort to present the Brahmins superior and unequal to others.

Brahmins' status is portrayed as superior to kings. For example, "know that a Brahmana of ten years and Ksatriya of a hundred years stand to each

38 C. J. Fuller, 13.

39 Vivekanand Jha, *Candala: Untouchability and Caste in Early India* (New Delhi: Primus Books, 2018), 105.

40 Abbe J. A. Dubois, *Hindu Manners and Customs and Ceremonies*, Reprinted (Delhi: Low Price Publications, 1999), 28.

41 B. R. Ambedkar, *Annihilation of Caste*, 53.

42 *Manu Smriti* 12:24.

43 *Bagavad-gita* 4:13.

44 B. R. Ambedkar, *Annihilation of Caste*, 53.

45 *Manu Smriti* 1:92.

other in the relation of father and son; but between those two the Brahmana is the father."[46]

Their food habits, although similar to others, are presented as distinct: "A Brahmana must never eat (the flesh of) animals unhallowed by Mantras; but, obedient to the primeval law, he may eat it, consecrated with Vedic texts."[47]

The religious rights for the Brahmains are performed earlier than others: "In the eighth year after conception, one should perform the initiation (upanayana) of a Brahmana, in the eleventh after conception (that) of a Ksatriya, but in the twelfth that of a Vaisya."[48] The list goes on.

2.10. Sudra-Fourth Varna

The Sudras are treated much unequally from the other three varnas. According to Manu "One occupation only the lord prescribed to the Sudra, to serve meekly even these (other) three castes."[49] Serving the Brahmanas 'is the highest duty of a Sudra, which leads to beatitude.'[50]

The first part of the name of a Sudra should express something 'contemptible'[51] and the second part 'denoting service.'[52]

Sudra is treated as a slave and hence, "No collection of wealth must be made by a Sudra even though he be able (to do it); for a Sudra who has acquired wealth, gives pain to Brahmanas."[53]

2.11. Dasyus and Chandalas

Those who are not part of varna are called Dasyus.[54] They have to live "near well-known trees and burial-grounds, on mountains and in groves, let these (tribes) dwell, known (by certain marks), and subsisting by their peculiar occupation."[55]

Candalas should live outside the village, 'they must be made Apapatras, and their wealth (shall be) dogs and donkeys.'[56] 'A Chandala, a village pig, a cock, a dog, a menstruating woman and a eunuch' are at the same level.[57]

46 *Manu Smriti* 2:135.

47 *Manu Smriti* 5:36.

48 *Manu Smriti* 2:36.

49 *Manu Smriti* 1:91.

50 *Manu Smriti* 9:334.

51 *Manu Smriti* 2:31.

52 *Manu Smriti* 2:32.

53 *Manu Smriti* 10:129.

54 *Manu Smriti* 10:45.

55 *Manu Smriti* 10:50.

56 *Manu Smriti* 10:51.

57 *Manu Smriti* 3:239.

The directions for their life is that "their dress (shall be) the garments of the dead, (they shall eat) their food from broken dishes, black iron (shall be) their ornaments, and they must always wander from place to place."[58] They were prohibited from walking in villages and towns during the night.

2.12. Untouchables

A worrying form of inequality in Hinduism is untouchability. Ambedkar argues that 'there is no racial difference between the Hindus and the Untouchables.' Before the arrival of untouchability, there was a 'distinction between Tribesmen and Broken Men from alien Tribes.' It is the broken Men who subsequently came to be treated as Untouchables.

Untouchability has no occupational basis too. It sprung from 'contempt and hatred of the Broken Men' and 'continuation of beef-eating. The Untouchables are distinct from the Impure. According to Ambedkar "while the impure as a class came into existence at the time of Dharma Sutras the Untouchables came into being much later than 400 A.D."[59]

The hereditary form of Untouchability 'has no parallel in the history of the world.' A polluted person can become pure by purification ceremonies, 'but there is nothing which can make the Untouchables pure. They are born impure, they are impure while they live, they die the death of the impure, and they give birth to children who are born with the stigma of Untouchability affixed to them, it is a case of permanent, hereditary stain which nothing can cleanse.' It is lamented that "there has never been a case of a people treating a section of their own people as permanently and hereditarily impure." Untouchability among Hindus is unknown to humanity in other parts of the world.[60]

2.13. The Position of Women

According to Manu 'a woman must never be independent'.[61] 'Nothing must be done by her independently, even in her own house.'[62] If her suitor is handsome and the same caste she should be married even before age.[63] Early marriage was to avoid mixing caste with the notion that women are more polluting.[64] Even, "though destitute of virtue, or seeking pleasure (elsewhere), or devoid

58 *Manu Smriti* 10:52.

59 B. R. Ambedkar, *The Untouchables: Who were They and Why They Became Untouchables,* Reprint (Delhi: Kalpaz Publications, 2017), v.

60 B. R. Ambedkar, *The Untouchables: Who were They and Why They Became Untouchables,* 21-22.

61 *Manu Smriti* 5:148.

62 *Manu Smriti* 5:147.

63 *Manu Smriti* 9:88.

64 C. J. Fuller, 22.

of good qualities, (yet) a husband must be constantly worshipped as a god by a faithful wife."[65] In this woman should not care about beauty, age and look.[66]

Men can be away from home and the woman should wait for him. It is said, "if the husband went abroad for some sacred duty, (she) must wait for him eight years, if (he went) to (acquire) learning or fame six (years), if (he went) for pleasure three years."[67]

Whereas men of the first three *varnas* undergo an initiation rite in early adulthood, women do not and, like all Shudras, women remain disprivileged in religious and legal terms.[68] They are not entitled to rites with sacred texts.[69]

They are considered as seducers of men. Therefore "one should not sit in a lonely place with one's mother, sister or daughter; for the senses are powerful, and master even a learned man."[70]

A wife is an auspicious, perfect Hindu woman only while her husband is alive. Whereas, a widow is inauspiciousness personified and epitomizes every negative quality. Widows cannot attend auspicious rituals, such as weddings.'[71]

2.14. King and Justice

Inequality has not spared the king and justice system. According to Manu, "the king has been created (to be) the protector of the castes (varna) and orders, who, all according to their rank, discharge their several duties."[72] Even the Gita says "it is far better to discharge one's prescribed duties, even though faultily, than another's duties perfectly. Destruction the course of performing one's own duties better than engaging in another' s duties, to follow another's path is dangerous."[73]

The king has to 'worship Brahmins'[74] and honor them with gifts.[75] Still further, "when a learned Brahmana has found treasure, deposited in former (times), he may take even the whole (of it); for he is master of everything."[76]

65 *Manu Smriti* 5:154.

66 *Manu Smriti* 9:14.

67 *Manu Smriti* 9. 76.

68 C. J. Fuller, 20.

69 *Manu Smriti* 9:18.

70 *Manu Smriti* 2:215.

71 C. J. Fuller, 22.

72 *Manu Smriti* 7:35.

73 *Bagavad-gita* 3:35., A. C. Bhktivedanta Swami Prabhupada, *Bagavad-Gita*, 40th Printing (Mumbai: The Bhaktivedanta Book Trust, 2014).

74 *Manu Smriti* 7:37.

75 *Manu Smriti* 7:82.

76 *Manu Smriti* 8:37.

but "when the king finds treasure of old concealed in the ground, let him give one half to Brahmanas and place the (other) half in his treasury."[77]

No great crime is known on earth than slaying a Brahmana.[78] Hence, no Brahmin should be given capital punishment irrespective of the crime: "Let him never slay a Brahmana, though he has committed all (possible) crimes; let him banish such an (offender), leaving all his property (to him) and (his body) unhurt."[79]

In contrast, if a Sudra insults a twice-born man with gross invective, 'shall have his tongue cut out.'[80] And "if he mentions the name and castes (jati) of the (twice-born) with contumely, an iron nail, ten fingers long shall be thrust red-hot into his mouth."[81] More severe is that "if he arrogantly teaches Brahmanas their duty, the king shall cause hot oil to be poured into his mouth and into his ears."[82] If 'a low-caste man tries to place himself on the same seat with a man of a high caste, he shall be branched on his hip and be banished, or (the king) shall cause his buttock to be gashed."[83]

Having reasonably presented the inequality in Hinduism, now we have to conclude whether Hinduism represents equality or inequality.

3. Concluding Lines

The concluding lines are inconsonant with the suggestions of Ambedkar. Innumerable Castes and embodiment of inequality are realities. India 'presents more survivals of primitive times than'[84] any other civilized society.

It is also held that 'India form a homogeneous whole' and 'possess cultural unity', therefore caste (inequality) thrives. In my view Hindu culture cannot be Indian culture therefore I am unable to identify the homogeneity and cultural unity.

Since endogamy is caste, (can be differed), 'the real remedy for breaking caste is inter-marriage' and the real enemy to fight with is the *Shrutis* and the *Smritis* which have inculcated the notion of caste.'[85]

It is hard to believe that inequality has taken the place of equality in Hinduism in the name of castes. It is harder that Hinduism has hated and pushed the least in the society to the most unimaginable position without

77 *Manu Smriti* 8:38.

78 *Manu Smriti* 8:381.

79 *Manu Smriti* 8:380.

80 *Manu Smriti* 8:270.

81 *Manu Smriti* 8:271.

82 *Manu Smriti* 8:272.

83 *Manu Smriti* 8:281.

84 B. R. Ambedkar, *Castes in India: Their Mechanism, Genesis and Development*, 14.

85 B. R. Ambedkar, *Annihilation of Caste*, 64-67.

even suggesting any measure to improve their plight. It is so painful that, in Hinduism, there is no 'consciousness of kind' except castes.[86] There is no appreciation of merits in a person unless a fellow caste.[87]

The notion that birth determines one's status is nowhere in the world and this is obviously behind the discussions on freedom of religion in India.

As long as the doctrines of (Gita) Karma, the soul is eternal and the body is not, punarjenma and the notion that one is suffering or enjoying the previous karma in the present life are even in the remotest part of the consciousness Hinduism's contribution to equality is doubtful. This, in fact, is, absolutely different from the vision of equality envisaged in the Indian Constitution.

86 B. R. Ambedkar, *Annihilation of Caste*, 41.

87 B. R. Ambedkar, *Annihilation of Caste*, 50.

15

APPROACHES TO PEOPLE OF OTHER FAITH

Selvindurai[1]

Indeed, it is a great honor and joy for me to join this editorial team to write this article. Rev. Dr. David Onesimu a man of God depending upon God and His guidance through prayer. I am also privileged to study through him and serve with him in MTSC. It a good time to be with him and serve god with ECI. I pray that God's continuous presence will be with him continually in all his endeavour.

Introduction

The search for the meaning of man's existence leads them to different horizons of understanding the Truth. They took separate paths to reach the same. Thus, there are various religions and each non-Christian religion is the result of the genuine thirst and its satisfaction by finding the Truth and Truth is God.

The Second Vatican Council in the "Relationship Church to Non-Christian Religions" puts it briefly, ancient times down to the present, there has existed among diverse peoples a certain perception of that hidden power which hovers over the course of things and the events of human life; such a perception and such a recognition instill the lives of the peoples with a profound religious sense. Religions bound with cultural advancement have struggled to reply to

1 *Rev. Dr. Selvindurai M.A. is an Associate Professor at Madras Theological Seminary & College, teaching in the Department of Missiology. At present he is the director of the Laymen Bible Training (LBT), a unit of MTSC. He is an ordained minister of Evangelical Church of India. He is also teaching at MTSC in the Department of Missiology.*

the same questions with more refined concepts and in more highly developed language.'

Our attitude toward other religions is one of respect, love and, appreciation. Vatican II put it this way, "The Catholic Church rejects nothing true and holy in these religions. she looks with sincere respect upon those ways of conduct and life, those rules and teachings which, though differing in many particulars from what she holds and sets forth nevertheless — often reflect a ray of that Truth which enlightens all men."

Reason for Dialogue

It is surely the fact that Christianity has been presented to these people in the form of western culture. It has never penetrated the inner life and thought of the East. Thus, it is left for us at the present day to face the next crisis in the history of Christianity, the extension of the incarnation to the East. Christ has become incarnate in Europe and America; He has still to become incarnate in Asia and Africa; Africa, however, does not present such a serious problem; But, the civilization of China and India are not only of greatest antiquity but also culturally the most profound which the Church has encountered since the first days of her mission in the Roman Empire.

This situation calls for a serious reflection on the real meaning of dialogue, self-understanding of faith from a dialogical perspective, a dialogical approach to people of other faiths and shaping of dialogical personality.

Definition of Dialogue

According to dictionaries, the primary meaning of 'dialogue' is 'talk' or 'exchange of view' between two persons. But, in a deeper sense dialogue implies intimacy of personal relationship, enjoyment of each other, and sharing of knowledge, experience, problems, sufferings, and resources. In this sense it initiates a process of healing, challenging, shaping and molding the personalities of its partners, their concepts and convictions as well. In Christian circles, particularly inter-faith dialogue is understood in terms of proper attitude, healthy-relationship, and mutual co-operation. From a missiological point of view, 'dialogue can be understood as being open to other religions, to recognize God's activity in them and to see how they are related to God's unique revelation in Christ. This understanding has taken different shapes in the ecumenical discussions on inter-faith dialogue.

The Spiritual Contemplative Approach

According to Rev. Murray Rogers, one of the pioneers in this dialogue is a readiness to listen to the other as other Rogers writes: "we may not listen in order to prepare our methods of approach, proclamation or attack, but with the awareness that Christ speaks to us from the other. Far from the expecting to despise or belittle what we hear we will be set to appreciate." For Murray Roger listening is not stopping of talking. To put it in his own words, to listen means far more than simply to stop talking, it demands silence in oneself in order to understand the non-Christian brother as he understands himself, a putting into brackets of my own Christian convictions.

The Four Stages of Inner Dialogue

Roger talks about four levels of inner dialogues, and four levels of external dialogues.

The inner level dialogues,

(a) The Christian needs to be unshakably rooted in Christ.

(b) He should so op himself in order that the non-Christian religious experience may begin to happen with himself." with the living Christ to hold us and a general grasp of the faith we can rather as a diver joined to his ship by the air-pipe and rope dive deeply into the non-Christian spiritualties."

(c) The Christian already deeply engaged in the Hindu spiritual experience becomes more deeply aware than ever of the irreducible uniqueness and transcendence of Christ, of Christian faith.

(d) The Hindu and Christian spiritualties are deepened together Preciously at this point Christian transcendence must manifest its concrete universality by showing that what it surpasses is not simply left behind but recapitulated gathered up drawn into the orbit.

The External Level Dialogues,

(a) The Christian knows that he meets his non-Christian friend in Christ. Long before being a non-Christian a Hindu is an image of God. Instead of asking what should I tell ask what does God tells me through His image in this Hindu friend.

(b) Now it is my turn to speak, to share with my Hindu friend in word or silence the results of my previous internal dialogue a Christian with his scripture and with his genuine spiritual experience.

(c) At the third stage like the Incognito Christ to the Emmaus road, the Christian helps the Hindu to see what his scriptures point to.

(d) Now the true face of the "Unknown Christ" hidden and so often deformed in religions of the world including the Christian religion is revealed. This is the movement of Conversion a work of the spirit when the risen Christ in whom the spiritual world of my Hindu, Pre-Christian neighbor is gathered up purified and transformed is seen known and Worshiped.

Fr. Monchanin, Dom Le Saux, Doth Bede Griffiths hold similar views. Swami Abhishiktananda, co-founder of Sacidananda Ashram and a member of the 'Circle' established by J. A. Cuttat, the former Ambassador to India recalls his experiences in the Circle, "Christian reading the Upanishads in the presence of Christ was to discover in ourselves in the secret place of the Rishis experience, and then under the inspiration of the spirit and by an existential process 'wholly' personal to each one, to allow the Christian expression and Trinitarian culmination of this experience to find its full development in us.

Two main conclusions the Swami arrives at are: (i) The lord is already in India... Our role is to help the holy seed been sown by the Spirit in the hearts and traditions of India to germinate". (ii) "India has received from her creator a very special gift of interiority, a unique inward orientation of the Spirit."

M. Mundaden sees in their writings a dialogue moving discussion of doctrines or common problems to a genuine personal encounter. The fruits of dialogue are to be Left work of the Spirit. The Christian must be willing to wait on the Spirit. The Christian must be able to enter a dialogue in the freedom of love-love which gives openness. Then there will be dialogue at the deepest level.

The Intellectual-Theological Approach

Some of the Theologians go to the sources of the non-Christian religions as the *Sruti* and *Smriti* literature of Hinduism. The great Indian philosophical systems and Schools of thought including the neo-*vedantic* and modern Christian writers are taken up by some others. They also may be used for an Indian interpretation of Christian revelation. Still, some others study the *margas* or a few terms as *Brahman, Eswara, Saccidananda* with the same aim. Already topics are presented as Trinity, God and the World, Christ and the Spirit, Church and Sacraments, history and fulfillment.

The Liturgical use of the Hindu Scriptures and its theological implication. of 'inspiration' are of interest to the theologians. Prof. Mathias writes: "Besides and objective historical, comparative study of the Old Testament and Hindu Scriptures, there is an attempt to interpret the inspiration of the Old Testament in such a way as to apply, it at in a limited way to the Hindu Scriptures.

R.V. de smet, J. H. Piet, Dr. S. J. Samartha have all attempted to have a philosophical dialogue with Hinduism. They have made their studies on Sankara, Siva Siddhananda philosophy and Hindu view of history. Modern Hindu authors are also widely studied by many. Raymond Panikkar, with his deep knowledge of Christian tradition in the west, his fairly good scholarship of Hinduism. And his wide interest in comparative religion has contributed the lion's share in the contemporary effort to build an Indian interpretation of Christian revelation or a Christian interpretation of Hinduism. Some of the topics he dealt with are; meaning of religion and its relation to actual religions;

the Eucharist is its relation to Hindu sacramental religion; the encounter of Hinduism and Christianity; The nature of faith; Christ and *Eswara*; Trinity and three *margas*.

In the work "Trinity and world religions" having criticized the spiritual contemplative approach of their phenomenological epoch or putting into brackets of one's own faith, he purposefully avoided the word *saccidananda* and found his clue in the three traditional types of spirituality or *margas* of Hinduism-*Janana, Karma, Bhakti.* He builds them into a triple Schema relating them to the special spiritualities of the Father the Son and the Holy Spirit respectively.

The conclusion is that one cannot ignore his fellowmen and act as if religion has given him complete assurance that he has no more to learn and nothing to change. He has to throw himself into the sea and begin to walk even if his feet are faltering and his heart failing. We have no right what so ever to stifle the growing seed to choke humble and personal buds to quench the smoking wick.

Socio-Political Approach

Christians happen to live in different socio-political atmospheres. They have socio-political duties as responsible citizens. Interfaith dialogue becomes very significant when socio-political discrimination against minority religious communities is felt. Country like India where secularism and religious persuasions are kept in tension, socio-political perspective in interfaith dialogue is very significant.

The social approach is an attempt to evolve a theology from the concentrate situation of evangelization India. The main focus of this theology is on communion and development. According to Prof. Mathias, the mission of the Church in terms of the proclamation of the gospel planting the Church cannot full justice to the present awareness of the Indian churches. Its context is "the richness of religious experience, the dynamism of a youthful nation, the bitterness and aspirations of the suffering and struggling millions. Hence, the evolving theology is woven around communion and development, focused on Christ the life in which all form a community of mutual sharing; Christ the Prototype of the New humanity the common end of all which is the concretization of communion.

Dr. Paul Devanandan is the pioneer in theological thinking. Dr. M. M. Thomas went further with it and made it much wider. R. Panikker and D. Amalorpavadas are partial supporters of this view. Catholic Church in India as a whole insists very much on social engagement. To fulfill the Church's mission an integral and total development of man and society is to be aimed at. The yeoman's work to promote this approach to Hindu-Christian dialogue has been done by the Christian Institute for the study of Religion and Society under the pioneering guidance of Devanandan and his associate M. M. Thomas. The main features of the theology fostered by the Institute are the following:

1) A growing appreciation of Christ's presence and activity outside the institutional Church, in the insurgent religions, movements, and struggles for a fuller human life;
2) Understanding of Christianity primarily as a new life, new creation, new humanity, inner change, a new order of being;
3) An understanding of salvation as social and cosmic, as something that embraces life in totality and all the realms of the created world;
4) A deep emphasis of the institutional growth of the Church understood in a traditional sense;
5) A readiness to cooperate with others in national reconstruction and other welfare activities;
6) A firm conviction that the best and the most relevant to present Gospel in today's India is to enter into a dialogue with the adherents of other faiths and ideologies in the context of the evolving new culture and struggle for a fuller and dignified human life."

Devanadan holds that Christian should join with those of other faiths In waging war against poverty, disease, and oppression. It is a "Christian mission to bring into Hinduism right view of history, of creation, of personality and community, for which the Hindu is searching... By understanding the inner working of Hinduism the Christian theologian may be able to show his Hindu friends that Hinduism can find its true meaning only in Christ."

Missionary Approach

The International missionary conference of Edinburgh 1910 people of other faiths have been mentioned in connection with the mission. A new awareness about them found expression in missionary consultations following the study of religions and their renaissance in various parts of the world. Christian thinkers called Christians to perceive the hand of god behind the renaissance of religions and Christ acknowledged in the process. Historically, the interfaith dialogue was an off-shoot of mission and evangelism. This was also the case in the world council of Churches when a study project within the unit on mission and evangelism led to the formation of a separate sub-unit on dialogue with living faiths in 1971.

The theological significance of the faith experience of the people of other religions attributed by the dialogians seems to indirectly ridicule the commission of Jesus to go into all the world and preach the gospel to every creature. In many Churches and ecumenical circles, evangelists and dialogians are allowed to function side by side.

Mission and dialogue are old allies unwilling to part with each other. A healthy tension between them may purify each other. They have both common concerns and different concerns as well. Their boundaries need to be marked. Proper communication should be the search for both. They should clarify a proper approach to the Bible, the meaning of conversion and the role of proclamation.

The Approach of Restoring the Culture

Culture is something so transparent in human life but so mysterious to understand its nature. Culture may have as many definitions as religion has. The term culture on the popular level is used to refer to a variety of things, language, behavior, arts, and national identity. There is no religion free of culture as religion has a social dimension. Every religion can evaluate its relationship with its culture related to it.

Restoring native culture is very important in the implication of the mission. There is a bad notion that Christian culture is Western culture. The concept of Swadeshi has to be developed. The native culture has to be restored, the indigenous way of worshipping, using the sacraments have to be practiced. The Gospel should not change the culture. Inculturalization, contextualization, and Indigenization should be addressed properly. "Culture shapes the human voice that answers the voice of Christ" said the Bangkok world mission conference in 1973. The Salvador conference strongly affirmed that "there is no way of being human without participating in culture, for it is through culture that is created."

Approach of Liberation

The basic text for the mission as liberation is well understood from the Nazareth Manifesto found in Luke $:16-21. When the gospel is preached to a person who is under the clutches of any kind of bondage or suffering or the oppressive structure of society the bask question which the oppressed or the sufferer or a slave raise is that, where is God in our suffering? Since there is no realization of God in their state of suffering the so-called God News or the Gospel or the message of Christ makes no sense. Therefore, when we talk about the Mission of God, it is not just giving them the message from the bible, but we should minister them, i.e., Instead of simply calling them to the church and be part of it at their cost of their daily wage, we should encourage them to earn their livelihood even on the Sundays and we should counsel them to come out of their sufferings and troubles whatever it may be. Therefore, the Gospel for a suffering person is to be out of their suffering state and be glad as the others do.

Conclusion

Dialogue with other religions really strengthens and Initiates Christian faith. And so there is no doubt about the necessity of dialogue. And for dialogue, some approaches it to propose herewith. We cannot say each approach is completely independent in itself and is mutually exclusive very often they complement one another. The approach to the people of other faith in a multi-religious context like India, we need to have our own stands of faith people and also it does not mean to convert them. The Church and Christian should set and follow the model of Christ.

Raymond Panikkar criticized the holders of the Spiritual Contemplative approach namely Swami Abhishiktananta and Murray Rogers for proposing the idea of a Phenomenological epoche' or putting in brackets' of one's own faith'. He considers such an epoche psychologically impracticable, phenomenological inappropriate, philosophically defective and theologically weak. But, their proposition to have an inner dialogue before the external or actual dialogue is accepted and approved by all.

The proposition that the theological implication of 'Inspiration' of O. T. must be applied at least in a limited way to other Scriptures may not be digestible for the conservatives. But, after Vatican II and "*The Declaration on the relationship of the Church to Non-Christian Religions*," the progressive thinking in this line cannot be absolutely denied Church exhorts her sons to enter into dialogue prudently and lovingly to promote moral and spiritual goods among men of all kinds. Vatican II says "The Church, therefore, has this exhortation for her sons, prudently and lovingly through dialogue and collaboration with the followers of other religions and in witness of Christian faith and life acknowledges, preserve and promote the spiritual and moral goods found among these men as well as the values in their society and culture.

Bibliography

Bosch, David. *Transforming Mission*, New York: Orbis., 1991.

C. Murrary Rogers "Hindu and Christian-A Movement Breaks," *Religion and Society*, Vol. 12 (1965).

Selvanayagam Israel, *A Dialogue on Dialogue*, The CLS Press, Madras-1995.

Vinay Samuel and Chris Sugden (ed), The Gospel Among Our Hindu Neighbors, Bangalore: Partnership in Mission-Asia, 1983.

X. J. Puthenkalam, "Christian Approaches to other Religions: For an Inter-Faith Dialogue," *The Living Word*. Vol. 87 (1981).

PART V

MINISTERIAL

16

THEOLOGICAL EDUCATION AND CHURCH PLANTING

D. Sundar Singh[1]

I praise God for the decades-long ministry of Rev. Dr. J. A. David Onesimu with the Evangelical Church of India in various capacities. On behalf of the church, I want to acknowledge and appreciate his significant contribution towards the growth of ECI. The infrastructural development he has brought about on the Madras Theological Seminary and College campus as its Principal is noteworthy. The seminary's Diamond Jubilee Hall, Diamond Jubilee Library Hall, Girls' Dormitory and a small Prayer Chapel were constructed during his tenure. Besides, he has been doing a marvellous job as Coordinator of Korean Partnership.

I am glad that my article is published in the Festschrift brought out to commemorate Rev. Dr. J. A. David Onesimu's 65th Birthday. I wish him many more happy returns of the day and pray that God will enable him to serve Him even better in the days to come for the growth of ECI beyond Chennai.

---

1 *The Most Rev. Dr. D. Sundar Singh B.D., M.Th. D. Min., the President–Bishop of the Evangelical Church of India is a compassionate Pastor, an eloquent speaker and writer. He is also a good counsellor and competent Bible Teacher and is regularly contributing articles to many theological journals and Christian magazines. The present paper is formerly published in Mission Mandate: A Compendium on the perspective in India, edited by M. Ezra Sargunam (Madras: Mission India 2000, 1992), 356-362.*

I. Introduction

Today the Church in India is passing through a period of theological confusion and ideological conflicts. Uncertain and ambiguous theological positions prevail everywhere due to a lack of clear-cut biblical teaching. In the name of evangelization, two sets of biblical imbalances have been set on foot. On the one hand, numerous Gospel Meetings, Healing Campaigns, Work Shops, and Seminars of various nature are conducted in an effort to reach the unreached. But at the same time, there is a noticeable danger in this, that at times the messages lack biblical centrality and adherence to hermeneutical principles. All kinds of theology are propounded by all sorts of preachers elucidating their individual experience which are sometimes contrary to the teachings of the Bible. Very seldom one hears a good biblical expository sermon these days. As a result, the faith of the church is weakened considerably and the believers get confused and are tossed to and fro and carried with every wind of doctrine.

On the other hand, some theologians who claim to possess superior theological scholarship, question the authority of the Bible and deny the fundamental tenets of Christian faith. They teach their students to believe that Christian salvation is simply liberating the oppressed and suppressed. In the name of maintaining communal harmony and tolerance toward other religious faiths, they have nullified the efficacy of the atoning work of Jesus Christ and thereby have falsified the very purpose of his incarnation.

It is here the responsibility of the Indian Theological Seminaries and Bible Schools becomes crucial. It is said there are about 500 Bible Schools and Seminaries in existence in India today. The purpose of this article is to analyse the present state of affairs of the Bible Schools and Seminaries as well as to propose certain guidelines to make theological education more effective in fulfilling the Great Commission.

II. Training for Church Planting — God's Unique Plan

Evangelism began in the heart of God Himself. When Adam and Eve sinned, they were separated from God. God wanted to restore man to Himself. And in the fullness of time, God sent His son born of a woman to redeem sinful humanity.

Great men of God like Samuel and leading prophets of the Old Testament had their Bible Schools and training centres. Our Lord and Saviour Jesus Christ had a "Mobile Bible Seminary" of his own. He trained 12 men in his close quarters. Apostle Paul conducted a 2-year Bible course by hiring the school of Tyrannus during siesta hours — very unusual and impractical time of the day to discuss Theology.

Early Church fathers like Origen and St. Augustine were great seminarians. During Medieval history, the common man was denied access to the Word of God and was deprived of reading and interpreting Scriptures. But then it was through a systematic study of God's Word, the great Reformation broke out under the leadership of Martin Luther. William Carey, the father of modern missionary movements laid much emphasis on "the training of Indigenous Leadership", which was one of his cardinal principles for evangelism and church planting. No wonder it was in William Carey's Serampore College, the first few indigenous leaders were trained. Hundreds of missionaries walked in his footsteps and followed his great example.

III. The Syndromes of Theological Education in India

1. Few Are Called But Many Are Chosen

There is a tendency these days among the seminaries to somehow "fill" their seminaries with boys and girls. "More students...more reports...more funds..." appear to be the basic philosophy. Admissions are given without sufficiently -verifying Whether one is called for full-time ministry or not.

On the one hand, owing to unemployment problems young people are rushing into Bible Schools without seriously considering their call for full-time ministry. On the other hand, seminaries are also like city buses and Bombay suburban trains trying to accommodate anybody and everybody just for the sake of a big number. Such trainees use Bible Schools as "Spring Boards" or as "launching pads" to other spheres and field of activities. Besides, a good number of them enter into the ministry considering it as a job through which they can earn their livelihood. For some, the attraction for theological training is an immediate appointment, a job guarantee, and other facilities.

2. More Theology Less Missiology

Dr. David J. Hesselgrave has stated that we are not interested in a Theology that does not missionize. Nor are we interested in a Missiology that does' not Theologized. It is imperative that Theology and Mission should go together. "Without Theology the Mission of the Church dissipates and without Mission, the Theology of the Bible stagnates."

Missionary training in India, for the most part, is a failure as far as producing evangelists and church planters are concerned because there is more theology and less missiology. Almost all the theological colleges are interested in training their students only in western theology which is scholastic, idealistic and hence dry. Unless Missiology finds its place in the curriculum theological education in India will not enable the seminaries to produce church planters. Ideally, Missiology should be integrated with the very theology of the Triune God. As the mission begins with God so Missiology should begin with Theology. Many Indian theologians think Missiology is an appendix to Theology. This must change.

3. Imported and Imputed Theology

Consciously or unconsciously we have got this into our mind anything comes from the West must be the best. Theologies ale imported or imputed into Indian theological schools from the West, therefore we teach a theology that is not born from our own experience and context. We have allowed others to articulate theology for us instead of articulating together for theological education in India. The tragedy is, the Indian Seminaries depend on the West not only for money but also for theology.

Andrew Kirk says, "Imitation of the Western academic ideal with its overemphasis on cognitive input in learning skill, threatens a really creative new approach to Theology. The task of exploring, synthesizing and continuing the first tentative beginnings of a new approach to the Theological task in the Third World still needs to be undertaken!" (Liberation Theology: An Evangelical View from Third World. John Knox Press, Atlanta, 1979. p. 206).

"Indigenization" and "contextualization" are the catch words of both the ecumenicals and the evangelicals. Today it is a fashion, to talk about indigenization and contextualization in theological seminaries. Some have gone to the extreme of identifying themselves with Hinduism, but of course not with Islam and Buddism as if Hinduism is the only religion existing in India. The so-called "Indian Christian Theology" represents only one segment of Indian society that is Hindus, so it cannot be called as the Indian Christian Theology but it can be called as Hindu converts' or Brahmin converts' theology because almost all the so-called Indian Christian Theologians are Hindu-Brahmin converts. The recent book on "Dalit Theology." is a counteraction against the work of Robin Boyd's "Indian Christian Theology." Again Dalit Theology represents only one segment of Dalits namely SCs and STs. Theologians who advocate Dalit Theology should know that "Dalits" are found in all castes including the upper castes. So, on the one hand, we face the problem of theologies being imported from the West, on the other hand, we face the problem of communal theologies coming out of the struggles of indigenization.

4. Rootless and Fruitless

Seminaries Some seminaries are started just for the sake of starting with-out clear-cut objectives. There is no linkage between the Bible schools and the church. In as much as seminaries are not rooted in a church, they are unable to bear fruit for the church. No roots, no fruits. In the modern days every Christian organization, particularly evangelicals including Pentecostals are very much interested in establishing their seminaries. In this way scores of seminaries have been established during the past ten years without proper planning. Classes are conducted as revival meetings in the church. They are neither academic nor practical but "spiritual". They never develop roots consequently bear no fruit. They hang "in-between." These are like *Dharmasala* for the unemployed youth. These seminaries produce theologically illiterate persons for the ministry. They are illiterate not only theologically but also practically. They do not know anything about their vocation for which they were called. This is why most of the graduates from this type of seminaries after graduation never become useful servants of God.

5. Experts without Experience

As R. E. Hedlund has rightly pointed out, "Perhaps one of the causes of the failure of missiological training as well as theological. studies in India is the penchant for appointing as lecturers persons who are academically qualified but inexperienced or incompetent in practical field ministries" (Evangelical Review of Theology, Vol.14—No.2. WEF, 1990, P.169). The world is full of church growth experts who have never planted a single church all their lives. So also our seminaries are full of teachers without pastoral experience. The need of the hour is experience-oriented Theological Education. Therefore, Seminaries need experts with experience. If we offer experience-oriented education, then the trainees will learn how to set short term and long term goals.

Theólogical education should be a pre-field training for those seriously called to serve cross-culturally on a long-term basis. Again this is possible only through experts with experience.

IV. Proposals for Effective Church Planting Ministry through Theological Training

1. Let us train as many as we can, engage as many as we can, win as many as we can when the doors are open for the preaching of the Gospel.
2. Let the seminaries be the "task-force" in a given area in fulfilling the Great Commission of our Lord, carrying the Gospel to the unevangelized towns and villages of India.
3. Enroll only those young men and women who are called and committed to the cause of evangelism and church planting. Let us get out of our mind that we train "Parish-priests." If seminaries have failed to give the students a vision for the lost, it is fairly impossible for them to get it when they are out of the seminary.
4. Appoint faculty members who have gone through the exciting experience of giving birth to a church themselves. If faculty members are not willing to accompany students on evangelism activities, it is not fair to send raw students out into the field. Church Planting can be taught effectively only by doing it.

5. Make sure that seminaries are idea-factories and Research centres which produce men of action and not just institutions of mere academic pursuit.
6. Establish more regional and rural Bible Schools and offer certificate level courses, for 80% of India's population live in 600 thousand villages. A graduate with B.Th./B.D. may not fit into the village situation.
7. Establish a clear and closer link and tie with the church. Seminaries should serve the church and not vice versa. Theological institutions must serve the needs of the church by producing pastors, evangelists and church planters. Where the Seminary goes, there goes the Church.

V. Conclusion

Both the Biblical basis and the historical survey of theological education reveal the fact that there is a close relationship between theological education and mission of the Church. For example, when Ziegenbalg started his mission in India, he had five mission principles, among those two were connected with training of indigenous pastors and teachers! Similarly, William Carey's missionary strategy included the training of youths for the Church and its mission. Therefore, later he founded Serampore College. Booth Tucker has rightly said that "one of his greatest achievements was the founding of Serampore College in 1819 for the training of indigenous church planters and evangelists." However, today we see theological institutions losing their original vision for which they were established.

Further history of the Church reveals many factors that have hindered the growth of the Church. One of the factors is the theological foundation relating to church growth. The apostolic and the post-apostolic Church, for example, believed in the lost-ness of man and the eternal punishment of man who is without faith in Jesus Christ. Unquestionably, the imminency of Christ's return also provided motivation for mission. These basic doctrines undergirded early missionary expansion and extension of the Church. Therefore, in order to produce church planters, theological education should be based on the right teachings of the Bible. 'The Scriptures were used by the early Church -as the divine instrument provided by the Holy Spirit for Evangelism. So, if our Seminaries want to produce church planters than they must give more importance to the Bible than theology.

17

PEOPLE GROUPS AND PEOPLE MOVEMENTS

***M. Ezra Sargunam*[1]**

I am happy to pen a few words of appreciation of Rev. Dr. J. A. David Onesimu, who served as the Principal of Madras Theological Seminary and College for 13 long years. I know him ever since he joined the Seminary in the year 1978. He was young with a lean body structure but with a smiling face. He was admired by everyone by Lecturers and students alike. My family loved him much because he sincerely and faithfully used to take tuition to our beloved daughters in the evening. His pastoral ministry started from ECI Vyasarpadi, Chennai, His devotion to the ministry made him popular in that area, among young boys who began to attend the church service with their parents. For them, he was their own elder brother of their family.

It was my privilege to recommend him for his studies in Seoul Theological Seminary (University) at the invitation of Korea Evangelical Holiness Church where he excelled in his studies as well as in learning the Korean language. He earned his Doctor of Philosophy (Ph.D.) from Asia United Theological

---

1 *The Most Rev. Dr. M. Ezra Sargunam M.A., B.D. D.D. (Lynda Vista Theological Seminary); D.D. (Senate of Serampore College) is an Evangelist, Church Planter, Pastor and the Father Bishop of the Evangelical Church of India. He is also a good writer regularly contributing articles to many theological journals and Christian magazines; and also the editor of the Mission Mandate (1992), and Mission Mandate II (2006). The present writing is a revised version of the article formerly published in the Mission Mandate, Bishop Dr. Ezra Sargunam (ed.), (Madras:Mission India 2000, 1992),180-199; and also in Mission Mandate II , Bishop Dr. Ezra Sargunam (ed.), (Chennai:Mission Educational Books,2006), 233-244.*

University, Korea; and also was awarded the Doctor of Theology, (Honoris Causa) from Kernel University, USA, in recognition to his contribution in the Pastoral ministry and the Theological education. During his tenure as the Principal of MTSC, he has added some basic infrastructures such as the Dimond Jubilee Hall & Platinum Jubilee Hall, as well as Prayer Hall, Faculty Residence, Vice-Principal's Residence along with Girls Hostel Extension, etc.

I am so happy that the Festschrift is published in honour of Dr. David Onesimu on the commemoration of his 65th Birthday. It is my prayer that God may add many more years in his life to serve Him wherever he is called to serve.

Introduction

Dr. Donald McGavran, whom I consider my *guruji*, 30 years ago said, "The fascinating story of the unique church planting ministry of ECI in India must be told everywhere in the pessimistic missionary world. What Dr. Sargunam and his colleagues have achieved during the last two decades, affirms that the Lord of the harvest is at work in several parts of India."

There are those considered to be great experts in church growth strategies who have written scores of books and produced volumes of literature on church growth principles but have never planted a church all their lives. We, from the Evangelical Church of India, do not consider ourselves as church growth experts. But, the good Lord has enabled us to be sensitive to the spiritual needs of receptive people groups and boldly go to them and work among them by evolving simple strategies of our own and adhere to the principles that we found were effective. One method that may be effective among one people group may not work among another people group.

So many church growth and mission conferences are held in our country every year. People involved in these conferences seem to exhibit a lot of interest in planting churches among the unreached people groups. But, one cannot learn swimming by just standing at the edge of a water-body gazing at it. The appropriate way to teach someone swimming is to persuade them to get into the water and as far as possible, urge them to learn the various strokes and breathing techniques on their own. The only essential rule in missionary enterprise is that the pertinent individuals or groups or mission organisations are "passionate" about their call and their "commitment" to the task of discipling and multiplying churches among the people groups of their choice is one hundred percent.

I. Friends Missionary Prayer Band: A Role Model

I have found this to be very true with leading indigenous mission organisations in the country. For example, most of the missionaries of Friends Missionary Prayer Band working in the mission-fields are not those who are necessarily trained in seminaries and have acquired degrees in the areas of evangelism, church planting, and church growth. Most of them do not have basic theological training. But, it is their faithfulness to the call for ministry and the deep sense of commitment to disciple the people group of their choice that has enabled them to win souls. It was the passion and commitment of a few Christian friends in Christ who had banded together with a serious concern for indigenous mission and had had several sessions of intensive prayer, which had given birth to one of the leading native missionary organisations of India. I don't think they would have fussed over choosing a name or having a formal inaugural ceremony for this mission agency. It was such a spontaneous movement that even today through their intensive fasting and prayer, their missionary enterprise moves forward with new doors of opportunity opening among the responsive people groups. Even today, all their prayer partners at the grassroots-level are banded together towards the ultimate cause of discipling people groups.

Therefore, it could be safely inferred that the scope for missions and church growth is not dependent on holding conferences and seminars, carrying out intensive studies on missions or writing myriad books on the subject, which sit on the shelves of libraries and bookstores gathering dust. Missionary enterprise is a serious business, entailing sacrifices for the cause of evangelism and church planting among various people groups of India.

Even today, despite the growing opposition to the preaching of the Gospel, it is possible to identify the responsive among the tribal and marginalised people and quietly carry out our church planting activities, if our hearts are ablaze with the passion for perishing souls and our commitment to evangelise them is absolute.

II. Ethnic Realities and Church Growth

1. Caste and Tribal Consciousness

Caste is a 'dirty word' in India. We should not be talking about it openly, but only practising it! There are many factors that separate the peoples of the world – language, culture, customs, and race. But, caste is the primary aspect that divides Indian society and is quite peculiar to it. The world over, even after conversion to Christianity, people continue to identify themselves with the racial, national or linguistic group they belong to. Then why do we think it is outrageous if people in India continue to be caste conscious even after conversion?

Some anthropologists and even Christian leaders have come to believe that caste is a necessary evil for the smooth functioning of society in India. Rev. J. W. Grant, an outstanding missionary had observed, "In the West, caste is commonly misunderstood and undervalued. The first-hand contact inspires considerable respect for the values inherent in caste. The caste serves in many ways as a brotherhood, exercising a moral discipline among its members and providing economic support for those who are in need. It offers the security that goes with a sense of belonging. It gives many of the satisfactions that North Americans seek by joining fraternal orders or service clubs. Exclusion from his caste is the worst disaster that can befall an Indian for it robs him not only of his material security, but also moral sanctions that mould him into accepted patterns of social living. The sudden disintegration of the caste system would probably result in moral chaos, for an Indian is not accustomed to making decisions as a self-contained individual." (J. W. Grant – God's people in India – 1959, pages 9,10).

2. Customs and Cultures

God desires to communicate with a given society through the channel of culture in which they are immersed. Man is fundamentally cultural. He is bound by the customs and cultures of his environment. Every group is very particular in fulfilling the customs and traditions existing within its ethnic unit. Evangelistic efforts should not in any way undermine or underestimate the age-long customs and traditional values within a particular caste or tribal group.

3. Family Ties

Another interesting feature of the people groups, more particularly the tribal groups, is the family and village ties. Village or family unity is also visible in the celebration of various religious ceremonies and rituals. Village unity plays a very important role in the basic overall unity and structure of the Indian village. Church planters would have to constantly bear in mind that they should not upset the structure of the village and family units in India.

4. Religiosity

Customs and cultures, literature, arts, and science or any kind of study, may it be astrology or astronomy, music or medicine, all are very much an integral part of the religious life of an individual and a community of Indian groups. This natural capacity for religion should be carefully handled in our attempt to lead an average non-Christian to the saving knowledge of Jesus Christ from his blind beliefs.

5. Conservation

People groups, whichever caste or tribe they belong to, are slow to discard their traditional customs and practices to accept new ways of life. Today, Indian societies are at a crossroads; the transition is fast affecting the thought and life of every group. Evangelistic action should aim at a change for a better hope and life in Jesus Christ.

III. Priorities in Discipling People Groups

A careful study of 'People Movements' among certain responsive peoples of India down the years reveals certain truths that set these movements in motion. Some of them are:

1. Animistic people are more open to a change of faith than people groups belonging to one of the major religions of the world.
2. Socially depressed groups dominated by an oppressive force – economic, political, religious or racial are looking for better answers to life and are often ready to accept the Christian solution.
3. Great motives for conversion are social and not theological. Rev. Vishal Mangalwadi in an interesting article (TRACI April 1981) has very vividly pointed out the fact that by and large, motivations behind conversions are social and economic rather than religious or theological.
4. People who have recently migrated are open to change and therefore to accepting a new faith. Refugees of war, flood, famine or oppression; migrating populations to newly irrigated land; rural people moving to the city in search of employment; college students away from home and servicemen; have all proved fertile fields for the Gospel.
5. Cities that are new and growing present better prospects for evangelism than old established ones. Those parts of the city that have transient or newly arrived residents have great church growth potential.
6. Certain isolated tribes, especially in mountainous or remote areas have proved responsive. They begin to realise their isolation and need to "catch up with the world." These natural desires are used by God to open their hearts to His Word.
7. The poor usually turn to God more readily than the rich, so Christian evangelists should pay special attention to the poor.
8. Those who take their non-Christian faith seriously are more approachable than the secularly-minded people to whom religion is unimportant. Rural, illiterate people often fall into this category more than their sophisticated, cynical urban brothers.
9. More conversions occur if we strategise web movements – by that we mean we encourage converts to bring the rest of the members of their families and relatives to Christ.
10. In the light of the great openness still extant among a good number of suppressed groups in our country, let us evolve a strategy to focus our attention on the responsive people to win the winnable. As Dr. Peter Wagner had told the participants in a Missions Consultation at Pattaya,

Thailand several years ago, "the people group approach is biblical, reasonable and manageable."

IV. The Missiological Factors Behind ECI's Growth

Dr. Ben Wati, the former General Secretary of Evangelical Fellowship of India made this striking statement about ECI's experiment in church planting several years ago: "There is no reason why this experiment (ECI) cannot be multiplied all over India to see much church growth in this needy land." Like Dr. Ben Wati, there are hundreds of others who feel that the ECI model and our experiment can very well be followed, and their efforts multiplied all over India, wherever people are responding to the Gospel of Jesus Christ.

I am outlining a few of the missiological factors behind the ECI Church Growth for the glory of God and to inspire others to follow this pattern.

1. Fulfilling the Great Commission in Toto

In the go...preach...baptise...teach Great Commission, our Lord has given us a package for evangelism and church planting. Many send...some go...and a few preach...but hardly anyone goes all the way and baptise the followers, continue to teach and shepherd them, gathering the new believers in groups to establish churches. ECI does that diligently and this is the secret behind our success story. We just do not confine to street-corner preaching, distribution of a tract here and a tract there or have relief and development projects just for the sake of it. We go all the way, not only in proclaiming the message but in following up the prospective enquirers to the extent that new groups of believers emerge and churches are planted. Preach...persuade...plant...is the slogan. We feel that God has given us a ministry, which is holistic and complete, in obeying the Great Commission in its fullness.

2. March of Faith

The most important factor in the ECI-OMS (initially Oriental Missionary Society, then OMS International and now One Mission Society, USA) movement is its founders, who were great men of faith, prayer patriarchs and men of vision and mission with highly cherished principles. Basically, ECI and our founding organisation OMS have had a clear vision and objective, as to our strategy in training national leaders, equipping them for the ministry, sending them to responsive peoples and planting churches.

3. Church Planting Seminaries/Bible Schools

Unlike the traditional seminaries that train 'parish priests for their denominations', the seminaries and Bible schools of ECI look beyond just producing pastors for established churches. With the closely-knit programme between the church and the seminary, the students are keenly monitored and disciplined and are made to fit into the ECI mould. Pioneer evangelism and church planting is a painful process. Not many organisations are willing to choose this; they rather opt for an easier path in the field of evangelism. We need called, committed and trained leaders to take up pioneer evangelism and church planting. While we should encourage cross-cultural evangelism, we must be able to strategise people movements only by training sons of the soil – indigenous leaders from various regions of India. We train our leaders through 3 Bible Seminaries and 10 Bible Schools run by ECI.

4. Focussing on the Responsive – the Oppressed and Suppressed

The oppressed and the suppressed people are really responsive. ECI has multiplied churches by the hundreds in the city slums amongst the scheduled castes and the villages amongst scheduled tribes. The people who are responsive today may not be responsive tomorrow. Like ECI, an all-out effort must be made by other mission agencies to disciple the most responsive.

For generations, the oppressed have always been responding to the message of the Gospel. The God of the Bible is the God of the slaves. ECI has always been identifying itself with the oppressed. Most of our churches are Dalit churches.

5. Church Growth through Transformed Lives

We have often heard pastors complain, "my church is not growing...nobody comes to my church because I preach the truth, condemn sin or any semblance of evil." But then, people could throng your church, if they sense that Christianity works in your church and they are delivered from their sins through heart-touching sermons. This is how every local church should be. The message of the Gospel becomes realistic and powerful when people see that it is operative in the lives of women and men.

6. Culture is Not a Barrier to Church Growth

ECI allows people to make a commitment and embrace the Christian faith without changing their social and cultural status, customs or traditions. Though casteism is not encouraged or promoted in the church, it is often ensured that caste does not become a barrier to people becoming Christians. It is the prime duty of the Christian evangelist to make sure that he does not upset the long-cherished customs and traditions, but effect conversions with the minimum of social dislocations. ECI strictly adheres to this principle.

It may be observed that the cross in the centre of the ECI logo is deeply entrenched in the lotus, which is supposed to be the seat of some Indian gods. The inference is that the historical Christ and the cross must ultimately take the seat of these mythological deities and thereby Christianity should become deeply rooted in the culture of India.

7. Church Growth through Power Encounter

Our Lord had ordained the twelve not only to preach but also to heal the sick and cast out demons (Mark 3.14,15). Multitudes followed Jesus because of the signs and wonders He did. The early Christians added thousands everyday to the church through miraculous healing, followed by sound preaching of the Gospel. The world is still looking for signs and wonders. The moment people see the power of God demonstrated, they begin to make a commitment and are drawn closer to Him.

When Christians go to the sick and express their love and concern for them and bring healing to them through prayer, they begin to put their trust in God. ECI gives much importance to the practice of divine healing both within the Body of Christ and among the non-Christians, where the ECI churches are located. Believers bring their ailing non-Christian neighbours to the church for healing. Childless couples are brought to the church and prayed for. In many cases, the prayers have been answered. God touches the womb and children are born.

8. The Urban Strategy – from Cities to Cities, Towns, Villages and Remote Tribal Areas

Missionary efforts, whether St Paul's or ours, when they begin in cities and towns and then spread out to the surrounding smaller villages, they make a lasting impact. By establishing churches in two or three urban centres, St. Paul claimed that he had evangelised the whole province. Ten years after he started from Antioch, he told the Romans that he had preached the Gospel of Christ from Jerusalem to Illyricum and that he had no more place to preach in these parts. The English missionary Roland Allen's comment about St. Paul, "He had really and effectively occupied the province" (Roland, Allen (1912). Missionary Methods: St. Paul's or Ours? London: Robert Scott, Page 19) justifies St. Paul's act of establishing the churches in important centres. This strategy has worked well with ECI too. People who move into the city are quite open to the Gospel in the first few years, as they look for fellowship. When the Gospel is presented to them, they are at least in a mood to listen and are also ready to make a commitment. When these young converts go back to their villages during vacations, they share their new faith with their friends and relatives. Before long, some of them show interest in the Christian faith.

This is how ECI has branched out from cities to towns and villages and has established contacts in remote areas and among the tribal people whose near and dear come to cities looking for better prospects and job opportunities.

9. Church Planting among the City Slums-Dwellers

In Chennai, Mumbai, and Kolkata, ECI has established a number of churches through day-care centres and relief and development projects by ministering to the city slum-dwellers and taking care of their temporal needs.

10. The National Missionary Arm of the Church - IMM

Every ECI believer is encouraged, challenged and motivated for direct involvement in the evangelisation of India. The Indian Missionary Movement was founded in the year 1974 with the sole purpose of serving as an indigenous mission agency for ECI. IMM sends native missionaries supported with funds raised mostly from ECI churches to the areas where the seminary students or the Every Community for Christ (ECC) teams are not able to reach. At the moment, there are more than 1000 IMM missionaries serving in 18 states of our country.

11. The ECI Partners

Another vital factor in the overall growth and development of ECI churches is the role played by some overseas and indigenous mission organisations who have been partnering with ECI for several years. ECI was founded by OMS, which continues to train leaders for the church through our seminaries in Allahabad, Chennai, and Kolkata and supports the ECI ministry through financial assistance towards the church planting activities of Every Community for Christ, the other missionary wing of ECI.

Over the years, the vision of ECI and its overall church planting capability and its holistic approach to missions have been recognised by a few other evangelistic mission organisations in the US and Korea like the Samaritan's Purse, New Directions International, International Coop Ministries, India Outreach Ministries, BILD International, Feed the Hunger, Grace Community Church, Arizona, and Korea Evangelical Holiness Church, who have been supporting the various ministries of ECI.

18

BREAKING THE 'DONOR-RECIPIENT' GODLESSNESS IN INTERNATIONAL RELATIONSHIPS

Stuart Brooking[1]

It is a delight to honour Dr. David Onesimu on the occasion of his sixty-fifth birthday by contributing to this volume. Overseas Council Australia has been a supporter of Madras Theological Seminary and Bible College for many years. It is in that context that I have come to know Dr. Onesimu and have appreciated him for the insights in his book on Dalit theology, but also for his leadership of the Seminary. It has gained in strength over the years of his incumbency.

As part of my doctoral studies and as a way to help my organisation, Overseas Council Australia, to think theologically and act in accordance with God's word I developed some key theological ideas by which to test our international relationships. While the contexts of discussion are different, I know that many of the issues raised here are ones that will resonate with Dr. Onesimu's views on the dignity of all people, and the difference that belief in our Trinitarian God makes in all relationships.

---

1 *Rev. Dr. Stuart Brooking is the Executive Director of Overseas Council Australia, a mission organisation which supports evangelical seminaries throughout the developing world with funding and consultancy. The aim is to assist each country to have a robust theological enterprise suitable to strengthen the church for mission. Dr. Brooking is also Head of Ministry and Practice in the Australian College of Theology. He has degrees in five fields and has published and edited works most recently in the fields of theological education and mission studies.*

It is too easy as a funding organisation, or indeed as an indigenous ministry, to set aside our proper status as organisational siblings in the Lord, and revert to a godless 'donor-recipient' way of relating. The 'donor-recipient' idea implies and fosters relationships that embody one organisation as greater and the other as having to be perpetually grateful.

I hope these ideas can be challenged by better theology so our thoughts, conversations, promotional material and actions are refined as we all seek to explore what our obedience should look like at the personal and organisational levels. I set forth three theological ideals to guide the assessment of our relationships. These theoretical issues are just one part of the story of course. There are many practical realities that need to be examined for us to truly submit all to the Lordship of Christ in the way we relate. Perhaps with an open conversation about these challenging ideas we can discover together how to better live as children of the same Heavenly Father, knowing the same Spirit in each of us.

1. Christology

The first of these theological concepts is Christological and has been best articulated by the Twentieth Century Dutch theologian Hendrikus Berkhof (Berkhof 1962/1977). In his seminal work, 'Christ and the Powers', Berkhof draws on the Biblical teaching, particularly in the Apostle Paul's writing in the books of Ephesians and Colossians, to enunciate a theory of institutional life. He proposes the concept that there is a supra-human dimension to organisations and institutions which can be analysed at two levels. From a philosophical materialist perspective, they display the characteristics of structures and processes which can be analysed with the tools of sociological inquiry. On top of this, however, is the concept that these institutions can take on a 'life of their own' which can work to either enhance life or dehumanise those within and without the institution. In the Pauline language, these are 'powers' and 'authorities' which can stand in opposition to the power of God. At the extreme, they become 'demonic', not only displaying the characteristics of self-justification and pretension but in their wake destroying the lives of those involved with them. The Biblical message in this context is to assert the authority of Christ over all powers. The irony of the assertion of power is embedded deeply in the Biblical rhetoric of surprise, inversion, and weakness. It is 'at the cross' that Christ subdues the evil of the world's institutions.

> "And having disarmed the powers and authorities, he [Christ] made a public spectacle of them, triumphing over them by the cross." (Colossians 2:15).

Numerous implications flow from this concept, but one implication of this Biblical theme is immediately relevant to our topic: Church leaders have the challenge to perceive the pretensions of all institutions including their own, to name their faults, and where possible, to work to make them life-affirming, not life-destroying.

In the context of the present topic, the implication of this Biblical theme will have a profound part to play.

By their very nature and purpose, one would hope that theological colleges, mission agencies, denominational organisations, and international Christian funding bodies would have at their core, a commitment to be self-analytical about the conduct of their relationships. Furthermore, one would hope that in their actual dealings with other institutions, they would have certain protocols of what to avoid and what to embrace so that the core reality of Christ's authority over these institutions is evident to all.

Such an approach to institutional activity is surely not mere idealism but reflects the consistency of core belief with outward practice. It would also reflect a commitment of the leadership of institutions to analyse not just the intent of actions, but the actual outcomes they produce. Thus, good intentions are necessary but not a sufficient criterion by which one would examine a Christian organisation's adherence to this theological concept.

Significantly, sadly, evangelicalism has been weak in the area of institutional analysis – the very task which is so needful this for this topic (Noll 2009) (p59). Historically, a critique of institutional life has been done by the theologically liberal elements of the church. In more recent decades, however, the Lausanne Movement has focussed its attention to redress this weakness and rebalance the evangelical part of the church towards this Biblical concept (Stott 1982).

In my thesis, I sought to assess the interrelationship of institutions across international boundaries so that the Western influences on theological colleges in the developing world can be critiqued. Are these relationships life-affirming? Or to put it in the theological language of Berkhof: do they submit to the lordship of Christ in the way these Christian institutions relate together?

2. Pneumatology

If the first underlying theme driving the research draws on the Christological concept of Christ's lordship over all powers, the second is drawn from a pneumatological concept. This theme seeks to draw out the implications of the Biblical concept that God's Spirit is to be understood as dwelling in each manifestation of the church. From a socio-historical perspective, it calls into question the hegemony of the Western church's dominance over all the church. This hegemony is the result of the success of its mission enterprise in the past two hundred years which sat alongside the colonising success of the West – first from Europe and then in a financial rather than classic form, from the USA.

The Biblical theme is summed up in the radical concept of the 'democratisation' of the Holy Spirit's presence among not just the leaders but all believers in Acts Chapter 2. This is part of the New Testament development in the Biblical story (Peterson 2009). This concept is frequently reiterated in the insistent use in the New Testament letters of the exalted language addressing Christians living in various places as 'saints' i.e., holy ones (e.g. Romans 1:7, 2 Corinthians 1:1, Ephesians 1:1. The implication is that their spiritual status is equal to all other believers even if, as is evident in the New Testament letters, their errant behaviour needs to be redressed.

In the context of the international relationships between Christian organisations, the danger is to hold to an implicit paternalism that traces its roots to the earlier colonial period. This institutional paternalism may be in contradistinction to more equal personal relationships between leaders from different countries, or it may, unfortunately, also be operating at that level. What is of interest is the numerous ways the West influences the theological enterprise of colleges in the developing world. The concern is that the Biblical concept may be affirmed at formal levels such as in publications and Memoranda of Understanding, but that the actual patterns of relationships may deny this idea of democratisation.

Over against a pattern of paternalism, one would hope to see evidence of mutual accountability and deference from both the Western and developing world institutions.

3. Theology

The third theological concept arises in the context of an ancient Biblical 'fund raising' program where a group of the first generation of churches were being encouraged to financially aid another group of believers. While the present topic is broader than merely the provision of funds from one group to another, that early funding drive nonetheless was based on a significant principle. The Apostle Paul wrote circa 48 AD to Christians in the Greek city of Corinth, as he explained why he wanted them to contribute funds that would be given to the poor churches suffering a drought in Judea.

> "Our desire is not that others might be relieved while you are hard pressed, but that there might be equality. At the present time your plenty will supply what they need, so that in turn their plenty will supply what you need. The goal is equality, as it is written: "The one who gathered much did not have too much, and the one who gathered little did not have too little." (2 Corinthians 8:13-15).

This third principle focuses on the perennial Biblical concept of the benevolence of God the Father who provides for his people. Indeed, Paul quotes from Exodus 16:18 reminding the Corinthian Christians when God provided for the Old Testament people in the time of their wilderness wandering, some 1,500 years beforehand. The former people experienced provision according to their need and this stands as an exemplar and confirmation of the pattern of the confidence that they should have, as they contribute to those with less.

This concept speaks deeply of the vagaries of history and for the present writer, the 'existential accident' of being a Western believer at the start of the twenty-first century. It speaks not only of the current personal responsibility of living in a wealthy country but also causes the anticipation, perhaps even the humbling expectation, that in some way there may come a reversal of circumstances in the years or decades ahead, whether in financial terms or on a broader front. This reflection is in some ways part of the background to Noll's recent book 'The New Shape of World Christianity' (Noll 2009). He seeks to explore what the experience of American Christianity and its mission activity has to say about other parts of the church throughout the world. He notes the extraordinary change in the world Christian dynamic and the success in church growth and mission in many parts of the developing world. As Noll explains, in some ways this is disorienting for American Christians who are so used to their own past religious hegemony.

As the Apostle Paul understands the issue, there is a universal commitment of Christian people around the world to act towards other Christians in a manner that provides for their needs. One element of this is that it is driven by a deep sense of equality before their beneficent heavenly Father. The sense of mutuality and humility is evident in the formulation of the obligation and thus ought to direct the characteristics of the international relationship seen in the fundraising activity in the first century AD. (The broader commitment of Christians to care for all people would be anchored in other Biblical texts such as in the teaching of Jesus and Paul regarding those in need e.g. Jesus' Parable of the Good Samaritan, Luke 10:25-37 or Paul's encouragements to wealthy people, 1 Tim 6:17-19).

Thus, these three theological concepts encourage us to seek a better understanding of the way a multiplicity of relationships function in the international theological scene.

The Christological concept enunciated by Berkhof encourages a profound examination by Christian leaders of their institutions and the ways they relate. The goal is to make the processes of institutions become life-affirming, not oppressively life-denying – being under the rule of Christ, not displaying demonic characteristics.

The pneumatological concept of democratisation encourages the recognition of the value of each expression of the church no matter in what country it is found. This concept works against paternalism in international relationships despite a history of colonial-style relationships over the past two hundred years. Rather it establishes a principle of mutuality and deference.

The theological concept of a beneficent heavenly Father leads to international relationships of mutuality and respect. This applies to financial interactions, but also speaks to the range of interactions between Western church organisations and developing world theological colleges.

So, my prayer is that this Trinitarian response will help give a Biblical framework to counteract godless 'donor-recipient' type relationships. Of course, the real challenge is not just to theorise what should be, but to analyse what is, and then have the courage to change what is wrong and establish new patterns. These patterns will be far more appropriate to a new era, but more particularly, appropriate to an old revelation. May we all have the courage to change the godless patterns in which we are tempted to exist.

Reference

Berkhof, H. (1962/1977). *Christ and the Powers.* Scottsdale, Penn., Herald Press.

Noll, M. A. (2009). *The New Shape of World Christianity: How American Experience Reflects Global Faith.* Downers Grove, Illinois, IVP Academic.

Peterson, D. (2009). *The Acts of the Apostles.* Grand Rapids, Eerdmans.

Stott, J. (1982). *LOP 21: Evangelism and Social Responsibility: An Evangelical Commitment, Lausanne Movement.*

19

EASY TARGET OR A PERSON WIDOWS AND SINGLE WOMEN IN INDIA

W. S. Annie[1]

Rev. Dr. David Onesimu is known to me from my student days. He is a soft-spoken person and a great Pastor at heart. He has contributed a lot to the growth and development of Madras Theological Seminary as a long-term Principal of it. He is an outstanding Evangelical theologian. His articles and reflections are widely used in ECI circles. It is a privilege to be part of this facilitation. I pray God to bless him and his wife, with long life, good health and all the blessings of life.

Introduction

For some time, I have been wondering, why a widow, a deserted woman, an elderly spinster, a single woman are not let to live in peace in our South Indian society. Probably, this is different in North East India and certain other areas[2] of our country.

---

1 *Dr. W. S. Annie completed her doctorate from Federated Faculty for Research in Religion and Culture, Kottayam - Senate of Serampore. Her book Globalization and Women's Subsistence Labour: A Third World Theological Perspective (Bangalore: SATHRI, 2009) was awarded the Frank Collinson award for the Best theological book of the year 2009-10. She has been in the teaching ministry for the past 24 years. Currently, she serves as Associate Professor at Union Biblical Seminary, Pune, India.*

2 A tribe in Gujarat never cares for their children. They don't have a family system. Children born to the women don't know their father. They are mostly cared by the grandparents. Another tribe in NEI, Assam, again has no family system. Children born to different men,

Case Study I: A woman who got separated from her husband, due to his infidelity, started to work, to fend for her family as her husband was not supporting her and their two children, a daughter, and a son. In her workplace, a male coworker who perceived her vulnerable condition planned to exploit her sexually. Following were the words he spoke to her to woo her into his trap.

1) *Purushan sathtetta vithavai enna peyaru. Purushan ellayana Thevidiya enna peyaru.*
   If your husband is dead, widow is your name. If you are not living with your husband (for different reasons), adulterous is your name. He also went on to question her,
2) Mother will give you food, clothing. But, for your needs of a husband (sex), can your mother help you?

Case Study II: A service staff (sweeper) who is a widow, had to work in a Christian campus from 9.00 a.m. – 5.00 p.m. She was assigned to sweep in front of the CEO's house at 9.00 a.m. Around 9.00 a.m. the CEO and his children had to go out of home, to their work. The CEO's wife (a post-graduate, retired headmistress) and her housemaid noticed the widow sweeping when her husband and children left the house to their work. They were agitated as it is a bad omen to see a widow when a person left the house for any purpose. They planned to stop the widow from doing her work on time, at 9.00 a.m. The housemaid was asked to inform the widow sweeper to come and sweep in front of the CEO's house only after the CEO and his children left home for work. Few weeks later, when the CEO found the widow sweeping at 11.00 a.m., he was furious (he always expected all his workers to do their work for him- the first). He shouted at the widow, go, go, go away! The widow understood the signal - never again, come, that late.

Case Study III: Four years before my brother passed away, leaving his wife with a six-month-old baby. Now, my sister-in-law never wears flowers on her head (protestant women don't wear *bindi*). She takes communion towards the end. This is to avoid, other women, having to face her. The belief is, if other married women, see her, they will soon become widows (lose their husband), like her.

The above three case studies are real stories. These stories raise many questions.

i. A female is an 'object' or a 'person?'
ii. Can't the society see a 'female as a person', independent, having her own rights, her own space, individuality, personality, autonomy?

---

live with their mother. They see Christianity as a religion, that looks down upon them and as a religion with superiority complex.

iii. Unfortunately, how much, marriage ruins a woman's life, for reasons, on which the woman absolutely has no control; the death of her husband in the case of a widow, and the perverted character of the husband (many other reasons) - in the case of the deserted woman?
iv. Who determines the needs of a woman? Why are others (men, other women, family, and society) so much interested in helping a woman, that too adversely?
v. How, the vulnerability (no moral support, to material and social support) of a woman is sexually exploited?
vi. Has education, Christianity - brought any change in the Brahmanic,[3] casteist psyche of our Christian communities?
vii. The above questions logically lead us to the very important, crucial question: 'what is' and 'what should be the space' of marriage in a woman's life? Can't a woman have an identity of her own, of herself, apart from her marriage?

The image of a female is ambiguous in our culture. Women are both held on a high pedestal as a goddess, on the other hand, they are trampled as a doormat. While the life of a woman is more celebrated than a male, it is the woman who is also despised and neglected. The first section of this paper deals with different celebrations related to a woman's life. The paper goes on to analysis the way widows and single women are understood and treated in our society. Indian widowhood is compared to western witch hunt. Banishing widows and single women are understood as the conspiracy of patriarchy. The second section deals with the Biblical understanding of widows and single women. Finally, the paper ends with a Christian reflection.

I. Celebrating Femininity

Celebrations are to do with the fulfillment, of the aspirations and dreams of an individual, family, community, different institutions, nations, etc. Also, a celebration is marked by an important occasion by doing something special. The onset of different phases in a women's life is celebrated in different parts of India, which we do not find in many other countries and cultures. The prevalence of these celebrations in our culture related with the fertility of a woman helps us to understand, how important these occasions are in the world view of these people

First Birthday: The first birthday of the first child (male or female) is celebrated thankfully.

---

3 Auspicious and inauspicious days, persons, times, taboos, omens, stigmas are part of the brahmanic ritualistic tradition.

Puberty celebration: Girls attain puberty between 12-16 yrs. The onset of puberty is welcomed with great festivity. The puberty celebration is an announcement that the girl is ready for marriage. It is the responsibility of the father to get his daughter married, to a man of the same caste as soon as possible. The age of marriage is also very crucial. Girls are expected to be married before they are 25 years old. If the age exceeds, the fathers of the girls are looked down, as an incapable father, who can find a suitable groom for his daughter.

Marriage: Weddings are again great celebrations. Culturally a women's life is geared towards this day when the woman is given to a man in marriage. Unmarried, single women are considered unlucky, unfortunate, etc., sexually dangerous, potentially disastrous. The single goddess Kali is also considered sexually dangerous and potentially disastrous.

Pregnancy: In fact, it is at this movement the purpose of a woman's life is fulfilled. The third-fifth, eighth months of gestation are considered auspicious when the pregnant woman can be taken to her maternal house for confinement. When a pregnant woman is celebrated, barren women are considered as 'cursed', 'fruitless' and are looked down upon and despised.

Motherhood: All religions glorify motherhood. Motherhood is a duty and the responsibility of a woman. Raising children becomes, by and large, the responsibility of the mother. Mothers are very often described as 'goddess.' In India where we have a very clear-cut division of labour, a widow mother's burden is doubled with the demise of her spouse. A woman who holds a job outside her home suffers from a 'double burden.'

Linguistic discrimination, Pejorative terms: Indian widows[4] have a very negative image in society. They are often regarded as "evil eyes", the purveyors of ill-fortune and unwanted burdens on poor families. Words in the vernacular are crudely pejorative: "witch", "*dakan*" and "whore." In Tamil widows are called as *mundachi* (headless corpse), in Punjabi, widows are referred to as randi, which also means prostitute. When *sumangali*[5] is the term used to indicate a married woman with husband and children, *amangali*[6] is the word used to refer to widows. Widows in India have a pronoun problem. The estimated 40 million women widows in the country go from being called "she" to "it" when they lose their husbands. They become "de-sexed" creatures. '*Vazhavatti*' is the term used to refer a single, unmarried spinster. Married life, for both men and women, with children is a fruitful life, the standard, the norm.

4 The feature film, by Deepa Mehta, 'WATER', clearly, depicts the plight of young and old widows, during the nineteenth century. This continues to be the plight of widows even today in many parts of India.

5 Fruitful, prosperous.

6 Unyielding, poverty ridden.

Anything other than married life, a different way of existence, is a fruitless life, a curse. Through, rumours and accusations, widows are often accused of being 'responsible' for their husbands' deaths, regarded as sexually threatening, and generally considered as inauspicious. They are assumed to have the ability to cast, 'evil eye', on others, that can bring ill fortune on others. In the case of widows, as they are deprived of a husband, they can bring ill fortune on married women.

Marriage as a sacrament: Marriage is an indispensable soteriological act. In the hierarchy of rebirths which includes the animals, the human, and the divine, a person's progress "up" (*moksha*) requires that he or she marry. Indeed, successful upward mobility implies that a soul has married frequently in past rebirths.[7] This explains the importance of marriage and the despised status of single and widowed women, in Brahmanic Hindu society.

Kali-The single (dangerous): The unmarried or independent *devis* have been described in slanderous and derogatory languages. Unmarried women are vulnerable to sexual harassment and they cannot raise a point of objection which might become counterproductive to their own moral integrity in society. Spouse *devis* are beautiful in physical and spiritual ideals. *Kali* does not fall into the patriarchal definition of beauty for the simple reason that She is not a spouse *devi*.[8] Unmarried or independent *devis* are considered to be unpredictable and dangerous. They have to be married to be kept in control. "He (Siva) must marry her (Minakshi) to tame her, to pacify her, to alleviate the threat she poses to the world order, to his order."[9]

Single women are the ones who choose to remain unmarried by choice or were not able to find a person to marry. Some women choose to stay unmarried due to health reasons (infertility, nagging physical inability). Single women are considered to be potentially and sexually dangerous. The other category of single women is transgender. Transgender women are the most ridiculed, ill-treated, deprived and sexually exploited human beings. They are stripped off their humanity and seen as lesser than cattle. Single women are assumed to cast an evil eye on other women, as they are deprived of all the joy of being a 'female.'

---

7 William P. Harman, *Sacred Marriage of a Hindu Goddess*, (Delhi, Motilal Banarsidass Publishers, 1989), 136.

8 Santanu K. Patro, A *Feminist Reading of Womanhood: 'Dark' Kali Tradition* (Delhi, ISPCK: 2005), 318, 322.

9 William P. Harman, *Sacred Marriage of a Hindu Goddess*, (Delhi, Motilal Banarsidass Publishers, 1989), 134.

Widowhood as 'social death:' Uma Chakravarty's[10] sociological analysis of widowhood examined the cultural and ideological construction of widowhood. Uma Chakravarty explored two related questions: why widowhood in India is constructed as social death (that is, why widows are treated as having no social, individual or sexual identity) and why, despite a common underlying ideology, different castes treat widows in different ways. Uma Chakravarty summarised the underlying logic of why widows are expected to remain celibate and chaste and to lead ascetic lifestyles in this way: widows, especially young widows, are seen as sexually dangerous (as having the potential to disrupt, pollute, and discredit their dead husband's lineage and society at large) and must, therefore, be 'neutered' or unsexed. The defacing of widows is particularly marked among the upper castes, such as the havik brahmans in Karnataka, in which women have no socially valued role other than their reproductive role. Among the lower castes. such as the chuhras in Uttar Pradesh, in which women are valued for their productive as well as their reproductive role, widows are allowed to remarry and remain incorporated in the social and economic order. Chakravarty concluded that the patriarchal formulations of appropriate behavior for widows of high castes and widows of low castes reflected, and were structurally integrated into the ideology and material relations of the caste system: a system in which the upper castes could restrict their own reproduction in order to reduce pressure on the physical resources under their control while encouraging the lower castes to reproduce (albeit while castigating the sexual mores of the lower castes) in order to increase the human resources under their control.

Building on Chakravarty's analysis, Abha Bhaiya offered a comparative perspective on widows and other single women based on an analysis of patriarchal control over women's sexuality, fertility, labour, and property and of patriarchal images and definitions of womanhood. According to Bhaiya, the patriarchal ideology which underlies the identity and construction of womanhood is mitigated by class, caste, and ethnicity but, primarily, by marital status. The purpose of patriarchy is to control women through the institution of marriage. When her husband dies, a woman's identity and situation change dramatically. Among the upper castes, where women are valued only for their reproductive role and where high fertility is not valued, widows have no legitimate identity. Among the lower castes, where women are valued for their productive role and fertility is more highly valued, widows, are needed for their powers of production and reproduction. However, Bhaiya argued, widowhood should not be allowed to overshadow the problems of women within marriage or the problems of other single women. All single women

10 Marty Chen and Jean Dreze, "Recent Research on Widows in India: Workshop and Conference Report", *Economic and Political Weekly*, 30 September 1995, 2437.

face common problems, including not being recognised as heads of their own households, being seen as available for domestic labour in the household in which they live and have no social or cultural occasions on which to come together.

Discrimination of Widows

India has the largest recorded number of widows in the world—33 million (10 percent of the female population, compared to only 3 percent of men), and the number is growing because of HIV/AIDS and civil conflicts. "Fifty-four percent of women aged 60 and over are widows, as are 12 percent of women aged 35-39. Remarriage is the exception rather than the rule; only about 10 percent of widows marry again." India is perhaps the only country where widowhood, in addition to being a personal status, exists as a social institution. Widows' deprivation and stigmatization are exacerbated by ritual and religious symbolism. Indian society, like all patriarchal societies, confers social status on a woman through a man; hence, in the absence of a man, she herself becomes a nonentity and suffers a social death. *Sati* (widow burning) is the ultimate manifestation of this belief. Widow remarriage may be forbidden in the higher castes, and remarriage, when permitted, may be restricted to a family member. Further, a widow, upon remarriage, may be required to relinquish custody of her children as well as any property rights she may have. If she keeps her children with her, she may fear they will be ill-treated in a second marriage.

Ritual and religious symbolism: Restrictions on residence, dress, diet and social intercourse force a widow to a life in the shadows affecting both her physical and mental health. Cruel mourning rites may confine the widow within a designated residence for many months or years. Life-threatening mourning and burial rites are prime examples of human rights violations that are justified by "reliance on culture" and "tradition."[11]

Inhuman, desacralising rituals: In few castes,[12] when the husband dies, on the funeral day, the womenfolk are not allowed to go to the burial, cremation ground. Meanwhile after the corpse of the husband is removed. The widow is decorated as a 'bride', flowers on the head, glass bangles are covered on hands, new *thali* (yellow thread with *mangal sutra*) is tied, new sarees are draped day after day for sixteen days. On the sixteenth day at 3.00 am, early morning the women folk gather. The bangles are smashed, the *metti* (finger rings in the legs) removed, the *thali* snatched, the colourful saree stripped, the bindi erased. After this ceremony, the widow is supposed to only wear simple earrings and chains. The plight of widows in brahmin families is the

11 World Bank, *Voices of the Poor. Case Study 9: Widows* (Washington, D.C., World Bank, 2000).

12 Certain families that are progressive forbid such practices.

worst. They are not allowed to attend the wedding and any auspicious, happy occasions. In contrast to this, a woman with her husband and many sons is put on a pedestal and worshipped. On the other hand, a barren woman, a widow is seen as 'unclean', 'garbage', 'inauspicious' in a community.

Thali (mangal sutra), flowers and *bindi* (red mark on the forehead) that a woman wears are a symbol of a married woman. A widow is deprived of all these symbols. In the 16th day ritual (*Karumari)* a widow is stripped off of all the symbols of a married woman.

European witch hunt and Indian widowhood: The medieval conception of women in Europe, shares much with the corresponding medieval conception of widows in India. In both cases, a perennial attribution of secret, bountiful, malicious "power," is made. Women are anathematized and cast as witches because of the enduring grotesque fears they generate in respect of their putative abilities to control men and thereby coerce, for their own ends, male-dominated Christian society. Whatever the social and psychological determinants operative in this abiding obsession, there can be no denying the consequential reality of such anxiety in medieval Christendom. Linked to the theological traditions of Eve and Lilith, women are perceived as embodiments of inexhaustible negativity. Though not quite quasi-literal incarnations of the Devil as were Jews, women are, rather, their ontological "first cousins" who, like the Jews, emerge from the "left" or sinister side of being.[13]

The medieval witch-hunts have long been depicted as part of a "war against women" conducted exclusively or overwhelmingly by men, especially those in positions of central authority. Deborah Willis notes that, "more polemical 'feminist accounts' are likely to portray the witch as a heroic protofeminist resisting patriarchal oppression and a wholly innocent victim of a male-authored reign of terror designed to keep women in their place."[14] In fact, the stigmatizing, victimizing, and murdering of accused "witches" is more accurately seen as a collaborative enterprise between men and women at the local level.

Historical studies on gender bias in science should, in turn, lead to a clearer understanding of gender bias in 'science and religion.' In *A World without Women*, David Noble describes the clerical ascetic culture that first came to dominance in the High Middle Ages as "a world without women..., a society composed exclusively of men, forged in flight from women, and intent upon remaking the world in its own half-human image." The scientific revolution of the seventeenth century in part represents a secular form of clerical authority. Though women finally entered the academic world in the nineteenth century, they were "only to be confronted by another clerical restoration, in the form

13 Katz, The Holocaust in Historical Context, Vol. I, 435.

14 Willis, Malevolent Nurture, 12.

of male scientific professionalism that betrayed the same misogynistic and, indeed, monastic habits of the clerical culture it superseded."

However, it must not be forgotten that many widows are enormously resourceful and resilient and go on to manage successful creative lives, both personally and professionally. Several widows and single women have become political leaders and even heads of State. Widowhood can, for some—prove to be a period of enriching economic independence and increased status. Female-headed households can be relatively well off, composed of younger generations of working men and women. An energetic entrepreneurial widow can gain respect as the main decision-maker, a role that she may never have enjoyed in marriage. Matriarchal households can be strongly self-supporting. Even in old age, few widows' economic contribution to the family as household managers and carers of grandchildren and the sick helps to protect them from the negative attitudes directed towards older women. The above, instances, helps us to understand that the stigmatizing and ostracizing widows and single women in India and other parts of the world was to keep women in their place.

Conspiracy of Patriarchy

1. *Uneasiness with Single Female:* In the Roman Catholic family, to dedicate one child, to the church ministry is considered a blessing. But, this practice is awfully criticized by non-Catholics. Catholics are accused of sending their daughters to ministry as the catholic families don't have enough funds to buy a groom. Letting, the daughter has a single status, by the parents, throughout her life, is seen with great contempt in the nearby family circles and society.
2. *Excessive romantisisation:* The film industry focuses on the 15 – 30 years age group. 80% of our movies are in romance. Cinema's romantises the relationship between a male and a female, that the women are carried away by its emotional character. Films that depict the sad facts of life, reality, are very less. I have just come across one mother who was not that enthusiastic about her younger two daughter's marriage. She was not enthusiastic as her first son-in-law who was a terrible drunkard committed suicide leaving his widow (22 yrs) and three sons, within four years of marriage. The mother didn't mind her younger two daughters remaining unmarried as her first daughter's life had already, turned tragic.

   Films, by and large, do not depict the reality of women's life. If films would show the reality of women's lives, the rush to get married, the uncritical marriage enthusiasm would go down. Women will be better prepared to face life, realistically, with all its difficulties, pain and sorrows.
3. *Women as carriers of Tradition:* From case study II, we can see how women happen to be the custodians of tradition. It helps women in two

ways. 1) To exert power over the 'other', in otherwise male-dominated church society and household, women are secondary citizens. In Tamil it goes well, 'edu pombalaiga vishayam." These are women's matters. In other words, it is to tell that men need not interfere into women's issues or women's space. 2). Power Over: It is interesting to note how married women can have an upper hand over widows (widows may have high economic, social and political power. But their religious status is very low). Both the CEO's wife and the housemaid had an upper hand over the widow. Though the housemaid had a lower status (job) than that of the sweeper widow, the married housemaid had an upper hand, religiously. These kinds of power-play go unnoticed, unchallenged, untheorized, very often. 3). The postgraduate, Christian woman, knows well, that, Brahmanic traditional notions such as auspicious day, person, time, taboos, omen, stigma are part of the brahmanic ritualistic tradition, that is rubbish and nonsense. But, she uses this against the widow, as a tool, to have power, control over the 'other', the 'vulnerable.' The housemaid who can never speak against the high status (job) widow, uses these prejudiced, discriminatory notions against the widow, for her advantage. These kinds of prejudiced, discriminatory notions become very handy. People can choose to use it against the 'other' or not to use it.

Unless the vulnerable, here the widows, have extra courage, boldness, perseverance, it becomes very hard for them – widows to digest it. (My mother, became a widow when she was just 32 years old. A Mudaliar man, who lived one house away from our house, used to work in the same factory, where my mum worked. He used to spit, when he saw her, when he was leaving his house. My mother did not understand,[15] why he did 'spit off' seeing her, being strange to the Tamil casteist culture and notions. Always, one feature that I noticed after a public gathering like a marriage, or a funeral or puberty celebration or birthday celebration was that, towards the end of the programme, we didn't know how it happened, but it did happen, the widows (5-6) got together[16] and discussed their matters. It was in one such gathering it was told to her, that the mudaliar man kept spitting at all widows. It was then my mother understood the disrespectful behavior of the Mudaliar towards her. The widows gathered, joined in cursing the Mudaliar who used to scratch his body, (under armpits, lower abdomen, and chest) due to high diabetics. They cursed him that he should scratch more, suffer more). Widows happen to be easy targets in our highly, patriarchal society. As a widow has no owner, everybody tries to exert control over her. These prejudiced

15 Deliberate Spitting, at the sight of a person, is to disrespectful the person.

16 Birds of the same folk gather together.

discriminatory notions against widow's works as an advantage for men. It helps patriarchy, as wives would like to have their husbands at any cost (even when they are HIV positive, STD infected, gangster, have extramarital affairs, addicts, gambler, etc). The inhumane treatment of widows and single women (case studies) informs other women to never assert their space, their rights. Many married women struggle in unhappy marriages, due to the above-seen stigma and prejudice, which they would dare not to face after divorce. Prabha Sridevan a former judge of the Madras High Court comments that "for this reason(s), the majority of women in India suffer in silence within an abusive marriage, even a severely abusive one."[17]

4. *Crippling effects of unfounded moors:* In case study III, the young widow did not want to face other married women. Widows do end up with more time (the time they share for, with their husband, husband's guests, etc) after the death of their husband. But, how will they spend and utilize their extra time? Any, job that happens to be of a leadership category involves facing people. These unfounded ideas cripple a widow, shy's her away from growing, making use of her potential, being helpful to people, etc. These theories are masterstrokes of Brahmanic patriarchy to keep widows (women) in place.
5. *Last to be hired and first to be fired:* Widows with children are considered a liability by the employer. As a widow has to shoulder the responsibility of both the parent, with which the widow struggles at the domestic front, employers feel a widow can't give herself 100% to the work. Thus, a widow happens to be the last person to be hired and the first person to be fired. Today, millions of the world's widows, of all ages, endure extreme poverty, ostracism, violence, homelessness, ill health and discrimination in law and custom. A lack of inheritance and land rights, widow abuse and the practice of degrading rituals and symbols make them the most vulnerable.
6. *Widows, Religious Fundamentalism and Vote Bank Politics:* In 1986, Rajiv Gandhi, with one eye on the fundamentalist Muslim vote, overturned a Supreme Court judgment that had granted monthly maintenance to elderly Muslim widow Shah Bano. The move was one of the major triggers for the rise of BJP.[18]

17 Prabha Sridevan, "In Search of the Ordinary woman", *The Hindu*, Chennai, 11 Oct. 2013, 14.

18 Times Tribute to an Uncommon Man, *Times of India*, 27 Jan. 2015, 11.

II. Widows and Single Women in the Bible

Widows in the Old Testament are said to be under the special care of the Lord. In Exodus 22:22 there is a strong warning not to afflict the widow. Old levirate laws are written for the protection of the widows. Isaiah exhorts people to plead for the widow and cries out woe upon them who make widows their prey (Jeremiah 7:6, 22:3, 49:11). Zechariah speaks comfort for the widow. Malachi says God will be a swift witness for those who oppress the widow.[19]

When we analysis the contribution of widows and single women in the Bible, their contribution has been more in the public sphere as they were spared from their domestic, private sphere of service, to serve in the public domain. It is a patriarchal conspiracy, of our age, to put the contribution of motherhood of women in a pedestal and glorify it, but to trample, brand widows and single women as witches, whores, beggars, dangerous, inauspicious, impure etc. This in a subtle way pushes women to take up motherhood as it is, looked high by society, on the other hand it also keeps widows and single women (by choice or force) to keep a low profile.

Though the Bible also puts motherhood on a pedestal, it doesn't demean widows, as we find in our Indian culture. Widows are well accepted and their service and contribution are well recognized.

Jephthah's daughter, Zelophehad's daughters: All these young, unmarried women are unnamed in the Bible. They have their identity through their father's. Jephthah's daughter is a crude example, where her life had to be cut short to fulfill her father's promise to God. The woman submits, but unwillingly. Zelophehad's unmarried daughters were given the inheritance of their father as they were considered as 'persons' worthy of a dignified livelihood.

Women of Midian: Women of Midian, after their men had been slain in the war, were taken as captives by the Israelites. Moses ordered that the women who had been married (now widows) be killed. But, the virgins be saved and given to the Israelites (Num 31:9). This story helps us see how women of antiquity were regarded not as persons but as things, just like cattle and flocks and household goods.

Lydia and Paul: Bible commentators believe that the the Bible does not say whether she was married or not, but it is easy to suppose she was a widow, who devoted herself wholeheartedly to her business. But, after Paul had come to Philippi, she had a new objective, and that was to learn more about the things of the spirit.

Phebe - A Deaconess at Cenchrea: Paul describes Phebe 'as 'our sister', 'a servant of the church which is at Cenchrea', 'a succourer of many', 'a

---

19 Edith Deen, *All of the Women of the Bible* (New York: Harper & Brothers Publishers, 1955), 350.

succourer of myself also.' In the early Church much was made of service, little of office, and it was more of an honor to be referred to as a servant than as a deaconess. Her goodness and sympathy, her loyalty and kindness, and her industry and trustworthiness marked her as a woman whose ministry inspired all who came into her presence.[20]

Philips's daughter: Philips's daughters were four unmarried daughters of evangelist Philip, who were also prophetesses. Because of their association with the greatest Christian leaders of their time and their own rare spiritual endowments, they became illumined expounders of God's words.

III. Christian Response

By and large, during the "Mass movements" in the nineteenth and twentieth centuries, it was the deprived sections of the Indian society that got converted to Christianity. After, two to three centuries of practicing Christianity, the Christian churches haven't outgrown the discriminatory practices like caste system, patriarchy, etc. Widow discrimination is one such that has received less attention in the academia and wider public. Though widows and single women are not that awfully treated, as in the Hindu communities, however, widows and single women are discriminated in the Christian communities also. Widows and single women have a negative image in society.

Ideal image of woman	Negative image of woman
Fertile female	Unfertile girls, transgender
Fair skinned	Dark skinned
Married woman	Unmarried woman, single woman
Married woman, with children preferably, with 'son'	Issue less married women
Married woman living with husband	Deserted woman, divorcee
Married woman is auspicious	Issueless woman, widows are inauspicious
Married woman	Widow

From the above observations, there are three different ways the widows and single women are treated in our Christian communities.

i) In humans: Brahmanic Hinduism treats widows as unauspicious.
ii) Indifferent: Christian communities struggle between Hindu traditional and Christian values. It is mildly harsh in the treatment of its widows.

20 Edith Deen, *All of The Women of the Bible* (New York: Harper & Brothers Publishers, 1955), 232.

iii) Considerate: Syrian Christians don't discriminate their widows, as widows. (Widows can continue to wear their thali, *mangal sutra* even after the death of their husbands. They are not expected to remove their thali, when Christian widows in many other parts of India are expected to remove their thali). Widows enjoy all the respect and privilege like any other married woman.

In a family, the responsibility of maintaining and sustaining the family is shared by both the spouses. But, when one spouse (male) suddenly disappears there is a vacuum in terms of emotional attachment, the unfinished responsibilities, day to day maintenance, social obligations income generation for the family, etc. One spouse can't fulfill all the duties. This requires external generous, non-exploiting, helping hands. During Biblical times, as women were much secluded from education, widows much needed extra care. This made the widows vulnerable, her fatherless children much more vulnerable. It is this vulnerability that makes widows a soft, easy targets. The biblical, partial God commands the Christian community to care for them, not to treat them as 'unclean, 'garbage."

The bible very clearly talks of widows, fatherless, strangers. The grain of the sabbatical year was meant for the widows. How is our church catering to the needs of the widows. Has the church questioned this evil practice on the Karumari day (16th day). Living in states like Tamil Nadu, Kerala and Andra Pradesh, I found the status of widows. unpleasing.

Hans Staffner gives a beautiful description of Pandita Rama Bai's life and how she lost faith in her Hindu Religion.

> "Our parents had unbounded faith in what the sacred books said. They encouraged us to look to the gods to get our support. But, the gods did not appear to us. After years of fruitless service, we began to lose our faith in them and in the books which prescribed this course and held out the hope of a great reward to the worshippers of the gods.'[21]

The next great disappointment came when she realized that the Hindu scriptures and Sastras gave no hope of salvation to women:

"My eyes were being gradually opened; I was waking up to my own hopeless condition as a woman, and it was becoming clearer and clearer that I had no place anywhere as far as religious consolation was concerned."[22]

Pandita Rama Bai left Hinduism because she found it useless to follow all that the Vedas asked them to do. Also, it was useless because women had no

21 Hans Staffer, *The Significance of Jesus Christ in Asia*, (Gujarat Sahitya Prakash: Anand, 1985), 158

22 Ibid., 158.

place in it. She had the courage to leave Hinduism and embrace Christianity. Christian church and its widows, single women should have the courage to undo inhuman superstitions of Brahmanic Hinduism, which has strongly encroached Christian minds.

1. *Baptism Versus Desacralising rituals:* Baptism is a ritual that symbolizies the purification of sins and makes him/her God's child, a member of the institutional church. Baptism is the initiation of a person into the body of Christ – the Church. On the other hand, in the desacralising ceremony the widow, becomes an inauspicious person, something equivalent to that of "unclean" in the Old Testament times. Acts chapter 10 teaches us that there is nothing called unclean in God's creation. Christian communities should prohibit such ceremonies. Widows should be treated with dignity.
2. *Citizenship Versus Purberty celebration*; Girls attain puberty between 12-16 yrs. The onset of puberty is welcomed with great festivity. The puberty celebration is an announcement that the girl is ready for marriage. All children when they are eighteen become full citizens of India. Citizens of India have all rights enshrined in the Indian constitution. The patriarchal traditions see women as an heir (son) producing, raising machine. The constitution sees women as a 'person' who has rights that they can choose to live by. Social reforms and collective action are much in place in our country.[23]
3. *Wedding ceremonies*: Wedding ceremonies, desecralising widowhood ceremony strip off all the dignity, personhood from a female (girl – woman). These celebrations can also become occasions that empower a woman. Puberty celebration can be an occasion when, a girl is taught, helped to take the responsibility of responsible adulthood. Weddings can be occasions were partnership is taught, to both the partners.
4. *Church - widows and single women:* Many single women face common problems, including not being recognised as heads of their own households, being seen as available for domestic labour in the household in which they live and have no social or cultural occasions on which to come together. This explains the reason, why women outnumber men in the church. Church is a space where they can come and be a participant

23 Social Reform and Collective Action: The recommendations from the session on social reform and collective action' included the following: (1) Women need an identity as autonomous individuals and as citizens of the country. (2) Women require a time and space at the grass roots level to meet, organise, and unleash their own power for change. (3) The state should support rather than oppose women who act as agents of change, and protect them from repressive violence. (4) Non-government organizations should be sensitised to examine the actions they are taking to support widows, their own role in perpetuating patriarchy. (5) Existing schemes need to be redesigned to include mechanisms whereby women have better control over resources.

irrespective of their identity. Widows and single women form a network among themselves that supports and helps them in crisis. Many churches also have projects and programmes for such women. The 16th day Prayer meeting, after the funeral, can be occasions where the widow is encouraged to lead a life on her own. Widows raise their daughters with much difficulty. But, during their marriage, it is some male relative (brides' brother or uncle) who gives the brides hand to the bride groom. Widows have to be honoured, being asked to give their daughter's hand, to the groom.

5. *Holy Spirit*: S. K. Datta thinks that, to a Hindu, the external world is unreal and that s/he is always oppressed by the idea that the consciousness behind what is seen and sensed is the unseen world continually exerting its influence *(dhosham)* upon the life of mankind.[24] Contrary, to this oppressive consciousness, Christians should have the consciousness that the Holy Spirit, a spirit of freedom, liberty, justice and peace guides, counsels its people in all circumstances of their life. There is no place for any influence *(dhosham)*, on people lead by the Holy Spirit.

   Marjorie Suchocki defines *sin* as a violation of relationships. In Christ's life, God's love was embodied and expressed. In him we see at work a transformative power stronger than death, a power that can bring reconciliation into our lives – that is *redemption*.

   The *goal of prayer* is openness and responsiveness to the divine call. The Spirit leads us in unexpected ways of healing our brokenness as individuals and as a society. Prayer can also be an occasion of wonder and gratitude for life as a gift and a time of self-examination and confession of our failure to respond to the call of inclusive love.

   Responsible selfhood avoids dualism (body/soul, matter/spirit, etc). Christian tradition has too often encouraged a negative asceticism, an alienation from the body, and a concern only for the salvation of the soul. But, process theology acknowledges our embodiment and asserts that bodily events enter into each moment of experience. Process writers encourage respect for the body but also assert human freedom, self-determination and the power of personal and social goals beyond bodily gratification. Responsible selfhood is a holistic concept that includes but transcends the body.

6. *Eucharist*: Sharing the bread and wine symbolizes sharing all the resources, by all in the community. It also symbolizes the equality of all who partake and are a part of the Body of Christ - The church. The

24 M. M. Thomas and P. T. Thomas, *Towards an Indian Christian Theology: Life and Thought of Some pioneers*, (Tiruvalla: CSS, 1998), 134.

unscriptural, cultural notions that a widow can bring misfortune on other married women, have to be challenged and eliminated. Instead, the Church should extend a helping hand, to women in need. The church should also make use of the enormous potential and contribution the widows and single women can offer.

20

HUMAN RIGHTS AND CHRISTIAN'S RESPONSIBILITY

Jacob Devadason[1]

I am happy to lay myself open to the charge that the Church is always on about rights in general and particularly in human rights. I will unashamedly talk about human rights in Church because when I read the Bible, I find that it is always on about human rights, social justice, and love. Rights, after all, has always been an instrument of the power equation. The more you talk about human rights the more you are talking about equality and justice; the less you talk about human rights then the less you practice justice and equality. So, it is little wonder that the Bible, which has so much to say about the use and abuse of power, has to say so much about human rights and social justice and how we handle it, both as individual Christian and as a Church.

This essay provides an account of Churches and Christians taking their faith seriously: drawing alongside people of God impoverished by the negation of their responsibility to give rights and space to their fellow believers and that attitude creates a crisis in our Churches and the minorities within the Churches become subject to exploitation and marginalisation. Exercising human rights and social justice shows the Biblical principles, and the Christ-like compassion, which are spurring so many into action.

If history teaches us anything whether it's slavery, whether it's women's right to vote, civil rights in the United States, Apartheid in South Arica, these

1 *Rev. Dr. Jacob Devadason is an Anglican priest, currently serving as an Incumbent/Vicar of St. Catherine's Church, Chester Diocese.*

struggles are only moving forward when decent men and women stand up and say: 'Enough is enough. No more. We are prepared to put our lives on the line if necessary. We are prepared to go to prison if necessary.'

But, within the secular world and the faith community, we have seen extraordinary levels of courage over the centuries, where people were willing to say: 'If it means I have to break an unjust law, I'll break an unjust law. I will carry that criminal record as a badge of honour.'

Power never relinquished itself to the oppressed. There is no example where those with power, substantial, structural power one day woke up, read the Bible, Bhagavad Gita or Quran, the Torah, and said: 'This is wrong.' Power is only ever relinquished when change becomes irresistible. We have witnessed such civil disobedience in Sudan recently, where people occupied the army headquarters and to leave until the dictator of many decades left. This was one of the most repressive societies – like Egypt under Mubarak. When the Egyptian revolution was happening in Tahrir Square in 2011, who would have thought that this regime was supported by the full might of the US state and the UK state? Mubarak had the distinction of meeting six presidents of the United States because he had been so long in power.

How can one describe the present India in history? The age of technology? The post-war period? The secular age? Postcolonial India? Emerging superpower? The global IT hub? For the great majority of people today it might be more appropriate to call it the return of the 'New Dark Age'. It depends on one's perspective, and often on one's experience. India is on the rampant of human rights violations which escalate under the present incumbency of the Central government. CAA and NCR are planned and designed and manufactured Acts to suppress minorities and especially aiming against the Islamic community.

Seen in terms of the promotion and observance of human rights, our nation indeed a dismal place. The Preamble of the Universal Declaration of Human Rights affirms that 'recognition of the inherent dignity and the equal and inalienable rights of all members of the human family is the foundation of freedom, justice, and peace in the world.' It recalls that in the years immediately before 1948 when the United Nations adopted the Declaration, 'disregard and contempt for human rights have resulted in barbarous acts which have outraged the conscience of mankind,' and calls for 'the advent of a world in which human beings shall enjoy freedom of speech and belief and freedom from fear and want... the highest aspiration of the common people.'

Since then, the world has not been, even for a week, free of war. What is called 'armed conflicts' these days have occurred less frequently in the developed countries, but elsewhere they have become more brutal, more destructive, more inhumane – and more mindless – than ever. It is not only individuals who suffer; entire peoples and nations are subjugated and pillaged by the powerful. Different forms and shapes of colonial rules continue in many places, neo-colonial domination is on the increase in post-colonial nations. More and more countries are ruled by democratically elected rulers turned out to be dictators which frequently declare a 'state of siege' or 'state of war' or other states of emergency which trend to become permanent. The 'enemy' in these cases is not a foreign invader but the people, who represent a threat to those who seek to maintain their position of power through brute force. In country after country, freedom of the press is replaced by absolute censorship or controlled by corporate companies who are part of the pro-government and most of the press become the mouthpieces ruling governments; press media and visual media both are competing with each other to serve as the propaganda secretaries for the ruling parties which is absolutely outrageous. Freedom of assembly is prohibited; freedom of movement is limited by strict curfews; arbitrary arrest is common; fair trails are replaced by summary tribunals; caste oppression is rampant; millions are unemployed, underfed and without minimal health care... This is indeed a 'state of war' – war against the common man, woman, child, aged and the vulnerable.

The preamble to the Constitution declares India to be a Sovereign Socialist Secular Democratic Republic and a welfare state committed to secure justice, liberty, and equality for the people and for promoting fraternity, dignity of the individual and unity and integrity of the nation. In different parts of India humanity lives under a reign of terror. Torture occurs more frequently and its more severe today than in the 'Dark Ages' and most recently when our nation was under British raj. It has become a systematic practice in many States of absolute control over people's ideas and actions. And it is not only the poorer areas of the country which are affected. Similar problems exist in the North-East regions of India. Racial, linguistic and cultural minorities and masses of foreign labourers are driven to see themselves as oppressed 'nations' within our societies. The law, as it applied, is often overwhelmingly at the service of the wealthy and influential. Technology has been provided easy means by which people's right to privacy is grossly violated.

Such is the state of our country. And in sharp contrast to the world envisioned in the UN Declaration. The nation is now crying for human rights and human dignity. In order to enjoy freedom, social justice, and human rights people are on the march of civil disobedience. Civil disobedience is necessary because our government and political leaders have a common medical problem, which is that they all have a problem of hearing. If you are going to get through their cognitive dissonance and their inability to see the facts – that we are running out of time, that inequality and violations of human rights are getting worst, levels of hate are rising – then it is incumbent on citizens to put pressure on them, first nicely though petitions, signature campaigns and so all and then when they' re not willing to respond, people have a moral responsibility to break up unjust laws that restrict the legitimate right of citizens to express themselves. The three freedoms, of association, assembly, and expression, are shrinking drastically.

To say that the Churches have a responsibility here is a bland truism. But what is the nature of the responsibility, how is it to be carried out? The Ecumenical movement has been concerned over human rights for decades, especially as regards religious liberty and rights directly related to it. However, it has become apparent that many of our traditional conceptions, approaches, and praxis models are hopelessly inadequate to cope with the dramatic situation the churches are facing today.

This does not mean that the ecumenical movement has been inactive. Christians and Churches in many countries are wrestling with this dilemma. In some of the worst national situations, they have emerged as the staunchest and most courageous defenders of the rights of the people. But one consequence of this is that leading Christians have sometimes become targets of repression and suppression. They are calling for a new sort of solidarity from churches and Christians in the ecumenical fellowship.

Some Churches and Christian human rights organisations have been engaged in a serious, critical review of quantitatively new human rights situation in the world, and of traditional Christian and ecumenical approaches and perspectives to human rights. Consultations are being held in cooperation with regional church leaders, and national seminars or study programmes developed on the initiative of the Churches and ecumenical bodies. Together they have represent a combined ecumenical effort to strengthen the Churches' capacity to identify human rights problems in their societies with greater clarity and to act upon them, and to discover new, more effective forms of active solidarity with fellow Christians and others particularly the minorities who require support in their struggle for greater human dignity and respect. The problems are great and frightening.

In these situations, how we as Christians can live and act. The Biblical way of living with our fellow humans is based on the truth… 'Love thy neighbour' is associated with the Parable of the Good Samaritan. Most of us are familiar with the story, which encapsulates naivety (the attacked man), violence (the bandit's actions) callous indifference (the priest and Levite), and compassion (the Samaritan). For me, the most pertinent sentence in the parable is the law expert's question: 'And who is my neighbour? There is little doubt that our 'neighbour' is a person (or people) in need. But how do we identify that person? And, what is the best way of assisting them?

The Indian government's hostile policy on CAA, NRC, and NPC led to the ongoing injustice to the minority communities has helped spur a spike in religious and race-related hate crime in our country. I want to know where the Church's voice has been in these matters. Our Bible is full of stories that God has raised human rights heroes; and prophets who have raised their voices and concerned against social injustice and political vendetta. Being a good neighbour involves affirming the diversity that exists in the genes on our Indian Churches and redoubling our efforts to ensure they become places where human rights, social justice, and equality exist within Church structures.

Human rights and justice are not just words but a praxiological concept which demands to be practically worked out in our Church life and Christians way of lived out their faith. As echoed by the prophets in the Bible, the absence of human rights and justice amounts to the absence of Yahweh God. The concept of human rights and social justice within the wall of our Christian community and families are not a postscript but the mainstay of Christian faith. As Jurgen Moltmann (Moltmann, 1998) expresses, the theology which emerges out of the passion for God's reign which is 'Just' cannot be restricted to doctrines, dogmatic and faith but is functionalised in everyday life in this very society, It should disturb and wake us up from the slumber. It should provoke us to move from a culture of silence to a culture of transformation. It should be the directive principle of our mission concretely realising the Kingdom of God in our midst. The Church as a community of disciples is a sacrament, which demonstrates a new liberated humanity as opposed to the oppressive, unjust and exploitative social, cultural, economic patterns and structures. It should foster human relationships and offer an alternative society of radical egalitarianism.

Moreover, we need to love our global and neighbours of friendly faiths – those who are part of our wider and extended family. It's true that 'charity begins at home' but it does not end there. If we truly follow Jesus' commands to love God and to love our neighbour, we must also acknowledge that the special relationship we have with the Almighty God must be replicated with one another, especially those in need our compassion. We as the Church of God called to challenge the evil regimes and structures and power which keep those who are made in the image of God in systemic poverty and injustice.

Church as a community must move towards building strong relationships. These strong relationships are the core to a successful route to implement human rights and justice which ultimately leads to peacemaking. Many believe that we just have to deal with the "issues" and causes of conflict, and then everyone will get along – but that is to overlook that issues in its totality. There will always be a difference, and that difference will sometimes lead to conflict within the Church – it is through good relationships and respect that we can learn to build a future together and learn from these conflicts rather than let them destroy the Church community.

Praxis of Human rights and justice are the practical work of building the Kingdom of God. God here on earth, in every place, every situation, and every relationship, we can reflect on the life of Jesus the ultimate model to learn how to give due rights and respect to others. The stories and things we've learnt come from the dual act of reading the Bible and learning from our community, and that is a practice I'd encourage all of us to undertake whatever situation we end up in. Violence, exploitation, oppression, injustice, and marginalisation are pervasive in our homes, communities, and Churches, in the systems and structure of our society and so many parts of the world – so we all have a role to play in being agents of human rights and justice our world so urgently needs. As we as a Christian step into this role we become the agents of change and transformation. I particularly love what St. John has to say about faith and social action, in his New Testament letter: "Let us not love with words and tongue but with actions and truth." I think we could all do well to read that, and then get on with it.

One of my favourite verses in the Bible is Micah 6:8 which includes the line: 'What does the Lord requires of you but to do justice, and to love kindness, and to walk humbly with your God?, We do this when we love our neighbour. By doing this we see God in the eyes of every human being we meet.

21

THEOLOGY OF MARRIAGE AND FAMILY CONTEMPORARY CHALLENGES FOR ITS SUSTENANCE

R. Paul Sigamony[1]

My association with Rev. Dr. J. David Onesimu began in 1981 when both of us were appointed as pastors in the Evangelical Church of India while he was serving in Chennai and I was ministering in Mumbai. God gave me an opportunity to work with him between 1989 and 1991 when he was made District Chairman of North Maharashtra District in Mumbai. He is a very humble servant of God, soft-spoken and friend of all. His heart for the ministry of the Lord and his passion for souls are appreciated. I acknowledge his servant leadership, willingness to serve, and honesty and faithfulness in all his responsibilities through my association and observation. His contribution to the church and the theological community is enormous. As he celebrates his 65th birthday, May the Almighty God be with him, protect him with good health and long life and use him more and more to achieve greater heights in his life. In this occasion, I am indeed happy and count it as a privilege to write an article under the topic: "Theology of Marriage and Family: Contemporary Challenges for its Sustenance."

---

1 *Rev. R. Paul Sigamony is an Assistant Professor at Allahabad Bible Seminary in the Department of Christian Ministry (Counselling). Currently he is a doctoral candidate at Sam Higginbottom University of Agriculture, Technology & Sciences (SHUATS), Allahabad.*

Introduction

In the post-modern era, humans have developed in various areas of their life and have achieved tremendous heights in all fields. People have become more literate and the economical level of most people has gone up. There have been significant changes in the field of communication and remarkable developments in the field of science and technology. At the same time, never before in the history of humankind, the institution of marriage faces challenges concerning its sustenance. The rise in the number of divorce cases substantiates it. There are various causes for this issue. This paper tries to find out some of the challenges which shake the sustenance of marriage in India

1. Understanding of Marriage

Marriage is a fundamental reality in human society irrespective of ethnic, religious or sociocultural backgrounds. Marriage in religious terms is the total union of two people in body, mind, heart, and spirit. Marriage may be defined as a lifelong and exclusive state in which a man and a woman are wholly committed to living with the other in a sexual relationship under conditions normally approved and witnessed to by their social group or society.[2] Marriage is a lifelong union of a man and a woman entered by their mutual and public consent.[3] Confucius said, "Marriage is the union of two different surnames in friendship and love."[4] It is being united and living together to grow in unity of mind, spirit, and body. Hence, the institution of marriage is of paramount importance in any society.[5]

Marriage can also be defined as a legally recognized social contract between two people, traditionally based on a sexual relationship and implying a permanence of the union. Marriage is considered to be divine in India.[6] Mazumdar defines marriage as a socially sanctioned union of male and female or as a secondary institution devised by society to sanction the union and mating of male and female for purposes of establishing a household for procreation and proving care for the offspring.[7] Marriage is a cultural universal

---

2 Lengmi Lungleng, *Interfaith Marriage: Pastoral Concern* (Delhi: ISPCK, 2019), 3.

3 David J. Atkinson, "Sexuality," *New Dictionary of Christian Ethics and Pastoral Theology*, ed. David J. Atkinson, et al. (Nottingham: Inter-Varsity Press, 1995), 77.

4 G. Felix, "Arbitration and Reconciliation in the Context of Pastoral and Marriage Dispute or Conflict", *Vaikarai* 18/ 1&2 (Jan-Dec, 2013), 192.

5 John Philip, "Marital Adjustment among the Wives of Alcoholics in Relation to Codependency and Selected Socio Demographic Variables," *TMAIC Journal of Counseling* 1/1(2014), 71-85.

6 Phanenmo Kanth, "Understanding the Shift in Contemporary Indian Family Life: Challenges for Family Therapy," *Sathri Journal* 8/1 (April, 2013), 13-38.

7 Abraham Christdhas, "Hindu Vivaha and Varna," *Marriage, Family and Church,* edited by Jesudason Baskar Jeyaraj (Bangalore: Christian Forum for Child Development, 2014), 152.

phenomenon. It exists in every society with varying forms. It is also the basic reason for the perpetuation and continuity of society and generation. Marriage is subject to the reciprocal influences of social, cultural and political forces.[8] People of all cultures and religions including those who do not believe in God participate in the institution of marriage.[9]

Sociologists are interested in the relationship between the institution of marriage and the institution of the family because, historically, marriages are what create a family, and families are the most basic social unit upon which society is built. Both marriage and family create status roles that are sanctioned by society. Human beings have the fundamental right to marry. This is considered natural by civil and religious authorities of all major religions since human beings are created in such a way that human life is ordered to the partnership of men and women and whoever is endowed with such givenness has a natural right to lead such a life.[10] J. C. Wynn defines marriage as, "A culturally accepted union of a man and woman in a husband-wife relationship as well as rules that recognize an order of sexual behavior and legalize the function of parenthood."[11]

Marriage is not just an escape route to sexual gratification, but a love relationship founded on mutually reverential respect, total mutual trust as its building, and on constant, mutual caring or concern as its roof.[12] Marriage in a way is a voluntary nature of coupling. The couples are in the marriage due to their own interest as for instance in India, women are on in marriage despite incompatibility between the spouses because in most cases wives are dependent on their husband for financial security. Women in India continue to be in marriage because traditionally they are expected to continue to be in the family, look after the husband, and children and if needed the parent-in-law even under the most deprived and cruel conditions.[13]

Marriage remains intact until one of the two people involved is separated by death. In other words, marriage is meant to be extremely strong and unbreakable and expected to be permanent and long-lasting.[14] Marriage is a

---

8 Alex Minichele Sewenet, Fasil Merawi Tessagaye and Getnet Tadele. "Interreligious Marriage: Social and Religious Perspectives," *Imperial Journal of Interdisciplinary Research* 3/6 (2017), 355-362.

9 Kostenberger J. Andreas, *The Bible's Teaching on Marriage and Family* (Washington: Family Preacher's Counseling, 2011), 3.

10 S. Appathurai, *Marriage is Forever* (Mumbai: St. Pauls, 2012), 23.

11 J. C. Wynn, "Marriage," *Dictionary of Pastoral Care and Counseling*, edited by Rodney J. Hunter (Nashville: Abingdon Press, 2005), 676.

12 S. Appathurai, *Marriage is Forever*, 247.

13 Manju Goel, *Marital Disputes and Counselling* (New Delhi: APH Publishing Corporation, 1997), 73.

14 P. K. Tandy, *In the Background of Marriage* (Delhi: ISPCK, 2006), 8.

social as well as a religious structure and is therefore subject to the reciprocal influence of social, cultural and political forces.

2. Types of Marriage

There are different types of marriages practiced across the world which depend on the cultural backgrounds and traditions of various societies and countries. India is a sub-continent with many cultures, customs, languages and ethnic groups. Hence, in each sphere of her life, we find diverse customs in practice. Marriage is also no exception to these generic norms. While one type of marriage is acceptable to one section of the society, it may not be accepted by another section due to their orientation and understanding of marriage. Few types of marriages are discussed here as i) *Polygyny* is that form of union in which a man marries more than one wife at a given time.[15] ii) *Polyandry* is a form of marriage in which a woman is married to two or more men at the same time.[16] iii) *Monogamy* is the practice of a man having one wife at a time. In such a system, one cannot think of having a second wife or husband as long as the life-partner is alive.[17] iv) *Polygamy* is the system where one person has two or more spouses at a time. A man is allowed to take another wife even when the first wife is still alive without divorcing his first wife or getting a divorce from his wife. This is the opposite of monogamy.[18] v) *Exogamy* marriage between individuals sharing a certain degree of blood or affinal relationships. This is known as exogamy which means marriage outside the group. A man must not only seek a wife out of his own clan but also must avoid the clan of the entire grandparent. It seems that in ancient times, people living in one household were not permitted to intermarry; but when the household broke up, the prohibited range of marriage was also contracted.[19] vi) *Endogamy* is marriage within the class. Endogomous is the custom of marrying only one's own group, such as clan and faith.[20] Sometimes, restrictions are imposed that the other partner is to be selected from the caste or class to which the first partner belongs. Hence marriage with out-of-group members is prohibited. Understanding of endogamy and exogamy differs from society to society. In some societies, endogamy connotes marriage within the ethnic group regardless of religious

---

15 K. M. Kapadia, *Marriage and Family in India* (Delhi: Oxford University Press, 1981), 97.

16 Salomon K, "Marriage; A Sociological Perspective," 29.

17 Phanenmo Kanth, "Understanding the Shift in Contemporary Indian Family Life: Challenges for Family Therapy," *Sathri Journal* 8/1 (April, 2013), 13-38.

18 Kanth, "Understanding the Shift in Contemporary Indian Family Life: Challenges for Family Therapy," 13-38.

19 Christdhas, "Hindu Vivaha and Varna," 154.

20 Lengmi Lungleng, *Interfaith Marriage: Pastoral Concern* (Delhi: ISPCK, 2019), 8.

differences of individuals.[21] vii) *Experimental Marriage* has been referred to as cohabitation. It allows two people to test their compatibility before they settle down as permanent life partners. By cohabitation, they can know each other intimately and can decide whether they can enter into marriage permanently or not.[22] This type of marriage is also called as a companionate marriage or trial marriage.[23] viii) *Same-Sex Marriage* happens between man and man or woman and woman. Some countries, even some staunch Christian countries, have legalized same-sex marriage. Homosexuals demand equal rights and opportunities just like heterosexuals including the right to marriage and cohabitation. The XIV General Assembly of the Synod of Bishops held from 4-25 October 2015 firmly stated that same-sex marriage does not even remotely resemble true marriage for various reasons. Recently, the Union Government of India has decriminalized article 377 by legalizing same-sex marriage in India.[24] ix) *Live-in-Relationship* is a phenomenon in recent decades that is spreading rapidly. Live-in-relationship is an arrangement of living under which the couples who are unmarried live together to conduct a long-going relationship similarly as in marriage. In this relationship, an unmarried couple lives together under the same roof in a way it resembles a marriage, but without getting married legally.[25] A live-in relationship is contrast to marriage and family values because young people come together to cohabit with someone before marriage or without marriage.[26]

As society keeps changing, understanding about marriage is also shifting. It differs from society to society, region to region, culture to culture, religion to religion and from tradition to tradition. Every type of marriage has its own scope and limitation in any given period and context.

3. Marriage and Religion

Marriage has a central place in any individual's personal life, social life and community life. Traditionally, marriages are arranged in religious and cultural settings. Many of the religious beliefs, rituals, and cultural practices are very

---

21 Alex Minichele Sewenet, Fasil Merawi Tessagaye and Getnet Tadele, "Interreligious Marriage: Social and Religious Perspectives," *Imperial Journal of Interdisciplinary Research* 3/6 (2017), 355.

22 Pradhan, "Marriage: Its Impact on Family Life," 64.

23 L. Sahayaraj, *Marriage and Family in the Plan of God: Reflections of Saint John Paul* (New Delhi: Christian World Imprints, 2014), 19.

24 Lawrence, "Family: An Agent of Evangelization," *Indian Theological Studies 53/1* (March, 2016), 109-121.

25 http//www.legalserviceindia.com/articlelive-in-relationship-211-1, html, accessed August 8, 2018

26 Richard P Olson & Joe H. Leonard Jr. *Ministry with Families in Flux* (Kentucky: John Knox Press, 1990), 84.

much linked with marriage ceremonies and customs.[27] Since most people of India are very much connected with one or other faith, religious ritual and ceremonies are always followed in marriage. Religious priests and leaders are consulted before finalizing marriages and fixing dates for marriage. At the same time, every religion has its own understanding of marriage.

3.1. Hindu Understanding of Marriage

According to Hinduism, human life has four stages or *asrama*. They are *Brahmacharya*- student life; *grahastha*- householder; *vanaprashta*-forest dweller and *sanyasas*-renunciant. Each successive stage covers twenty-five years. The four ends of human beings are righteousness (Dharma), prosperity (*artha*), sensuous pleasures (*kama*) and spiritual liberation (*moksa*).[28] To demonstrate the centrality of marriage to this whole structure, they must understand the concept of *sanskaras* or sacraments in Hinduism. Despite the differences in the sacramental duties of the various classes of Hinduism, marriage is common to all.[29] A man who has not taken a wife has not fully perfected his personality and must be regarded as incomplete and imperfect. For the Hindu, marriage is also a sacred institution whereby man and woman become one spirit. Hindu marriage is also a social duty and in the Vedic period, it was a moral religious obligation as well. Marriage and the offspring of male children was the only possible way in which a man could repay his debt to his ancestors.[30] According to the Vedas, "Marriage is a union of bones with bones, flesh with flesh and skin with skin, the husband and the wife become as if they were one person."[31]

3.2. Islamic Understanding of Marriage

There are two main terms used to refer to marriage in Islam: nikah and zawaj and both are found in quran. The difference between the word nikah and zawaj is linguistic. As far as the usage of the word nikah and zawaj in Quran and sunnah is concern both words are used with the same meaning. Nikah incorporates the meaning of the act of physical union between spouses as well as the legal and social institution.[32] The Arabic word for marriage is 'nikah' which refers to contract. It is not merely an ordinary contract that people

---

27 L. E. Sahanam, *Belonging but not Believing: Interfaith Marriage* (Delhi: ISPCK, 2009), 15.

28 Arvind Sharma, "Marriage in the Hindu religious tradition," *Perspectives on Marriage: A Reader*, edited by Kieran Scott and Michael Warren (New York: Oxford University Press, 1993), 412.

29 Raj Bali Pandey, *Hindu Sanskaras* (Delhi: Motilal Banarsidass, 1969), 154.

30 Selvanayagam, *A Second Call: Ministry and Mission in a Multifaith Milleu*, 299.

31 Manju Goel, *Marital Disputes and Counselling* (New Delhi: APH Publishing Corporation, 1997), 65.

32 S. S. Waheedulla Hussaini Quadri Multani, "The Islamic Institute of Marriage," 17-25.

have in normal and ordinary transaction. This is because the Qu'ran uses the terms 'Mithaqun Khalitun' which denotes a contract of marriage. The words 'Mithaqu Khalitun means a strong covenant or agreement.'[33] According to Islamic view point, marriage is basic to family formation and Muslims are encouraged to marry, because not only marriage practiced by prophet, but God has instructed people to marry.[34]

Celibacy is discouraged and marriage is encouraged in Islam. For example, 'Marriage is of my way," the prophet is reported to have taught, as well as, "When a man has married, he has completed one half of the religion", and "Whoever is able to marry, should marry." Such stimulus from religious teaching has made marriage the goal of every Muslim and caused a considerable amount of social pressure to achieve the end of every member of the society.[35] Hence, it is very clear that Islam advocate marriage for its community members. The Qur'an permits a Muslim man to have four wives provided he has the means to care for them and the mind to treat them equally.[36] However, only a small portion of Muslim men practice polygamy.

3.3. Christian Understanding of Marriage

God created man and woman. Male and female he created them and he named them Adam, which means humankind. After making Eve from the bone of Adam, God united them as husband and wife. Adam told that Eve was bone of his bone and flesh of his flesh. The purpose of God was to make them one body.[37] Yahweh told them to be fruitful and multiply and fill the earth.[38] Hence it is clear that the institution of marriage was ordained by God himself. Marriage is not a purely human institution despite the many variations it may have undergone through the centuries in different cultures, social structure, and spiritual attitudes. These differences should not cause the couples concerned to forget the truth and the meaning of Christian marriage. For Christians, marriage is more than a natural institution; it was created by God and elevated

33 Zahidul Islam, "Interfaith Marriages in Islam and Present Situation," *Global Journal of Politics and Law Research* 2/1(2014), 36-47.

34 BelkeisAltareb, "The Practice of family and Marriage Counseling in Islam," *The Role of Religion in Marriage and Family Counseling,* edited by Jill Deba Onedera, (New York: Routledge Tailor and Francis Group, 2008), 91.

35 Lois Lamya Ibsen al Faruqi, "Marriage in Islam," *Perspectives on Marriage: A Reader*, edited by Kieran Scott and Michael Warren (New York: Oxford University Press, 1993), 398.

36 Selvanayagam, *A Second call: Ministry and Mission in a Multifaith Milleu*, 307.

37 Genesis 1:28; 2:22-23.

38 Michael G. Lawler, "Marriage in the Bible," *Perspectives on Marriage: A Reader*, edited by Kieran Scott and Michael Warren (New York: Oxford University Press, 1993), 11.

by Christ himself as the symbol of divine and human love. Hence, marriage is sacred and it is a gift of God.[39]

The aim of Christian marriage is to become one flesh. This involves both the leaving and the cleaving to one another. "One flesh" talks about the unity, equality and oneness in every way of their life which includes mental, physical, emotional, social, spiritual, economical and psychological of their day to day life until death separates them from this world. In the sacrament of marriage a baptized man and woman mutually and exclusively give themselves to each other in an act of irrevocable consent. Through their vows, they are joined by Christ in union that will be marked forever by respect, concern, compassion and commitment.[40]

3.3.1. Marriage as Covenant

Marriage is a sacred covenant between a man and a woman, which is instituted by the Creator. It is a visible sign of God's love and commitment to his people.[41] Once this marriage covenant is brought into existence through the act of giving and receiving the consent in freedom before two witnesses in the form required by the law, it is exclusive and permanent.[42] Sexual relationship is a meaningful part of marriage and it is meaningful only within marriage. Both parties have conjugal rights and responsibilities. In marriage a man and a woman enter into a fully personal union, not just a sexual or genital one. They enter into a union which establishes not just a legal relationship, but a blood relationship which makes them one person.[43] Since it is a covenant, without personal consent of both man and the woman there is no marriage. This consent cannot be imposed, but the mutual exchange of consent must be a free act of the will on the part of the spouses.[44]

3.3.2. Theology of Marriage

The family has its origin in marriage and it is the ultimate fulfillment of the aim of marriage. In primitive time, the emphasis was on the family as a community, the only aim being the continuation and the growth of the greater community, and the individual was almost entity absorbed into the family at the cost of his own identity. In the early centuries, Christians lived and moved within the traditional religious and social milieu of the place and marriages

39 Antony Chundelikkatt, *The Marriage Covenant* (Mumbai: St. Paul's, 2013), 66.

40 Jill D. Onedera, "The Practice of family and Marriage Counseling in Catholicism," *The Role of Religion in Marriage and Family Counseling*, edited by Jill Deba Onedera, (New York: Routledge Tailor and Francis Group, 2008), 41.

41 Ephesians 5:31-32.

42 S. Appathurai, *Marriage is Forever*, 250.

43 Michael G. Lawler, "Marriage in the Bible," 11.

44 Pinto, *Law of Marriage and Matrimonial Reliefs for Christians in India*, 7.

were conducted according to the local customs and laws. So, there was no distinctive church practice as we see today.[45] Marriage becomes a sacrament or means of grace not by any external ritual but by becoming instruments of the saving love of Christ through mutual love, sharing and submission. The husband and wife are growing, sanctifying, loving, and bearing witness together, for which marriage is assign of reality.[46] The primary purpose of God creating family is human companionship. It is in other words, the wellbeing or welfare of the spouse. They should not only be able to satisfy their physical and emotional needs, thereby, but they should also be able to understand each other well, relate to each other, surrender themselves to each other fully and share the responsibility with each other well.[47] Although the church recognized the sanctity of marriage right from the apostolic period, its understanding of the institution has developed as a pastoral response to particular theological and cultural challenges.[48] For Christians, marriage is a sacred covenant, which has to be observed and maintained throughout their lifetime. Hence faith life has a lot to do with sustaining marriage and family under all circumstances.[49]

3.3.3. Jesus' Understanding of Marriage

Jesus spoke of marriage in Mark 10:2-12 and affirmed that in the light of God's intention, marriage is a significant institution which must not be taken lightly. Thus Jesus expressed that marital relationship is fulfilling God intention on human beings.[50] Even though Jesus has not directly dealt with the institution of marriage, the church teaches about marriage on the basis of Jesus' view on family and marriage that is expressed in the Book of Genesis.[51] It is the will of God that man and woman should become one.[52] The early church remained faithful to the teachings of Jesus Christ, who said about the permanence of marriage. This concept of mutuality does not allow one to sexually exploit the other; it demands respect for the desires needs and emotions of the other. Since

---

45 Chundelikkatt, *The Marriage Covenant*, 103.

46 Kuttiyil, "Marriage as a Sacrament," 24.

47 Lawrence, "Family: An Agent of Evangelization," *Indian Theological Studies* 53/1 (Bangalore: St. Peter's Pontifical Institute, March, 2016), 109-121

48 Chundelikkatt, *The Marriage Covenant*, 104.

49 Varghese, eds., *A Study Book on Counseling*, 155

50 Richard P Olson & Joe H. Leonard. Jr, *Ministry with Families in Flux* (Kentucky: Westminster/John Knox Press, 1990), 14.

51 Genesis 2:18-24.

52 George Mathew Kuttiyil, "Marriage as a Sacrament," *Christian Family in Transition, Continuity and Discontinuity*, edited by Koshy P Varughese, (Faridabad: Dharma Jyoti Vidya Peeth, 2012), 23.

marriage is a command from the Lord it is permanent from its conception until the death of one of the partners.[53]

4. Marriage in the Indian Civil Code

India is a diverse country. Therefore it has several laws under which marriages are solemnized. In addition to various legal provisions amendments were added taking into consideration of different religions in India.[54] Marriage and divorce in India are governed by personal laws of the various religious groups. There are three main religious groups in India: Hindu, Muslim, and Christian.[55] When the Indian constitution was adopted in 1950, the government also adopted a non-interference policy in the personal laws of its religious communities. Indian government tolerates it as a result of its constitution guaranteeing the freedom of religion to all citizens and groups. However, in concern with the age it is the same in all religious groups. It says, "The age of the man intending to be married shall not be under twenty-one years and the age of the woman intending to be married shall not be under eighteen years."[56] Moreover, with the impact of modernization, the existing laws were given new outlooks and freedom of the individuals is given utmost importance over communitarian aspects.[57]

The Christians in India are a minority community and the church is governed by different personal law. Therefore the Christians in India to a large extent have to rely on the codified law such as, 'The Indian Divorce Act, 1869', 'The Indian Christian Marriage Act, 1872', 'The Indian Succession Act, 1925', and 'The Indian Special Marriage Act, 1954.'[58] Justice K. T. Thomas, Supreme Court of India in his forward to the book Laws applicable to Christians in India observes that, "The Indian Christian Marriage Act and The Indian Divorce Act was enacted to meet the needs of the British subjects of European domicile who were residing in India and the same could be available by the Christian in the country as a whole." According to him, both the laws were defective in Indian context and the efforts made by the Government of India for the Revision of Law relating to marriage and matrimonial causes in respect of Christian have not been successful until the Special Marriage Act 1954 was made. The Indian Christian Marriage Act strictly follows monogamous marriage. Therefore according to Christian Marriage Act, when the second

53 Chundelikkatt, *The Marriage Covenant*, 66.

54 Thomas, "Sociological Challenges of Marriage and Family in India," 166.

55 Pinto, *Law of Marriage and Matrimonial Reliefs for Christians in India*, 13.

56 Ibid., 265.

57 Thomas, "Sociological Challenges of Marriage and Family in India," 150-172.

58 Pinto, *Law of Marriage and Matrimonial Reliefs for Christians in India*, 14.

marriage is solemnized by the church authorities, it is void if one of the parties in the so-called marriage has a spouse alive.[59]

5. Marriage Breakdown and Divorce

Marriage is a divine institution. Bible says, Marriage should be honored by all."[60] Yet with all this, when one make a critical analysis of the present status of marriage and family life, it is distressing to note that the very bases of both the institutions are called into question. Today, families and marriages find themselves in profound crisis due to erosion of fundamental values such as permanence of marriage, unity and sanctity of family life.[61] According to God's plan, man and woman together form the most fundamental unity of humanity the family, based on marriage, togetherness, companionship, mutual help and parenthood are part of God's for marriage.[62] But today more than ever, broken marriage is a common problem. Even though the divorce rate in India seems to be less in comparison with international statistic, yet it is on increase.[63] Though causes for the marital breakdown are many, Civil Law under the Matrimonial Causes Act of 1857 for the first time recognized dissolubility of marriage on the ground other than adultery. It was realized if marriage can be dissolves on account of adultery, causes such as cruelty and desertion could also be valid grounds for divorce. Accordingly, grounds for various reliefs in marriage are provided both in Cannon law and Civil law.[64]

The Indian Divorce Act 1869 has taken up guilt or fault theory of divorce. On the other hand, divorce by mutual consent is provided under the Special Marriage Act 1954. Breakdown theory has also been put forth as a third alternative for dissolution of marriage. In the irretrievable breakdown of marriage, the criterion is of non-resumption of co-habitation after a decree of judicial separation or non-compliance to a decree of restitution of conjugal right for certain duration.[65]

---

59 Pinto, *Law of Marriage and Matrimonial Reliefs for Christians in India*, 8.

60 Hebrews 13:4.

61 Lawrence, "Family: An Agent of Evangelization," 109-121.

62 Christine Gomes, *The Bible and your Family* (Chennai: New Leader Publications, 2014), 29.

63 Lawrence, "Family: An Agent of Evangelization," 109-121.

64 Pinto, *Law of Marriage and Matrimonial Reliefs for Christians in India*, 50

65 J. Dominion, *Marital Breakdown* (London: Darton, Longman & Todd, St. Paul's Publication, Indian Edition), 1988.

6. Family

The word family is derived from the Roman word 'famulus' which means 'a servant.'[66] In Roman law, the word denoted the group of producers and slaves and another type of servants as members connected by common descent or marriage. Family is a group defined by a sex relationship sufficiently précis and enduring to provide for the procreation and upbringing of children.[67] Family is a community of people living together in an environment which is a centre of healing, a place where one can live, where one can admit one's frustrations, stupidities and anger to people who do not have to retaliate.[68] Family is a unit of interacting and communicating persons enacting the social role of husband and wife, mother and father, son and daughter, brother and sister.[69] The role is defined by the community, but in each family they are powerfully reinforced by sentiments, partly traditional, and partly emotional arising out of the experience.[70]

Family is the first cell in the social structure, the very first union, which is indispensable and without which there are no children, men, women and even no human society.[71] Family is the most significant and basic institution of any society.[72] Family is the first school of learning about love and life. Family is the a where one experience hardship, tragedies, joy and happiness that prepare him/her for a better human being, who can understand one another, love one another and pave for a better future life. Family is a nurturing place where people learn about their abilities, practice giving and receiving love, care and dare to dream what they might become.[73]

Family is a unique institution that has various functions directed towards evolving persons, communities and society at large.[74] Family has always been at the functioning of Indian society and even contemporary people continue

66 Evangelin Laji, "Family and its Mode of Communication," *Kerala Theological Journal* 10 (June, 2018), 82-93.

67 Christdhas, "Hindu Vivaha and Varna," 148.

68 Marie Mignon Mascarenhas, *Family Life Education and Value Education in the New Millennium* (Bangalore: Centre for Research Education Service & Training for Family life Promotion, 1999), 8.

69 Bryan Strong, *The Marriage and Family Experience: Intimate Relationship in a Changing Society* (Belmond: Thomson Wadsworth, 2008), 43.

70 S. Appathurai, *Marriage is Forever,* 22.

71 Mascarenhas, *Family Life Education,* 8.

72 George Mathew Kuttiyil, "Marriage as a Sacrament," 22.

73 Mascarenhas, *Family Life Education,* 9.

74 Joseph George, "Marriage and Family Counseling," *A Study Book on Counseling* (Tiruvala: Christava Sahitya Samiti), 78.

to take pride in the centrality of family life.[75] In the midst of great social, economic and political changes over the centuries, India has a long heritage of stable family life and structure.[76]

According to the document of The Second Vatican Council, "Family is the primary and fundamental school of humanity". Pope Francis says in his encyclical Gaudium Evangelii: "Family is the fundamental cell in society where we learn to live with others despite our differences, and to belong to one another; it is also a place where parents pass on their faith to their children." Mother Teresa said, "What can you do to promote peace? Go home and love your family."[77] Hence it is clear that family is the source of peace and harmony in the society. Everybody comes from a family, and family is the first natural society with un-derived rights. Society is transformed by the family.

7. Challenges

In the midst of great social, economic and political changes over the centuries, India has a long heritage of stable family life and structure. The spirit of family solidarity has remained a sustaining power, which has provided meaning to the daily lives of our Indian people.[78] However, in the age of electronic media, television and computers in remote areas, the Indian family is being exposed to ideas, ideals and lifestyles that are challenging the structure and stability of the contemporary family unit. Today's Indian families are encountering complex and disturbing problems that include rampant poverty, disease, overcrowding, water and air pollution, migration of families and individuals, lack of available employment and vocational opportunities, and a gradual weakening of age-old traditions and erosion of values among the individuals. More recent challenges that Indian families are encountering include, marital strains and dissolution, parent-child conflict, various forms of violence both inside and outside family, substance abuse, and so on.[79]

---

75 Rita Choudhury, "Understanding Family Life in India," *Family Life Education in India: Perspectives, Challenges and Applications*, edited by Aparajit Chowdhury, et al. (Jaipur: Rawat publications, 2006), 32.

76 Mascarenhas, *Family Life Education*, 9.

77 Lawrence, "Family: An Agent of Evangelization," 109-121.

78 Marie Mignon Mascarenhas, *Family Life Education*, 19.

79 Aparajita Chowdhury," Family Life Education in the Indian Socio-Cultural Context," *Family Life Education in India: Perspectives, Challenges and Applications*, ed. Aparajita Chowdhury, et.al, (New Delhi: Rawat Publications, 2006), 3.

7.1. Lack of Intimacy

Intimacy means the state of being closely familiar with another person.[80] When Gen 4:1 says that Adam knew his wife, it is understood as having known each other intimately and had sexual intercourse. One of the purposes of Christian marriage is to satisfy one another's emotional and sexual feelings. Marital love has to be supported by conjugal love.[81] Conjugal love involves a totality, in which all the elements of the person enter-appeal of the body and instinct, power of feeling and affectivity, aspiration of the spirit and of will. Marriage would be empty and dysfunctional when it no longer contains and manifests their love with one another in a more intimately.[82] The husband and wife are intimately bonded to each other. They have to care for each other, trust, love, respect and enjoy each other to grow in intimacy.[83] After getting married, very often the priorities of the couple changes and their love become cold, which leads to lack of intimacy in their family life.

7.2. Mismanagement of Finance

Money is very essential in the day to day activities of the family life. In the traditional family system mostly, husbands were the breadwinners and the wives were home makers who did not have income of their own. As the transformation has taken place in the family system to nuclear families and migrated to towns and cities, it became inevitable that both husband and wives need to work and earn to meet all the family needs. In this situation, if husband and wife have a mentality of 'my money', and 'money', problem would arise. The economic issues concern who earns, who will spend, how to spend, how much to spend and how to budget must be decided by both of them. Problems can be from any ankle of the economic sector causing deep or trifling distress.[84] Economic stability is an important factor for marital harmony. There need to be a guarantee to supply the essential marital needs. Unmet needs bring about frustration and are quickly reflected in all sectors of marital life.[85] Plans for future investments, purchasing of house, buying expensive things for home, and going for a tour must be decided by both to reduce tension and unwanted disagreements in the family life. Lack of common planning about the use of

---

80 William Stewart, *Making the Most of Your Relationship,* (Mumbai: Better Yourself Books, 2007), 120.

81 Antony Chundelikkatt, *The Marital Covenant* (Mumbai: St. Pauls, 2013), 111.

82 Antony Chundelikkatt, *The Marital Covenant* (Mumbai: St. Pauls, 2013), 137.

83 Vernon Vaz, Yolande Pereira, *Creating a Happy Family,* (Bangalore: Asian Trading Corporation, 2005), 31.

84 D. John Antony, *Types of Counseling* (Nagercoil: Anugraha Publications, 1996), 117.

85 Gideon Sobhanam, *United to Adjust: A Sacramental Theology of Marriage for Marital Counseling* (Delhi: ISPCK, 2007), 96.

money and property, lack of basic knowledge of the facts about each other's earnings, are areas of economy which cause tension and need to be talked out If money matters are not dealt properly in the family, the very sustenance of marriage itself will be at the danger.

7.3. Non-Priority to Family Members or Not Spending Quality Time with their Spouses

For the daily sustenance the couple may work but the amount of time spent even after the office hours on the official work may be an indication for the other spouse, perhaps wrongly, that the other has no consideration for his or her interests. Again apart from work, the time of recreation spent outside the house individually will raise suspicious in the mind of the spouse.[86] Couples who know each other before marriage and have spent time with one another either over mobile, social media or face to face may also feel that after getting married they have come cold. Many spouses complaint that their spouse do not spent value time with him or her any more as they used to in the beginning of their relationship. That can create a kind of suspicious or doubt on their partners. They may even doubt whether they have married a right person or not. People who are in the ministry may involve in more spiritual activities and church related matters forgetting their spouses. They may have time for everything but not to their spouses. Even if they do unintentionally also need to be set right with their spouses. They need to express by their attitude and action that how their spouses are more important to them than others.

7.4. Lack of Communication/Openness and Sharing

Good communication helps build a healthy and functional marriage. Communication is the life and blood of any relationship. The health of a marriage largely depends on the quality and quantity of their communication.[87] Couples who communicate very well in the beginning may become cold and fall prey to *communication deficit model of marital distress.*[88] Even though we live in the world where communication has developed a lot, it is possible that people do live in a same house but live without having proper communication with one another. They are connected with the whole world through social media, but not connected with the spouses living with them in the same house and in the same room. Many marriages have come to an end because of lack of communication. Spouses are busy in their own work, struggling without communicating their wants, desires, and their emotional feelings to their life partners. Women express their feelings more freely than men. Men are very

86 D. John Antony, *Types of Counseling* (Nagercoil: Anugraha Publications, 1996), 119.

87 Santhosh John, *Spirituality of Marriage* (Delhi: ISPCK, 2011), 150.

88 Gideon Sobhanam, *United to Adjust*, 72.

tight-lipped about their feelings, and like to resolve their own problems and issues by themselves.[89] Conflicts arise out of simple situations like when a husband does not pay attention to what the wife is saying or when a husband fails to remember their wedding anniversary and like many other occasions.[90] If the husband and wife fail to develop a strong bond, friction can occur at any stage.[91] Neglecting this may lead to disastrous situation in the later years and shake the very sustenance of the family.

7.5. Conflict in Family Relationship and Support

Very often the main factor for the conflict in the marital relationship is interference of in-laws. The relationship between mother-in-law and daughter-in-law is often problematic and remains a controversial subject in India. In the traditional join family system, the central figure of the household is the mother-in-law.[92] She is the disciplinary figure and the implementer of family rules and regulations with the newly wedded bride. A newly married woman has multiple roles to play in the family. As a wife, daughter-in-law and sister-in-law, she occupies a central place in the extended family system. However, in the modern society, the traditional joint family system has mostly turned into nuclear family system. The problems of in-laws are minimized, but conflicts can still occur due to the matters connected with the in-laws in different form.[93] Conflicts can be reduced if husband and wife talk together and plan together about all the matters in connection with their parents and decide how to support them and take care of them when they are fragile and weak.

7.6. Inter-Faith Issues

Since the growth of industrialization and urbanization, people migrate from place to place in their own country and internationally. While they live and work with people of other faith it is possible that young people do get marriage selecting partners from other faith. When people of different religious background marry, the dominant spouse has the say as to the practice of religion together. The submissive spouses usually yield to the wishes of the dominant spouse and when not willing to budge quarrels ensure. Very many times problems start not until child rearing starts. Now the couple become alert as to which is the correct religious orientation and in what orientation the child

89 Vernon Vaz, Yolande Pereira, *Creating a Happy Family* (Bangalore: Asian Trading Corporation, 2005), 47.

90 Vernon Vaz, Yolande Pereira, *Creating a Happy Family,* 43.

91 Beulah Wood, *Families in the Plan of God,* (Bangalore: SAIACS Press, 2011), 134.

92 Rita Choudhury, "Understanding Family Life in India," *Family Life Education in India: Perspectives, Challenges and Applications,* ed. Aparajita Chowdhury, et.al, (New Delhi: Rawat Publications, 2006), 52.

93 Marie Mignon Mascarenhas, *Family Life Education*, 227.

is to be reared.[94] However, it is the children who experience serious problems in such marriages.[95] Celebration of the religious festivals of the partners of another faith also may cause problems, which are aggravated when family members of the partner insist on following the tradition, customs, rites and rituals of their own religion. Issues such as these and other similar ones can cause an internal strife leading to a conflict of one's own conscience, loss of faith and alienation from other partner's family.[96] Not all interfaith marriages are shaky. They strive in the midst of divergence and differences only when in their relationship there is a union of body, mind, heart and spirit.[97] Since, both of them had decided to get married and establish their home with having understood their differences, they must not allow any kinds of differences to come on their way to shake their married life.

7.7. Other Issues: Technology - Social Media

A newly wedded woman told her husband, "Instead of marrying me you should have married a mobile phone." These words would have come from her out of frustration. Science and technology have developed a lot. That is a gift for human beings. Technology has reduced human workload in many ways. It helps people to connect with anyone anywhere in the world in no time. It's so helpful in various ways. People are connected with one another through social media and internet very easily. The media which connect people often become an instrument to disconnect families and end their married life. There are spouses who never allow even their spouses to look into their mobiles.

There are many other issues such as alcohol addiction, Drug abuse, domestic violence, dowry, extra-marital relationship, and pornography do affect marriages of many people.

8. Result of Unresolved Issues

The marriage is called union because of its very being and its end has to be a permanent union. Permanent means that it is a union intended to last for the joint lifetime of the partners themselves.[98] However, when married couples have unresolved issues in their family life, their union doesn't lose for long. When they are not able to solve their problems, they must seek help from family members, friends, pastors and counselors to set their home right. If it is not done in a proper way in the proper time, their marriage vows to come

94 D. John Antony, *Types of Counseling* (Nagercoil: Anugraha Publications, 1996), 121.

95 Marie Mignon Mascarenhas, *Family Life Education,* (Bangalore: Centre for Research Education Service & Training for Family Life Promotion, 1999), 228.

96 Vernon Vaz, Yolande Pereira, *Creating a Happy Family*, 55.

97 Vernon Vaz, Yolande Pereira, *Creating a Happy Family*, 62.

98 Marie Mignon Mascarenhas, *Family Life Education*, 229.

to an end. There is nearly unanimous opinions among social scientists and anthropologist that the number of divorces in the most part of the world is increasing day by day in comparison with the number of marriages that are registered.[99] Even though the divorce rate in India is low compare to some western countries, one cannot deny that the rising divorce rate in India is alarming. According to a report released by World Press, there were 1 or 2 cases of divorce per year in the 1960s. In the 1990s, the divorce cases increase more than 1000 per year. In the Family Court of Mumbai alone, there were 7200 divorce cases filed. It is evident through a study that in most of the Indian cities the number of divorces is on the rise. Another report says that 25 out of every 1000 marriages in India end up in divorce.[100]

9. Practical Suggestions to Overcome the Issues

At the time of marriage, the bride and the bridegroom declare that they will remain husband and wife and will live together until death separates them. Hence it is both of their responsibility to work out some solution for the permanence of their marital life. Few practical suggestions are given for them to consider:

- Respect one another's individuality.
- Try to understand each other's strength and weakness.
- Be open and have healthy communication.
- Listen to one another.
- Encourage one another.
- When disagreements arise instead of blaming their partners and justifying their own actions, they need to accept their own faults and shortcomings.
- They must learn to build self-esteem by using words that support and motivate rather than criticize one another.
- In order to reduce stress in the relationship, the spouses should be sensitive to each other's needs, aware of other's feelings and be cooperative.[101]
- Take counsel from pastors and trained counsellors whenever it is necessary.

Conclusion

Marriage is never plain sailing for anybody, but for some, it may unfortunately very stormy. Constant adjustment and adaptation are required between the spouses for the marriage to be successful. A strong and supportive relationship

99 S. Appathurai, *Marriage is Forever*, 75.

100 S. Appathurai, *Marriage is Forever*, 79.

101 Santhosh John, *Spirituality of Marriage*, 151.

between partners and their families can make uncertainties tolerable, and can make successful adaptation to marital life easier. When two individuals are joined in marriage, the difference will always exist between them. They are two people often from widely divergent families, who have come together. They should learn to respect and accept each other's culture, tradition, habits, individuality, and their families. Before getting into a marital relationship, one should know about married life, the changing trend of the society about family life. Above all, they must try not to talk about their spouses and the issues between them to others rather try to talk with one another with an open mind and confidence to overcome all the challenges they face for the sustenance of their marriage with the providence and guidance of God.

22

AN ABSTRACT ON THE STUDY ON MISSION STRATEGY OF INDIA FOCUSED ON EVANGELICAL CHURCH OF INDIA

Lee Byung Sung[1]

In 1985, when I was studying the final year in High school, first I met Rev. Onesimu in our church high school student's retreat in Korea. I was 16 years old then. One night Prayer, I heard his testimony in the retreat. In his testimony, he said, "God loves India more than Korea." At first, when I heard that I felt uncomfortable. In my opinion, I thought 'God loves Korea more than India, for the passion towards faith is greater in Korea.' Rev. Onesimu continued, "Because the population in India is much more than Korea." Further, he says India is in the Bible (Esther 1:1) after hearing this, I thought 'Yes, that's right. If God values one life more than the world, God might love India more.' Right then, I made a promise to God, "I will become a missionary to do ministry in India."

I became a KEHC missionary to India 20 years later and settled in Pune and Rev. Onesimu was the president of MTSC and a pastor of the local church in Chennai and finally, we met in India. He always treats people humanly and manages his ministry prudently. He makes people comfortable by hearing them out and leads the organization smoothly. In other words, he has a servant leadership. Rev. Onesimu is a good man.

---

1 *Rev. Dr. Lee Byung Sung, Ph.D. Post-Graduate School of Theology, Seoul Theological University Bucheon, Korea.*

He speaks fluent Korean, also he translates the Korean sermon to Tamil and English nicely. KEHC has supported his studies in Korea and encouraged his ministry, we are proud of him. He gets praised whenever he says greetings in Korean language at the Annual Assembly Meeting of KEHC. As Korea Evangelical Holiness Church trusts him, many ministers and believers visit India from time to time and decided to give financial support to ECI because he maintained a good relationship with them. Rev. Onesimu provides a clue for the missionary work for KEHC and he manages the practical work for ECI in action. Moreover, when there is a matter of opinion between ECI and KEHC, he acts as a mediator and a coordinator.

The opportunity that I got to meet him is one of my happiness. Thanks to him, I became a missionary, worked with him, and till now Rev. Onesimu and I are praying for Korea, India and the kingdom of the Lord. Our friendship is like Jonathan and David in the Bible. He is my brother and my co-worker. I wish him good health, a good future, and good ministry in ECI.

This research aimed to analyse a history of the Evangelical Church of India (ECI) and its mission strategy and to propose a future mission strategy and policy of ECI.

Evangelical Church of India rapidly grew by practicing the principle of receptivity. The Church has focused on lower caste and backward caste. It is also distributed mainly in some states like Tamil Nadu and Andhra Pradesh of South India and focused on a few tribes. Also, the Church tends to financially depend on foreign funds.

The Church needs a more modern and applicable mission strategy. ECI needs to widen from lower caste to higher caste and from part to the whole. The mission strategy has to be designed by indigenous people who are accustomed to the need and emotion of Indians, not by foreign mission societies or missionaries.

This research takes the method of review of the historical literature. In particular, the General Assembly Report, statistics date and Monthly Report are the primary sources to be able to evaluate the practice process of the mission strategy of ECI so far. However, there are cases to be a direct quotation because of unpublished sources and rare mission sources to India. The reason is that the sources are not sorted yet and so there is a limitation in expressing them.

Because there is almost no study on the mission strategy of the Evangelical Church of India so far, instead, I have tried to evaluate a few studies on the mission strategy of the mission strategy for India. However, it has limitations in analyzing the mission strategy of ECI with it.

In chapter one, this paper deals with the problem statement, the purpose, the method and the scope of research, the previous studies and terms definition. In chapter two, this paper periodically divides a history of the Evangelical

Church of India and its mission strategy and studies on the importance of India mission and its mission strategy and limitations. In chapter three, this paper deals with a history of the Korean Church's India mission and its mission strategy and proposes a mission strategy through it. In chapter four, this paper deals with Korea Evangelical Holiness Church's role for India mission and analyzes the Evangelical Church of India's mission strategy and its results. In chapter five, this paper ends with the summary and the proposal for the mission strategy of ECI.

Evangelical Church of India proposed the mission strategy as follows; the first is an image strategy. ECI has to continue to plant church and made symbolic Christian constructions. The second is a homogenous class focused strategy. It is a strategy to use castes. Converted people go and proclaim the gospel to their homogenous people. The third is a family unit mission strategy. It can be effective for Indians who have a strong family kindred consciousness. The fourth is a local connected mission strategy. It is to connect with local church and mission society and to share possible information through development cooperation with local government. The fifth is a power encounter mission strategy. It is to use the proof of God being among many religions including Hinduism. The sixth is to use immigrated urban people mission strategy. It is to plant a church for people who migrated to cities and for them to go to suburban areas and close village and plant a church. The seventh is an inculturation mission strategy. Indian church has to proclaim the gospel through Indian culture and language which can communicate with Indians. The eight is whole generation mission strategy. All church congregation, pastors and laypeople, all generations have to participate in the mission.

Therefore, the mission strategy of ECI can gain the effective results by practicing an image strategy, a homogenous class focused strategy, a family unit mission strategy, a locally connected mission strategy, a power encounter mission strategy, immigrated people mission strategy, and inculturation mission strategy, whole generation mission strategy.